Let's Understand Social Security and Stimulate Investment

Let's Understand Social Security and Stimulate Investment

or
Separating Economic Voodoo from the Truth

Loren Meierding

iUniverse, Inc.
New York Lincoln Shanghai

Let's Understand Social Security and Stimulate Investment
or Separating Economic Voodoo from the Truth

iUniverse books may be ordered through booksellers or by contacting:

iUniverse
2021 Pine Lake Road, Suite 100
Lincoln, NE 68512
www.iuniverse.com
1-800-Authors (1-800-288-4677)

ISBN-13: 978-0-595-37153-2 (pbk)
ISBN-13: 978-0-595-81551-7 (ebk)
ISBN-10: 0-595-37153-1 (pbk)
ISBN-10: 0-595-81551-0 (ebk)

Printed in the United States of America

TABLE OF CONTENTS

PREFACE

I have been an avid follower of the political scene for many years and have been disturbed by the arguments on the left on economic matters. But the propaganda and nonsense surrounding the current discussion of fixes for Social Security takes the cake. Reactionaries opposing any change in Social Security have thoroughly confused and misled the public. A reader who reads the first 8 chapters of this book carefully will have a good grasp of the issue of adding personal retirement accounts to Social Security and should see through the present confusion and propaganda.

The importance of fixing the long-term problems of Social Security by introducing personal retirement accounts was evident before the 1983 Greenspan Commission supposedly "solved" the funding of Social Security for the next 60 years by raising FICA taxes. Had a real solution that introduced personal retirement accounts been instituted at that time, most baby boomers would be enjoying several hundred dollars more per month in retirement income. Because fixing Social Security is now under discussion I would like to help move the argument forward so that the children and grandchildren of baby boomers may at least do better.

I offer this book to the public for three basic reasons. First, economists have produced a massive amount of analysis of the Social Security system during the past three decades. Their analyses are too complex for the average person who wants to understand the issues, especially the issue of personal retirement accounts. Comments by politicians are highly misleading. This book will enable the average person to understand and compare the financial future of Social Security, if it is not reformed, to a reformed Social Security system with personal retirement accounts. Second, few people seem to understand the negative impact corporate income taxes have had on our economy for the last three quarters of a century. I lay out evidence to make a case for eliminating the corporate income tax as a step toward eliminating taxation of savings and investment. Third, I experienced the operation of government bureaucracies at first hand in air traffic control, air defense, and transportation and provide arguments for reducing intrusion of bureaucrats in our economy

My background and qualifications for writing this book include the following. I entered Yale College at age 16 and graduated with a BA in philosophy in 1967. After a year studying mathematics at the University of Montana, I was drafted and ended up in Korea for thirteen months. After completing active duty in the Army I earned a Ph.D. in philosophy at the University of Texas in 1978.

I worked for two years as an actuarial assistant for a pension consulting firm in Los Angeles. It was my job to analyze the assets of small pension plans, determine the present value of future benefits and to fill out the government forms required, in particular the forms for the IRS. Working in the pension field for two years, passing three actuarial exams, and having made some models of the Social Security system gives me a good background for writing about the Social Security system. I also spent about 10 years using all my spare time to study the U.S. economy.

For twelve years I worked for Hughes Aircraft Company in Fullerton, California as a systems engineer involved in the design of air traffic control, air defense, missile defense, GM trucks, and transportation systems. My work involved developing simulation models of these systems. Work on projects for the FAA and foreign defense departments gave me understanding of the way government bureaucracies function (waste money on a grand scale).

I spent a couple of years doing consulting primarily developing a database application. After that I began writing several books and moved back to Montana to take care of my elderly mother.

CHAPTER 1

Economic Voodoo

Voodoo Economics

During the campaign for the Presidency in 1980 Ronald Reagan advocated a "supply-side" approach to Federal tax policy. Reagan believed lowering personal tax rates would increase government revenues. By allowing Americans to keep more of their earnings they would save and invest more which would cause greater production and a greater supply of goods and services.

Opponents called the supply-side approach "voodoo" economics. The reigning approach to economics policy for the previous 50 years had been Keynesian demand side economics that assumed increased government spending would stimulate the economy producing greater investment and productivity. Greater spending by government increases demand for goods and services presumably increasing prices and profits to produce increased investment and increased supply. However, if demand increases with insufficient new investment to produce adequate supply, the increased demand may cause greater inflation. This was a chronic problem during the 1970's.

Fixing Social Security

Both sides of the economic policy debate over the past few decades have claimed their opponents espoused voodoo economics. Nevertheless if there ever has been a target justifying the label of "voodoo economics" it is the current claims by Senators Reid, Baucus, and Schumer that our existing Social Security system is "solvent" until the year 2045 or that only minor adjustments will be needed, as the AARP states. The most egregious distortions and deceptions recently have surrounded President Bush's attempts to fix the long term problems of Social Security. Many specious arguments are brought forward to confuse the public and show why Social Security does not need fixing. The ignorance, obfuscation, and disingenuousness in their claims about Social Security has reached new levels. These claims are economic voodoo. Politicians and pundits frequently participating in cable news shows have made many highly misleading and wrongheaded claims about Social Security and the U.S. economy over the past 25 years. The same shopworn economic ideas are repeated over and over again. This book was written to bring out the foolishness and absurdity of many of these claims. It will illuminate the Social Security and tax and spending policy discussions and indicate some of the fallacies of reasoning involved.

As someone who has worked in the pension actuarial field, the necessity for introducing personal retirement accounts with Social Security has been obvious. The changes to Social Security made in 1983 solved near term income shortfalls primarily by raising taxes. The reforms failed to fix the long-term problems. A proper solution would have produced increased investment and economic growth rather than decreased investment and economic growth. Now over 20 years later, the baby boomers will receive several hundred dollars a month less from Social Security than they might have received, and nothing yet has been done to fix the problems. If nothing is done for another 20 years the children and grandchildren of baby boomers will also receive much less than they should receive.

President Bush has initiated a proper and principled push to fix the Social Security problems while they can be fixed. This process has stalled but the problems with Social Security are not going away and the earlier they are dealt with the better. Unfortunately those responsible for creating, modifying, and maintaining Social Security as it currently exists have presented the Social Security retirement system in a manner that is highly confusing to the public. By creating a so-called Social Security "Trust Fund," Congress and the Social Security Administration have misled the public to believe that Social Security does not need much fixing. The subject seems more complex than it really is. Consequently most people have a simple faith in the Social Security actuaries' analysis published in the annual Trustees' Reports. They claim the system is solvent until the 2040's. One of the techniques the Social Security actuaries use in the annual Trustees' Report is to denominate annual Social Security retirement (OASI) income and benefits in terms of percentage of covered payroll instead of billions or trillions of dollars. This makes understanding the implications of future trends of Social Security more difficult. In this book Social Security income and spending estimates by Social Security actuaries were converted to dollar amounts.

This book will enable people to understand the current debate over personal retirement accounts and the need to fix Social Security. Perhaps it will also encourage reduction in taxes on investment and in government intervention in the economy. Our long-term economic benefit, especially the welfare of the lower income workers depends on improving investment and reducing regulation so that greater productivity and greater economic growth will be realized.

In the following chapters the arguments against changing Social Security and against reducing the tax burden are examined and refuted. The underlying assumptions and implied principles are indicated. Chapters 2 to 8 provide anyone an excellent understanding of the true state of the Social Security system and the consequences of a reform that will include personal retirement accounts. An attentive reader of the seven following chapters will be able to separate the "voodoo" from the truth. The analysis will show why reforming Social Security to incorporate personal retirement accounts is warranted. Chapters 9 to 13 cover other issues concerning deficits, taxes, and government intervention in the economy. Some of the most significant assumptions or principles deserve the label of "principles of voodoo economics." Labeling them in this way may increase awareness of how truly wrongheaded they are. Thirteen principles of economic voodoo are discussed. The list is not exhaustive. There are many others that politicians and left leaning pundits believe.

Taxation and Deficit Spending

Pundits for the Democratic Party are still denigrating the Reagan tax cuts for supposedly causing large deficits and increasing the Federal deficit to over $4 trillion. Chapter 9 takes up this claim and shows that during the Reagan Administration the official national debt increased significantly. Yet it is not evident that any significant increase in the true debt accrued during the 1980's, if unfunded liabilities previously excluded from the official debt are included. Critics of Reagan who castigate him for deficit spending are engaging in voodoo economics when they maintain that the increase in official national debt during his administration was so harmful. Moreover the Democratic House of Representatives refused to cut spending and must share any blame for deficits.

It has also been a staple claim by politicians and pundits in the Democratic Party that the perceived prosperity of the 1990's was due to the Clinton tax increases of 1993. The increases supposedly brought about a balanced budget. However, anyone who cares to investigate will find that in 1993 President Clinton was predicting deficits for another ten years. It was the Republican takeover of Congress in 1994 and subsequent "government shutdown" that caused cutbacks in spending and spending trends that led to a balanced budget. Claims that tax increases would bring about prosperity are simply more economic voodoo. Chapter 10 examines claims about the economic prosperity of the 1990's separating economic voodoo from the truth.

Desirability of Reducing Taxation and Government Intervention

The Federal income tax has become exceedingly complex. The code is so complex that the IRS itself is unable to satisfactorily help people fill out their tax forms correctly. The U.S. income tax has numerous other problems as well. It puts U.S. corporations at a disadvantage in competition when foreign corporations pay lower profits taxes. More economists are recognizing that better economic growth and greater prosperity will result from taxing consumption rather than income. Personal income is either consumed or saved and invested. Taxing income not only taxes consumption, but also saving and investment. Reducing saving and investment by paying excessive income taxes reduces growth in productivity and long term economic growth. The same problem applies to levying corporate income taxes. Profits are the best source of funds for productivity growth. Profits are not taxed by a consumption tax.

Consumption is taxed very simply by sales taxes. Hence a national sales tax that replaces the Federal income tax is the ideal solution. When the burden and complexity of income taxes is removed, U.S. corporations will have an advantage in global competition. Saving and investment will not be penalized but encouraged and economic growth will be promoted, especially since corporations will be able to retain all their earnings and invest them. While a national sales tax is the best approach to tax policy, there are formidable obstacles to realizing it. Many people hate corporations, believing that they are rolling in money from exploiting their customers and employees and need to be punished by taxation of profits. There is a natural resistance to sales taxes. However one of the virtues of the sales tax aside from the simplicity and ease of collection and reduction of government snooping in personal affairs is that people have a clear understanding of the amount of taxes they are paying. People cannot easily cheat on sales taxes either. Everything is simple and clear and easily monitored.

Probably the major obstacle to replacing income taxes, especially corporate profits taxes with sales taxes, is that the existence of income taxes provides Senators and Congressman with the power to change the rates at anytime. Congress can offer special exemptions and subsidies to corporations at any time. They can also at any time increase the rates. Because corporations live under the threat of changes that will benefit or harm them, they are motivated to contribute significant sums to the campaign funds of Senators and Representatives. If a sales tax replaced income taxes, corporations would not have the same motivation to contribute. It would be more difficult for Senators and Representatives to raise campaign funds from corporations. This problem of course could be solved simply by greatly increasing the limits on personal contributions to campaigns. The limits on individual contributions have forced politicians to depend more on special interests and corporations as their source of campaign funds.

There is a simpler step than passing a national sales tax to replace income taxes in order to improve saving, investment, production, and economic growth. It might not be easy politically either but is very simple to implement. This step is to *abolish the corporate income tax*. The presence of the corporate income tax reduces competition and reduces saving, investment, and economic growth. By eliminating it we could increase economic growth and living standards over the long term. Chapters 11 and 12 show why less taxation and regulation is desirable. Chapter 13 specifically shows the desirability of eliminating the corporate income tax as a quick, simple, and very significant reform of the tax code which would have significant results. The amount of revenue collected from the corporate income tax is not great. The greater economic growth from its removal would in a short period generate increased revenues from personal income taxes. These new revenues would replace the revenue currently produced by the corporate income tax.

Free Markets

The United States had a relatively *laissez faire* economy during the Nineteenth Century. But at the beginning of the Twentieth Century progressives believed that corporations were engaged in unethical activities that could only be stopped by government regulation. This led to the passage of many laws that set up Federal and State regulatory agencies. Also in 1909 corporate income taxes were introduced and gradually increased until the rates were confiscatory during World War II and for some years after. Since that time they have been reduced but still have an effective rate of about 40%, and a higher rate of 60% on investment from retained earnings and on the manufacturing sector.[1] The Social Security pay-as-you-go funding method has almost certainly reduced saving and investment in our economy.[2] Other kinds of meddling with the economy, for example the Federal Reserve's handling of the money supply over the years, has often reduced economic growth. I believe that one can argue that had our economy remained *laissez faire* we would have experienced an extra 1% per year in economic growth for the last 80 years. A one percent annual growth doubles in 80 years. So our economy could be double what it is with the average worker making over $70,000 per year. Most people should be driving a car of the quality of a Lexus.

Free markets are far more resilient than most intellectuals give them credit for being. Imperfections tend to get fixed without government intervention. Elites would need to be omniscient in economic matters to fix the problems they point out. Perhaps some believe that they are. They believe that there are economic free lunches when there are none. Theory may be fascinating, but one must pay careful attention to the evidence. Above all one should not assign bureaucrats the task of fixing anything when all their incentives push them toward failing. Bureaucrats who succeed see their budget and empire go away. Bureaucrats who fail will gain more money and a larger bureaucratic empire after the next budget. A *laissez faire* economy would promote a far better life even for the poor than economies with extensive government intervention.

Many persons with a purely naturalistic world view are dismayed by a world that has great disparities in income and wealth. They want equality of material possessions. They want everyone to enjoy the same share of what is produced whether they receive a large or small share of all goods and services available. They want socialist or partially socialistic transfer redistributionary schemes to be implemented to bring about full equality or at least much greater equality.

For them a laissez faire capitalistic system with people selling their labor in the marketplace is objectionable. Employees receive significantly different wages and salaries depending upon their knowledge, skills, and propensity to work hard. The socialist wants to achieve much greater equality of income and wealth. To some extent this goal can be achieved by a progressive income tax and Social Security retirement benefits distributed with lower income workers receiving a much higher percentage of pre-retirement income than high income workers. In addition government can provide various services to all. However in the long run much greater wealth accrues to members of a laissez faire system.

In the real world different people have a wide range of talents and interests. Some have religious beliefs or interests that do not lead them to seek wealth of material possessions in this life. The consequence of different interests and abilities means that there is a natural tendency to have differences in material wealth.

There are a number of problems that come with introduction of socialist redistributionary and transfer schemes. First an elite must oversee the implementation of socialist transfer programs. This always produces unfairness because elites demand special privileges. Second, redistributionary systems with heavy taxation significantly reduce rewards and incentives for producing abundant goods and services for the public good. Thus both pure socialistic schemes and less onerous redistributionary schemes introduce disincentives to be productive. The result is that many very productive people realize that they are not being rewarded adequately for extra work they perform. Many of them will reduce their work effort and spend more time enjoying leisure time instead. The economic pie of goods and services provided will accordingly tend to shrink. Nearly everyone will be poorer.

Third, when corporations have their profits heavily taxed they have less ability to invest and increase production. Competition is reduced, because potential competitors have less resources with which to compete. Fewer workers are needed. The least skilled and least productive workers are laid off. Greater unemployment results. There are greater disparities in income and greater inequality. Attempts to introduce socialism and redistribution are actually counterproductive. Imposition of heavy taxation on corporations actually increases concentration of economic power in the largest corporations and produces additional inequality.

There is a principle implicit in the views of socialists and others on the left desiring to put more of the economy under the supervision of bureaucrats:

Voodoo Economics Principle #1: Elites (legislators, lawyers, and bureaucrats) know how to invest capital better than entrepreneurs.

This principle is of course quite false, but Democrats operate as if it were true.

Chapters 2 through 8 will examine Social Security and personal retirement accounts exposing the propaganda and economic voodoo presently surrounding the issue. Chapters 9 and 10 will examine the U.S. economy of the 1980's and 1990's and point out some of the economic voodoo surrounding claims about the consequences of government debt and taxation. Chapters 11 to 13 will examine the consequences of excessive taxation and the desirability of eliminating or greatly reducing taxation of corporate profits.

CHAPTER 2

Theoretical Potential for Social Security

President Bush has proposed fixing future problems of funding Social Security by incorporating a system of personal retirement accounts. Senators Reid, Baucus, and Schumer and other Democrats argue that a personal retirement accounts system would *reduce* benefits. They and the AARP claim only minor adjustments to Social Security are needed prior to 2044. Claiming that the transition to a personal accounts system will reduce benefits is a scare tactic. The cogency of their argument depends on our current Social Security system maintaining current levels of benefits until 2044. But we shall see in this chapter and Chapter 4 will again demonstrate that Social Security as presently constituted will require significant benefit cuts many years prior to 2044.

Overview

In Chapters 2 through 8 we will examine the long-term consequences of Social Security if it were to remain as currently constituted. We will contrast it with several possible approaches permitting all or part of the retirement part of Social Security (OASI) to be deposited in personal retirement accounts. The questions to be answered are:

- which approaches should produce the most retirement income?

- what costs are expected during transition to a system of personal retirement accounts?

- what benefits are expected during transition to a system of personal retirement accounts?

The key basis for making these comparisons requires computing the replacement income after retirement as a fraction of the income earned just prior to retirement. After retiring and foregoing regular working income, workers need to have income from pensions and other assets that replace a large amount of their working income. It is generally believed that retirees should have at least 70% of their pre-retirement income replaced.

This chapter will examine the theoretical possibilities of pay-as-you-go transfer schemes like Social Security. It will show that a pay-as-you-go transfer system like Social Security with a 2 to 1 worker to retiree ratio holding far into the future, cannot replace more on average than about 28% of pre-retirement income at retirement. Chapter 3 presents a reasonable estimate of a worker's replacement income if the entire amount contributed by employee and employer for Social Security retirement were invested in personal retirement accounts and earned a reasonable return. Chapter 4 shows the replacement income a worker might expect if the amount contributed by employee for Social Security retirement, that is ½ of current FICA deductions for retirement were invested in personal retirement accounts and earned a reasonable return. The calculations also assume Social Security benefits are cut in half. A Social Security system with personal retirement accounts could come close to replacing 70% of pre-retirement income. An unreformed Social Security cannot come close.

Chapter 5 evaluates the consequences if nothing is done before 2045. Democratic Senators and the AARP assure us that only minor adjustments are necessary. We will see that they are wrong. Social Security will need to borrow $14 trillion from the public by 2045 if nothing is done. Chapter 6 examines a Social Security system with personal retirement accounts. It assumes an average of 4% of covered payroll contributed to personal retirement accounts. It shows the amount of investment produced and the amount of borrowing necessary for the years 2005 to 2060. Chapter 7 provides a comparison of transition costs and investment for our current Social Security as analyzed in Chapter 5 with the system of personal retirement accounts analyzed in Chapter 6. Comparison is made for the periods 2005 to 2018, 2019 to 2035, and 2035 to 2060. Chapter 8 sums up the results from comparing the transition costs for the two systems. A system with personal retirement accounts will have a very positive effect on investment. It will improve economic productivity and growth during the transitional phases far more than pay-as-you-go Social Security.

Historical Background

Social Security was instituted in 1935 during the Depression. It was designed as a pay-as-you-go system. Taxes deducted from employees' wages were matched by employers. The receipts were then spent on paying retirees' benefits. Any income above the amount paid out for retirement was spent on government programs. Because it takes a few years to qualify for benefits, in the initial stages a pay-as-you-go system has a very small amount of benefits to pay relative to its income. So FDR used this income to fund many of his social programs. Initially the rate of taxation was a total of 2% for employee and employer on the first $3000 of income. By 1965 the combined total for retirement from employer and employee was 6.75%. With the addition of Medicare in 1966 the total combined FICA for Social Security and Medicare increased to 11.7% of covered payroll by the mid-70's. This increase of about 4.5% seemed innocuous to economists who blamed most of the economic problems during the 1970's on the oil shortages. Yet an increased tax of 4.5% of payroll is a very significant amount. It *directly* reduces saving considerably by reducing income.[1] But it also has a strong *indirect* influence on saving. If people expect their retirement to be covered by Social Security and Medicare, they will save much less than otherwise. The historical FICA tax rates for OASI are shown in Figure 2.1. The bars do not include Disability, Medicare, or SSI which bring the total deductions up to 15.3% of covered payroll.

Percent of Covered Payroll

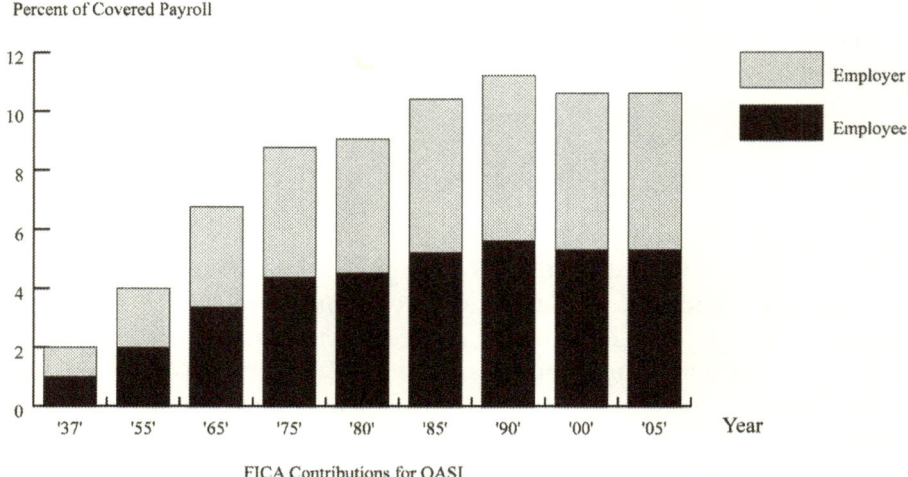

FICA Contributions for OASI

Figure 2.1 Employer and Employee OASI Contributions

By 1980 the rate for the retirement portion (OASI from employee and employer) of Social Security had increased to 8.66% on $25,900 of payroll. Despite the frequent increases in tax collection, by 1983 Social Security was paying out more than it took in. A commission was formed to determine what needed to be done. The full retirement age was raised by up to 2 years for younger workers and the OASI FICA rates were increased in several steps to 5.3% each for employee and employer (the total employee contribution for retirement, disability, and Medicare is 7.65%). It is very tempting to raise taxes to keep the system functioning but at some point this approach will lead to excessive taxation and reduced economic growth. It also causes reduced saving. The extra income not needed for paying retirements is "borrowed" and spent by the federal government. In return for borrowing and spending money which should have been invested for retirement, the Treasury department gives special Treasury bonds to the Social Security Administration. Additional bonds are given to cover accrued interest. The special bonds comprise the so-called Social Security "Trust Fund."

A pay-as-you-go funding system does not invest money to fund retirement liabilities. Because the baby boom was followed by a birth dearth Social Security has a very large unfunded liability of over $11 trillion.[2] When the Federal Government carries a very large unfunded liability the savvy bond traders know that Congress is likely to follow the path of least resistance and force the Federal Reserve to create inflation. As a protection against future inflation, real long-term interest rates in the U.S. have tended to be one or two percent higher than they historically should be.[3] This has produced a significant cost to the economy. *Further it has weakened our economy over many years, caused workers to have lower wages and salaries than should have occurred, caused higher unemployment than would have occurred, and caused higher deficits than might otherwise have occurred.*

Democrats believe that Social Security and its pay-as-you-go financing scheme are wonderful and must be preserved at all costs. They are committed to a second principle of voodoo economics:

Voodoo Economics Principle #2: Socialist transfer schemes must be implemented and preserved at all costs.

This is voodoo because socialist transfer schemes make people poorer.

The retirement benefits funded by invested FICA contributions should be compared to what our current Social Security system could provide. If benefits are maintained at the level defined by the current benefit formula they will replace an average 2/5 of pre-retirement income. If 25% or 30% reductions in benefits will be necessary the benefits will replace an average 2/7 of pre-retirement income. Despite the claims of Democrats in Congress that little needs to be done until the 2040's, it will be clear that the second alternative must be implemented.

As we will see below, our current Social Security system cannot in the future provide more than about 28% of pre-retirement income for the average worker without increasing the FICA taxes. Democrats believe that it is essential to preserve Social Security without combining it with personal accounts apparently because it is so wonderful and yet it will only be able to pay at most about 28% or 2/7 of pre-retirement income for the average worker. *How can it be rational to prefer a system providing no more than 28% of pre-retirement income to a system that can produce more than double that proportion of pre-retirement income?*

Why should Democrats be so committed to preserving Social Security as it is? In Chapter 3 we will see that if the entire OASI contribution of 10.6% were deposited in personal retirement accounts, the average worker could expect, by utilizing tried and true saving and investment, to replace about 2/3 of pre-retirement income. Currently our pay-as-you-go Social Security system offers about 2/5 of pre-retirement income for the average worker and in the future will replace about 2/7. Figure 2.2 shows these fractions visually. The "Current SS" bar represents the proportion of pre-retirement income preserved if Social Security continues to pay benefits through 2045 using the same formula presently used. The "Reduced SS" bar represents the proportion of pre-retirement income obtained if Social Security must cut benefits before 2045. The "Account(10.6%)" bar indicates the percentage of pre-retirement income earned at 6.5% returns if employee and employer OASI contributions for retirement are invested.

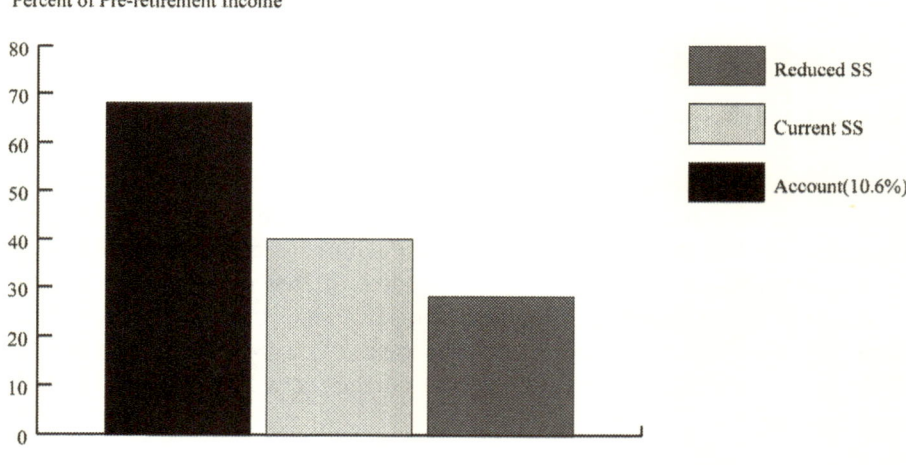

Figure 2.2 Replacement of Pre-retirement Income.

Commitment to preserving Social Security with little change and by so doing cheating workers out of one-half or more of their possible retirement income means that most Democrats are heavily committed to socialist financing schemes, although they go to extraordinary lengths to deny it. As the analysis of this chapter and of Chapter 4 shows there must be cuts in benefits in the relatively near future. If someone were truly concerned with the welfare of our younger workers now in their twenties and thirties, they would want to see the average worker able to realize 68% (Appendix 1, Table A1) of pre-retirement income instead of 28%, and for higher income workers, 68% instead of 19%. The active members and leaders of the Democratic Party claim their party is the party of the people. Yet they demand that the Social Security transfer system be preserved as it is, even if average workers will be condemned to reductions to 28% of pre-retirement income without any compensation. If benefits are going to have to be cut, does it not make sense to allow workers to start saving now?

Nature of Pay-As-You-Go Social Security

The analysis of Chapter 6 will show the potential for a personal retirement accounts system utilizing the traditional way to provide for retirement. Consistent and regular saving makes large quantities of money available for investment by companies to build new factories or invest in equipment or training that will pay off in greater production over a long period of time. The investment helps to improve the productivity of the individual workers and of the economy as a whole and compounds returns to the investor. Moreover, by utilizing the virtues of traditional investing with about 10% of one's income, Chapter 3 shows it is possible to replace about 2/3 of one's pre-retirement income.

Social Security will not be able to do nearly as well. The current benefit formulas cannot be maintained to 2045. This follows from the *very nature of the current pay-as-you-go Social Security*. Social Security is a transfer scheme. It does not invest anything and does not rely on the growth of the investments to produce income after retirement. It does not depend on, but taxes current workers and transfers the taxes to workers on retirement. This kind of scheme can provide a decent replacement of pre-retirement income with OASI FICA contributions around 10% if a ratio of workers to retired persons is 4 : 1. Then current Social Security benefit levels with an average replacement of about 40% of pre-retirement income is feasible on a permanent basis. If the average number of years working is in the 35 to 45 years range, then an average life expectancy of no more than about 10 years after retirement will keep the ratio of workers to retirees at about 4 : 1.

Transfer schemes like Social Security are very tempting to implement. The requirements to qualify for retirement benefits limit the number of retirees at the beginning of the program so that the ratio of workers to retirees is very high. With a very high ratio like 40 : 1 the initial tax on earnings can be small. When Social Security was implemented, workers and employers were each taxed 1% of workers pay for OASI. It was also the case when Social Security was implemented that most retirees had spent many years at hard physical labor and life expectancy at retirement was very short—only a few years. At that time in the 1930's it would have seemed that a ratio of 10 : 1 for workers to retirees could be maintained indefinitely.

In the initial stages of a transfer system with very few workers on retirement and workers living on retirement for only a few years, surplus contributions accumulate. They can provide funding for government programs. By passing Social Security FDR obtained money needed to fund many of his New Deal Programs. With the taxes at very low levels of only 1% and promises to provide retirement "insurance" and a supplement to retirement income, the program was very popular. The benefits at retirement were based on a progressive scale that returned a higher proportion of pre-retirement income to those with lower incomes than to those with higher incomes. As an income transfer scheme that a) is progressive giving greater proportions to the lower income workers, and b) transfers income from one generation group to another generation, it clearly redistributes income in certain ways and is a socialistic scheme.

Ponzi schemes, including chain letters and pyramid marketing schemes, have been declared illegal in all 50 states. The people who start them tend to make considerable amounts of money. The latecomers pay in and get nothing back. The returns are not based on earnings from investments. Surprisingly Social Security operates like a Ponzi scheme. The initial retirees pay very little in and get a return that vastly exceeds what they paid in. Returns on FICA contributions dwindle with each generation. They now are running equivalent to about a 1% return for average workers. This is greatly inferior to highly conservative savings accounts which return 3 or 4 percent. *For many higher income workers the returns are negative—they pay in more than they will ever receive back* (compared to 6% returns if invested conservatively). Future generations will do even worse. So the U.S. Government requires everyone to join a kind of Ponzi scheme when they are illegal in every state.

A Theoretical Future Replacement Rate

Let us understand the implications of some obvious facts. This is not "rocket science" or anything close to it. Social Security is a "pay-as-you-go" system that only transfers money between generations It does no saving. It reduces the need for saving for retirement, does not invest in assets that can produce a return for many years, and reduces economic growth. The demographics now are such that the average retiree lives about 18 years past age 65 and because many workers spend years in school and often do not get into the workforce until around age 30, they are likely to work about 35 years if not less.

With a working life about double the time in retirement, and because the working population is not likely to increase at a rate even close to 1% per year anytime soon, and life expectancies at age 65 are expected to increase, there is no reason to expect that during the next century or so that there will be any more than 2 workers supporting 1 retiree under a "pay-as-you-go" system transferring part of the earnings of workers to retirees. Since the employee and employer contributions to OASI contribute 10.6% of covered payroll with 2 workers contributing to 1 retiree, on average, the contributions of 2 average workers will be about 21% of the wages of an average worker. Hence, theoretically a "pay-as-you-go" system will not provide the average worker a retirement income of very much more than about 21% of their average wages at retirement.

For various reasons it is possible to do a little better than 21%. Benefit payments could be arranged to provide lower income workers more than 30% of pre-retirement income and to provide higher income workers less than 20%. Because Social Security benefits will surely have to be cut by about 30% in the future, the system, due to its very nature as a transfer between generations, cannot provide more than about 28% or about 70% of the current average Social Security replacement income of approximately 40%. This is an insufficient amount. The capacity for Social Security to replace pre-retirement income is confined by a theoretical result governed by the 2 to 1 worker to retiree ratio. Because in the past there were 4 or more workers per retiree, the average worker could receive 40% of his or her pre-retirement income. In the future that same level of replacement of earnings would only be possible if the total OASI contribution were increased by about 50% which would provide an unfair burden on workers. Social Security could also be retained in its present form if the normal retirement age were changed to about age 77. This would reduce life expectancy after retirement by 10 years. It would cut the years of paying retirement benefits in half. Baby boomers will not accept long extensions on retirement age, however.

Social Security Administration Projections

The analysis by the Social Security Administration actuaries projects that in the 2030 to 2080 period the *income* of OASI increases from 11.35% of covered payroll in 2030 to 11.52% of covered payroll in 2080. It is projected to be 11.42% of covered payroll in 2045 and 11.46% of covered payroll in 2060.[4] These numbers differ from the 10.6% contributions because they include estimates of income from taxes on Social Security benefits. The estimates for *benefit* payments in the 2004 Trustees Report increased from 14.51% of covered payroll in 2030 to 16.82% of covered payroll in 2080. The projection is for 15.37% of covered payroll in 2045 and 15.87% of covered payroll in 2060.[5]

We see that if we divide income percentage by benefits to be paid percentage, we find that income is 78% of benefits in 2030, 74% of benefits in 2045, 72% of benefits in 2060, and 68.5% of benefits in 2080. These percentages are plotted in Figure 2.3 and basically indicate the percentage of current Social Security benefits that can be paid if benefits are not to exceed income.

Percent of Current SS Benefit Formula

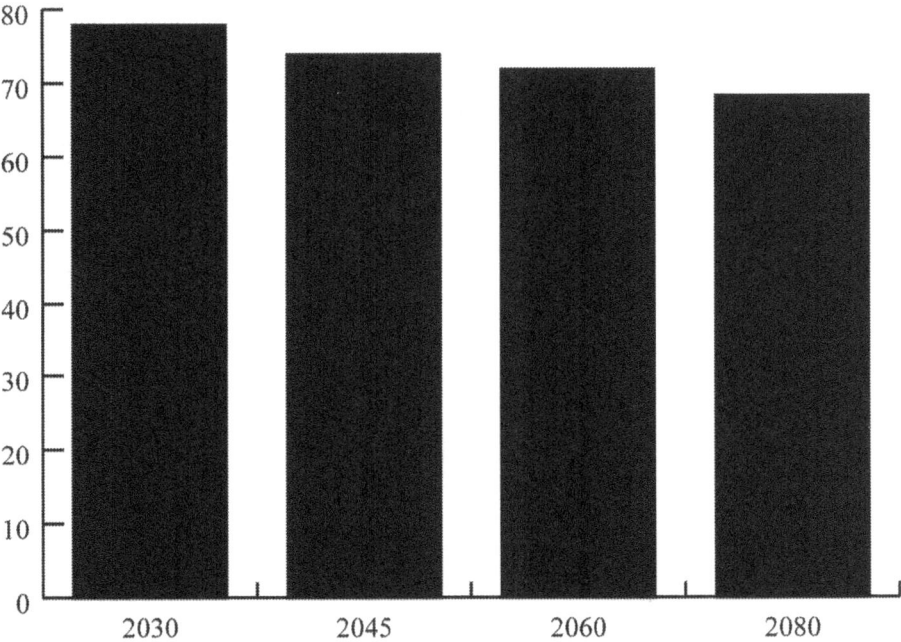

Percent of Current SS Benefits Payable in Future Years

Figure 2.3 Decline of Income to Pay Benefits

The implication of these numbers is that unless the deficits are covered by borrowing or additional new taxes, the benefits promised by the current Social Security system must be cut over 20% by 2030, by about 27% in the 2045 to 2060 time frame and over 31% by 2080 as projected by Social Security actuaries. A 30% average reduction if applied evenly over the range of incomes would reduce the replacement of pre-retirement income for average incomes at retirement from 40% to 28% of pre-retirement income, roughly agreeing with what we concluded from a purely theoretical point of view.

Actually of greater importance is the income for early retirement.

> *For the person retiring early at age 62, as most now do, the retirement income would be 20% of pre-retirement income. If we reflect on the fact that the average worker in the future will spend about half as many years in retirement as he or she spent working and the worker will be supported by the OASI 10.6% contributions of two people, we know that 28% is surely the maximum income replacement to be expected if borrowing or increased taxes are avoided.*

It is certain that reductions in benefits cannot be avoided. *With expected trends in demographics over the next century, a pay-as-you-go system can offer no more than about 28% of pre-retirement wages as compared with the 40% replacement of earnings that Social Security has offered workers until now.* Democrats want to do nothing because the system is supposedly solvent until 2044. As will be shown in Chapter 5, if benefits are not reduced, the U.S. Treasury will have to borrow about $13 trillion by 2044 or have income taxes raised to produce that amount over the 26 years from 2018 to 2044. The average deficit for 2018 to 2045 is about $500 billion. With about 70 million retirees, there is an average annual shortfall of about $7000 per retiree or about $600 per month per retiree. Benefits could be cut by an average of about $600 per month per retiree to eliminate the shortfall. If a system is not put in place to help younger workers, they will be left with retirement reductions without compensation. If we act now, younger workers can have compensation that should fully restore the necessary reductions they will face. The choice is between *reductions without compensation* and reductions with full and more than full compensation. The scare tactics of saying that the transition to a personal accounts system will reduce benefits while implying that they will not be reduced by the current *status quo* Social Security system is quite misleading. This is voodoo economics. They must be reduced in either case, but only a Social Security system with personal accounts will enable workers to avoid reductions and replace more than 40% of their pre-retirement income.

The important point to remember is that nothing like the status quo can be maintained until 2044. It is not possible to continue as is, past 2018 without making significant changes. The AARP claims only minor adjustments are needed. Senators Reid, Baucus, and Schumer and other Democrats claim that a personal retirement accounts system would reduce benefits. Well, if that argument makes any sense, it must be based on maintaining benefits at levels required by the current method and formula for calculating benefits. So

Democrats must be planning to borrow or raise taxes by $14 trillion by 2045 for paying Social Security benefits. What else will they want to raise taxes for or borrow for from future generations? But despite their claims to the contrary, raising taxes for Social Security will be very difficult by 2018 and borrowing from future generations will be morally wrong and extremely difficult to support politically. So benefit cuts after 2018 are virtually certain to happen. If we wait until workers now age 25 are nearly 40 before doing anything, they will lose out on an opportunity to have savings that adequately compensate for the reductions in benefits they will surely experience.

CHAPTER 3

The Power of Saving and Investing

Democrats believe that Social Security with its pay-as-you-go financing scheme is wonderful and must be preserved at all costs. But the consequences of socialism and socialist transfer schemes are always the same. By taking part of the rewards for producing from more productive workers and giving to many who are not producing for the presumed social welfare, the incentives to produce are reduced and less is produced. The pie of goods and services available to a society becomes smaller. When divided more equally, although shares may be more equal, most of the members have less than if the rewards for producing were not undermined and productivity were left unhindered. Over a period of many years the disparity in the amount and quality of what is produced becomes very great.

The socialist ideal is to make everyone equal with equal material possessions. It in fact tends to make everyone equally poor. Socialists depend on a principle of wrongheaded egalitarianism:

Voodoo Economics Principle #3: It is preferable for everybody to have equal shares of a very small pie than shares that are not exactly equal of a much larger pie.

The underlying belief must be that equality of material possessions is so important that it is worth having the great majority of people receive smaller shares of material possessions than they might otherwise have received. By reducing incentives to be productive, jobs are destroyed as well. This is voodoo economics.

The key concept for purposes of comparing transfer schemes with investing approaches is to determine the fraction or percentage of *pre-retirement income* that is *replaced* by pension and investment income. The pre-retirement income is the amount of income a worker earns just before retirement. It is generally believed that a retiree should expect to have at least 70% of pre-retirement income available from pensions and investments.

In order to understand whether there is any merit to the contention by Democrats that the U.S. should preserve the Social Security pay-as-you-go transfer scheme without change, it must be compared with the old-fashioned investment approach that invests money growing at compound interest. *So we will compare the benefits of a defined contribution pension plan which invests the same amount of wages or salary deducted for Social Security retirement with the benefits that same amount of money will provide under the current Social Security benefit formula.* In view of the analysis in Chapter 2 (and more detailed analysis in Chapter 5) that shows that Social Security benefits will have to be cut by 25% to 30% within about 20 years, it is particularly important to compare the benefits FICA deductions would provide if invested, to current Social Security benefits reduced by at least 25%.

This chapter will examine the probable benefits if the full 10.6% of covered payroll contributed by employee and employer were invested. There are four cases to compare with a system with personal retirement accounts:

- retiring at regular retirement with Social Security benefits at current levels

- retiring at regular retirement with Social Security benefits realistically reduced 25%

- retiring at early retirement with Social Security benefits at current levels

- retiring at early retirement with Social Security benefits realistically reduced 25%.

The last case is actually the most important since most Americans start drawing Social Security benefits at age 62.

Chapter 4 will examine the probable benefits of a mixed system that invests only the 5.3% contributed by employees and uses the 5.3% contributed by employers to fund ½ the Social Security benefits under the current formula. In this chapter and the next comparisons will be made with current benefits and with Social Security benefits reduced by 25%. The comparisons will show that the more money invested rather than provided by Social Security, the better off everyone will be. Remember, however that any system implemented will be voluntary; participants can stay under the current system.

Investing FICA Deductions Compared to Current Social Security

The FICA rate for employee deductions for OASI (Old-Age and Survivors Insurance—the retirement portion of Social Security) is 5.3% of payroll up to the maximum amount (now at $90,000). The employee portion is matched by the employer for a total of 10.6% of covered payroll. Suppose that 10.6% of one's earnings were put in an account and invested in good and relatively safe investments. What could an average worker expect? Let us look at an average worker now age 25 who retires at age 67 after working for 42 years. At retirement the worker has an average salary projected to be about $161,700 at age 65 assuming growth at the Social Security Administration intermediate assumption annual wage growth of 3.9%.[1] An average wage or salary in 2005 of $35,000 at 3.9% growth for 40 years makes the average wage about $161,700 in 2047. Examination of wage growth data for different age groups from U.S. Census Bureau data shows that wages and salaries grow at about 5 and 1/3 percent per year from age 25 to age 50 and at rates around inflation after that. If we start with a wage rate of $27,800 in 2005 and have it grow at 5.33% for 25 years to age 50 and then at 2.9% until age 65, the salary reaches $161,800 in 2045. This is a monthly income of about $13,500 at age 65. For the calculations and numbers used here consult Table A1.1 in Appendix 1.

The Social Security Administration has studied the matter and concluded that personal retirement accounts can expect to return at least 6.5% if invested in safe equities.[2] If 10.6% of the salary at each year from 25 to 67 were put in an account that experienced 6.5% interest for the remaining years until age 67 the account would grow to a total value of about $1,388,000 at age 67(see appendix Table A1.1).

> *The estimated sum would produce a monthly income at 6.5% of about $6,940 per month. One could purchase a life annuity at age 65 offering $9,250 per month for that amount. The annuity would provide 68% of the $13,500 income at retirement. Thus a 25 year old in 2005 retiring at age 67 in 2047 could expect to replace 68% of his income at retirement, if he or she were able to deposit the money contributed to FICA for retirement in a personal account.*

The percentage calculated holds for low, average, and high income workers if their wages and salaries for their lifetime grow at the rates indicated in the previous paragraph.

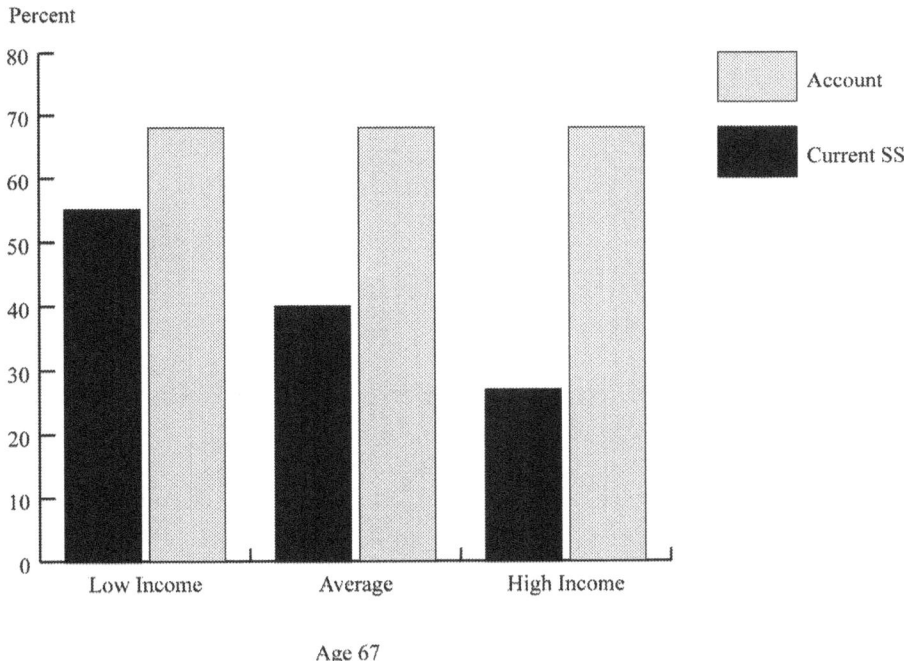

Age 67

Figure 3.1 Comparison for Regular Retirement

If a person retiring in 2047 with average income were to receive benefits under the current Social Security benefit formula, the formula is designed to provide retirees with about 40% of retirement income. For our example, earning on average $13,500 a month before retirement requires about $5100 per month to replace 40%. *Thus the calculations show that if the OASI FICA taxes were invested, a person retiring with average income could expect to do about 70% better in terms of replacement income than under our current Social Security system and benefit formula.* The comparisons are shown in Figure 3.1.

The Social Security benefit formula currently tends to replace:

- about 55% of retirement income for low income workers

- about 40% of income for average income workers

- about 27% of income from high income workers (with maximum income subject to the tax).[3]

Thus if Social Security maintains its current level of benefits, then relative to what they could expect to receive if all of their FICA OASI contributions and their employers went into a personal investment account:

- low income workers can expect to receive about 20% less from Social Security at retirement

- average income workers can expect to receive about 40% less from Social Security at retirement

- high income workers can expect to receive about 60% less from Social Security at retirement.

Some schemes for fixing Social Security advocate placing the burden of the cuts on higher income workers by indexing their benefit calculations to inflation instead of wages. But a 27% return on contributions which could very well earn 68% is already rather unfair. This is only about 40% of what could be earned if the money were put into investments.

Many workers may work for nearly 50 years. The extra years they have worked—the Social Security benefit is based on a maximum of 35 years—do not count for Social Security. But an extra 6 or 7 years of contributing to a private account before age 25 could easily add an extra 10% to the percent of replacement income. This would yield a replacement income of nearly 80% of pre-retirement income. Under the present system those extra years do nothing to increase retirement income.

It is important to understand that the estimated 68% of pre-retirement income applies to all who worked 42 years. It is based on the assumption that an average worker would experience increases of wages and salaries of about 5.33% per year to age 50 and then 2.9% to age 67 with earnings of 6.5% per year on contributions throughout the period. Even low income workers retiring at age 67 with 55% pre-retirement income under current Social Security would expect to receive more income in retirement than under current Social Security. The average worker could earn 50% more than under current Social Security. The high income worker can expect to receive more than double earnings he will receive under the current Social Security benefit formula.

> *Everyone should expect to do better and higher income workers should expect to do much better. A system with private accounts that put all the OASI money in private accounts would provide greater retirement income than current Social Security for virtually everyone and much better for higher income workers. It would be much fairer to higher income workers.*

Early Retirement

The majority of Social Security retirees elect to begin receiving their Social Security benefits at age 62 rather than waiting until their retirement age of 65 (age 67 for young workers in 2005). Using the assumption that personal accounts will earn 6.5%, we find that the full 10.6% OASI contributed for 37 years from age 25 would yield about 51% of pre-retirement income at retirement (calculated at age 62—see appendix Table A1.2). Let us compare this with retirement benefits from the current Social Security benefits formula. Under the current system:

- the low income worker retiring early in 2042 at age 62 will see his 55% replacement of pre-retirement income reduced by 30% for retiring 5 years early to a 39% replacement of pre-retirement income.

- the average worker retiring early in 2042 at age 62 would see his 40% replacement of pre-retirement income reduced by 30% for retiring 5 years early to a 28% replacement of pre-retirement income.

- the high income worker retiring early in 2042 at age 62 would see his 27% replacement of pre-retirement income reduced by 30% for retiring 5 years early to a 19% replacement of pre-retirement income.

The comparisons with current levels of Social Security benefits are shown in Figure 3.2.

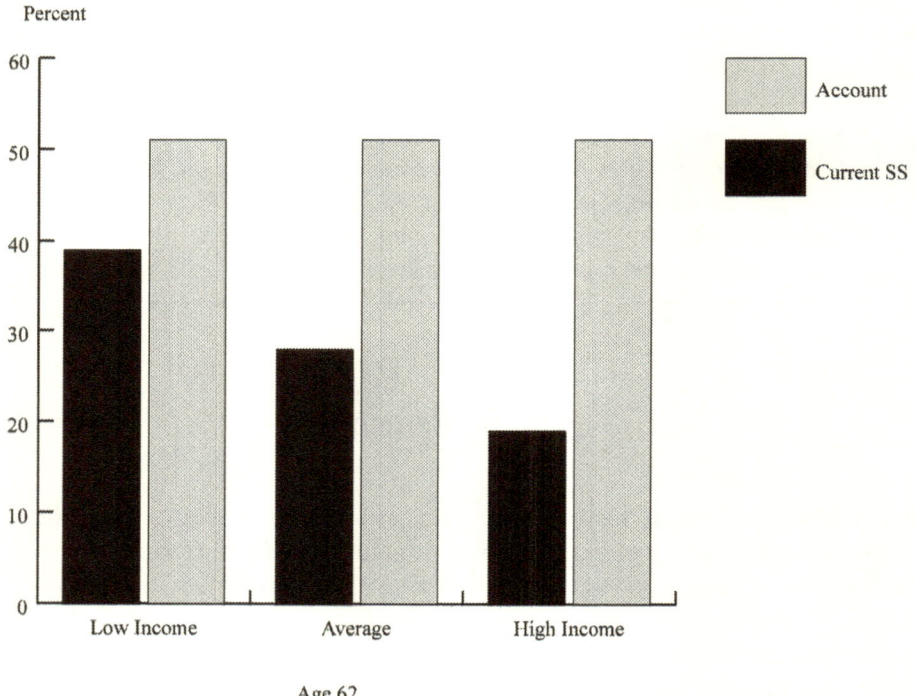

Age 62

Figure 3.2 Comparison for Early Retirement

Thus if Social Security should succeed in paying the current level of benefits by borrowing or higher taxes compared to realistic expectations if all of their FICA OASI contributions and their employer's went into personal investment accounts, early retiring

- low income workers can expect to receive about 25% less from Social Security at retirement

- average income can expect to receive about 45% less from Social Security at retirement

- high income workers about 63% less than they could expect to receive

When high income workers receive less than half what they might have received if they were permitted to put the same amount of money contributed to Social Security into an investment account, it seems that the system is beginning to treat them unfairly. Further cuts in benefits levied primarily on the higher income workers by indexing their benefits to inflation rather than to wages without doing the same for lower income workers, as has been proposed, is surely unfair.

The Comparison If Current Social Security Benefit Formulas must Cut Benefits

Thus far we have been making comparisons on the unrealistic assumption that Social Security will be maintained essentially as is, as if Democratic Senators and the AARP were right in insisting that only minor adjustments are needed.

> *The comparison thus far already shows that a transfer scheme with current Social Security benefit levels does poorly in comparison with an investment approach. The comparison is far worse for Social Security with benefit reductions that are certain to occur.*

Social Security actuaries project $400 billion Social Security retirement deficits by 2028. As we showed in Chapter 2 and as Chapter 5 will make even clearer, Social Security will require cuts on the order of 25% to 30%. The cuts will have to begin long before 2044.

Personal retirement accounts utilize the traditional way to provide for one's retirement. Consistent and regular saving and investing of an appreciable amount of money, which in turn is used by companies to build new factories or invest in equipment or training, pays off in greater production over a long period of time. The investment helps to improve the productivity of the economy and compounds returns to the investor. By utilizing the virtues of traditional investing with about 10% of one's income, a person can expect to do considerably better than current Social Security even if current benefit levels could be maintained.

> *The comparison does not count additional improvements in productivity and real wages produced by the monies invested through personal retirement accounts.*

The comparison is much worse if the current Social Security benefit formulas cannot be maintained to 2045. We can expect reductions of at least 25% for everyone retiring after about 2025. The comparison is shown in Figure 3.3. If the 25% reductions are spread evenly across income levels:

- low income workers should see a reduction from 55% of pre-retirement income to 41%

- average income workers should see a reduction from 40% of pre-retirement income to 30%

- high income workers should see a reduction from 27% of pre-retirement income to 20%.

Thus

- low income workers would receive about 40% less

- average income workers would receive about 55% less

- high income workers would receive about 70% less

than they would receive if the 10.6% OASI deduction were placed in an account earning 6.5% until retirement.

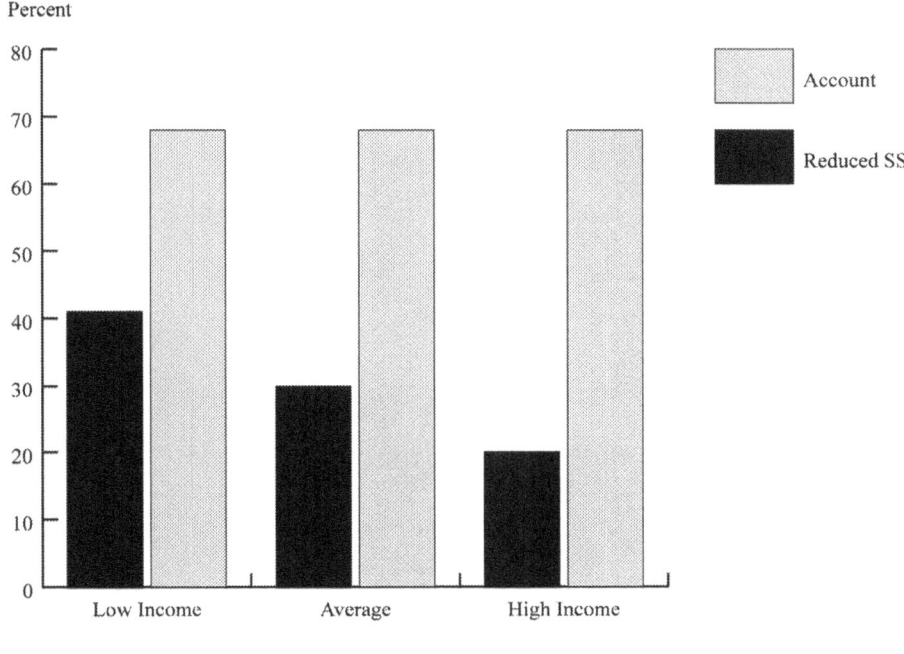

Reduced SS Age 67

Figure 3.3 Replacement Income with Social Security Reductions

The Most Important Case: Early Retirement with Social Security Benefits Cut

Most Americans apply for Social Security benefits when they are 62. This makes the early retirement comparison most important. Also the most important comparison includes Social Security benefits cut by at least 25% because the cuts are sure to happen to almost everyone under 60 today. The comparison is shown in Figure 3.4. As noted above, early retirement reduces the retirement income from investments from 68% to 51% of pre-retirement income. In the case of early retirement when the benefits are reduced by 25% and spread evenly across income levels:

- low income workers should see a reduction from 39% of pre-retirement income to 29%

- average income workers should see a reduction from 28% of pre-retirement income to 21%

- high income workers should see a reduction from 20% of pre-retirement income to 15%.

Thus

- low income workers receive 43% less

- average income workers would receive about 60% less

- high income workers would receive about 72% less

than they would receive if the 10.6% OASI deduction were placed in an account earning 6.5% until early retirement.

Percent

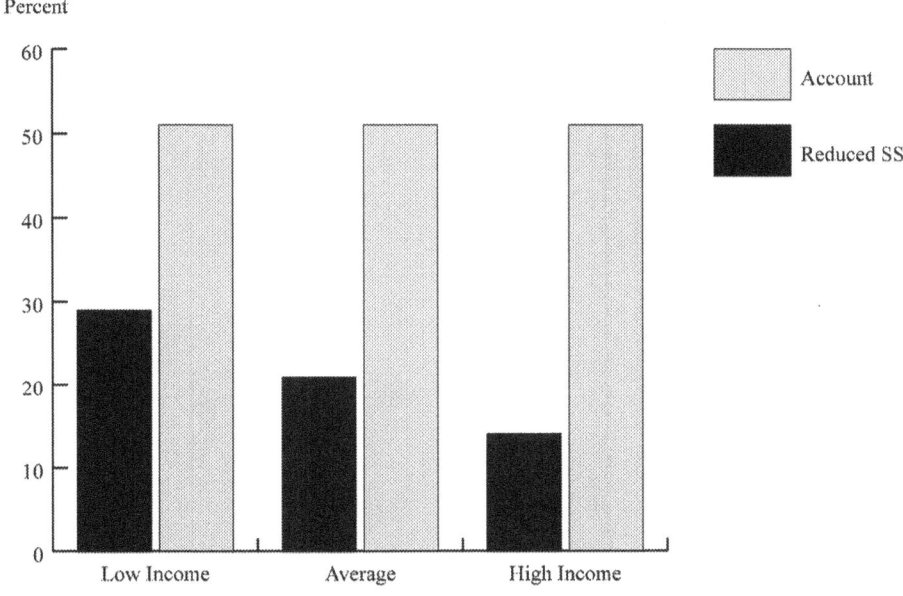

Reduced SS Age 62

Figure 3.4 Early Replacement Income with Social Security Reductions

What if the Returns are Poor?

Of course there is some risk. If returns were only 4%, the invested OASI contributions would accumulate to 40% of pre-retirement income which is just about what the current Social Security benefit formula provides for the average worker (see appendix Table A1.4). By limiting risky investments there is little likelihood, unless a major economic catastrophe occurs, of returns as bad as 4%. Of course, *such an economic catastrophe would wreak havoc with pay-as-you-go Social Security as well.*

Conclusion

The comparison in Figure 3.4 is the most important because it shows the levels of pre-retirement income replaced by Social Security benefits most retirees will probably receive, if action is postponed. The results all show that everyone could expect to do better with saving and investment of FICA (with returns of 6.5%) than with the Social Security benefits they can expect to receive in the 2030's and 2040's.

It should be evident that it is unfair to higher income participants to apply most of the benefit cuts to them when they are receiving only about 30% of the benefits they would expect to receive if all their FICA contributions went into private accounts.

Remember also that the comparison has not taken into account extra increases in wages and salaries from the increased economic growth resulting from investing the money. An extra 1% per year in economic growth would yield 40% higher incomes for nearly everyone over a 40 year period.

CHAPTER 4

What about a Half and Half System?

A Half and Half System

Chapter 3 compared the potential results for investing the 10.6% FICA contribution by employee and employer to our current pay-as-you-go Social Security system. In Chapter 6 we will examine a more potentially feasible case of a Social Security system with personal retirement accounts. In this chapter we compare a half and half system with ½ the Social Security benefits and the employee share of FICA of 5.3% contributed to personal retirement accounts. We can use the same figures used in Chapter 3. The calculations merely require cutting the Social Security benefits in half and the 10.6% investment accounts in half and adding them together. The calculations again are based on a worker now age 25 who retires at age 67 after working for 42 years. At retirement the worker will have an average salary projected to be about $161,700. The calculation assumes wage growth at the Social Security Administration intermediate assumption annual wage growth of 3.9%.[1] An average wage or salary in 2005 of $35,000 at 3.9% growth for 40 years reaches about $161,700. Wage growth data for different age groups from U.S. Census Bureau data shows wages and salaries grow at about 5 and 1/3 percent per year from age 25 to age 50 and at rates around inflation after that. If we start with a wage rate of $27,800 in 2005 and have it grow at 5.33% for 25 years to age 50 and then at 2.9% until age 65, the salary reaches $161,800 in 2045, a monthly income of about $13,500 at age 65 (see appendix Table A1.1). Calculations showed that 10.6% of income earning 6.5% yielded asssets producing 68% of pre-retirement income.[2]

This chapter will examine the probable benefits, if the 5.3% of covered payroll contributed by employees is invested and after retirement they receive ½ their Social Security benefits based on the current Social Security benefit formula. There are four cases to compare with a system with personal retirement accounts:

- retiring at regular retirement with Social Security benefits at current levels

- retiring at regular retirement with Social Security benefits realistically reduced 25%

- retiring at early retirement with Social Security benefits at current levels

- retiring at early retirement with Social Security benefits realistically reduced 25%.

The last case is the most important since most Americans start drawing Social Security benefits at age 62.

What Happens if 5.3% is Contributed to Private Accounts?

The FICA rate for employee deductions for OASI (Old-Age and Survivors Insurance the retirement portion of Social Security) is 5.3% of payroll up to the maximum amount. The employee portion is matched by the employer for a total of 10.6% of covered payroll. Suppose that 5.3% of one's earnings were put in an account and invested in good and relatively safe investments. What could an average worker expect?

First, investing 5.3% of covered payroll will produce ½ the retirement income from investing 10.6% or 34% of pre-retirement income. Second, suppose that we allowed ½ of the OASI contribution (all the employee OASI) contribution to go into private accounts. Suppose also that we cut current benefits by 1.25% for each year up to 50% so that a worker contributing 5.3% to personal retirement accounts for forty or more years would experience the maximum reduction in Social Security benefits of 50%. Then from regular Social Security and private accounts:

- low income workers would receive ½ of 55% or about 28% of pre-retirement income plus 34% from private accounts for a total of 62% of pre-retirement income

- average incomes workers would receive ½ of 40% or about 20% of pre-retirement income plus 34% of pre-retirement income for a total of about 54% of pre-retirement income

- average incomes workers would receive ½ of 27% or about 14% of pre-retirement income plus 34% of pre-retirement income for a total of about 48% of pre-retirement income.

Thus Social Security retirees could expect to do somewhat better than if the current Social Security were able to maintain its present benefit formula to the year 2047. For this case they will not do quite as well as for the case with all 10.6% OASI going to personal accounts. It is, however still considerably better than the 55%, 40%, and 27% returns for low, average, and high income workers receive under current Social Security benefit formulas. The results are shown in Figure 4.1.

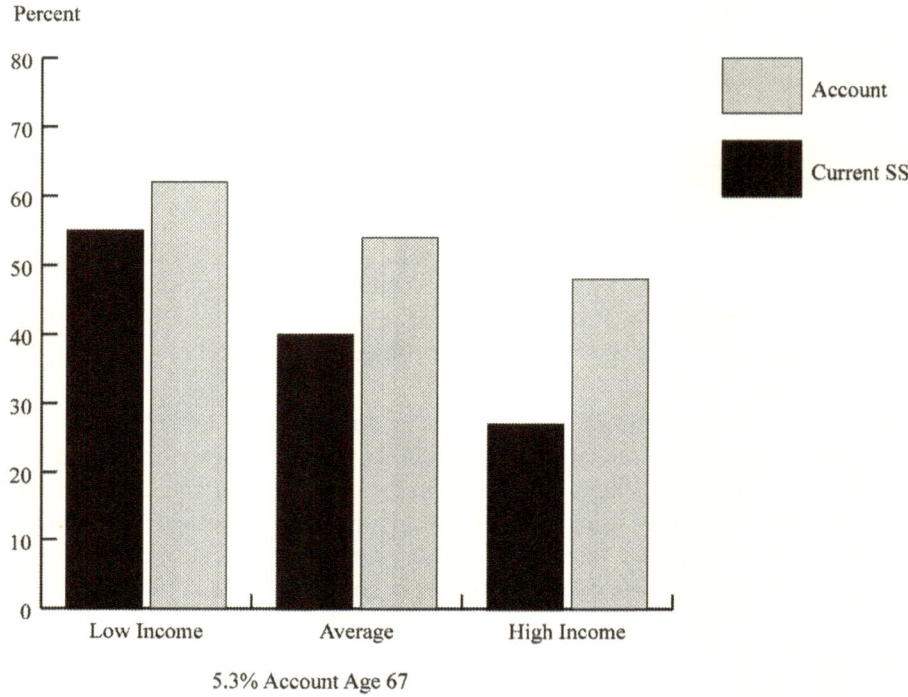

Figure 4.1 Comparison for Regular retirement with 5.3% Contributions

Figure 4.1 is based on Social Security continuing to pay benefits at current levels as implied by Democratic Senators and the AARP. However, Chapters 2 and 5 show Social Security benefits must be cut by about 30%.

Early Retirement

The most important case to examine is early retirement because most retirees elect to begin receiving Social Security at age 62. Contributions to personal accounts amounting to 5.3% of covered payroll would then yield about ½ of 51% (see Appendix table A1.2) or 25% of pre-retirement income. Workers retiring early in 2042 at age 62 will see their Social Security benefits reduced by 30% for retiring 5 years early. The Social Security benefit formula is designed to give low, average, and high income retirees about 55%, 40%, and 27%

respectively of their pre-retirement income at regular retirement. Consequently 30% reductions for early retirement yield 39%, 28%, and 19% respectively for low, average, and high income retirees.

If workers have their Social Security benefits reduced by 46% at 1.25% per year for contributions of 37 years to a personal account, workers would receive 54% of their Social Security benefits. Thus early retiring workers contributing 5.3% to personal retirement accounts would receive replacement of pre-retirement income from Social Security as follows:

- low income workers would receive .54(39%) = 21% of pre-retirement income from Social Security

- average income workers would receive .54(28%) = 15% of pre-retirement income from Social Security

- high income workers would receive .54(39%) = 10% of pre-retirement income from Social Security.

Thus if we add the 25% of pre-retirement income from the personal retirement accounts to the income received from Social Security we find that

- low income workers would receive a total of 21% + 25% = 46% of pre-retirement income

- average income workers would receive a total of 15% + 25% = 40% of pre-retirement income

- high income workers would receive a total of 10% + 25% = 35% of pre-retirement income.

Thus low income workers retiring early in 2042 at age 62 could expect an extra 7% replacement of income or 18% more benefits than current Social Security would provide if current benefit levels could be maintained. Average income workers can expect an extra 12% replacement of income which is 43% more benefits than current benefit levels of Social Security would provide. Early retirement high income workers should have an extra 16% replacement of income or 84% more benefits than provided by current Social Security benefit levels.

The comparison is shown in Figure 4.2. But remember the benefits for Social Security were not reduced as Chapters 2 and 5 demonstrate must surely occur.

Percent

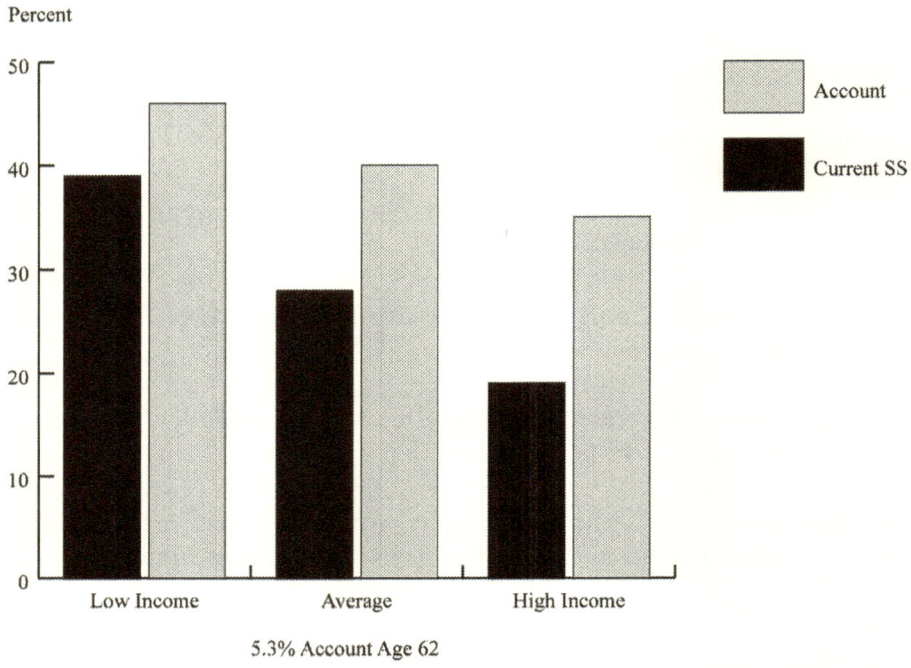

5.3% Account Age 62

Figure 4.2 Early Retirement Comparison for 5.3% Personal Accounts

Comparison If Current Social Security Benefit Formulas are Cut?

The most important comparison is the case of reduced benefits for Social Security. As pointed out in Chapter 2 the comparison is much worse for unre-formed Social Security if the current benefit formulas cannot be maintained to 2045. This will be shown with more detail in Chapter 5. If Social Security benefits are cut 30% across the board, the current levels of replacement income provided by Social Security of 55%, 40%, and 27% for low income, average income, and high income workers respectively become:

- 39% of pre-retirement income for low income workers

- 28% of pre-retirement income for average income workers

- 19% of pre-retirement income for high income workers.

The estimates for replacement income for retirement at regular retirement age from a half and half approach were:

- 62% of pre-retirement income for low income workers

- 54% of pre-retirement income for average income workers

- 48% of pre-retirement income for high income workers.

Thus

- the 62% of pre-retirement income low income workers could expect represents a 59% greater retirement income with a half and half system than they can expect if Social Security is not soon reformed

- the 54% of pre-retirement income average income workers could expect represents a 93% greater retirement income with a half and half system than they can expect if Social Security is not soon reformed

- the 48% of pre-retirement income high income workers could expect represents a 153% greater retirement income with a half and half system than they can expect if Social Security is not soon reformed.

The comparison of the half and half system with necessary reductions in Social Security benefits for retiring at retirement age 67 in 2047 is shown in Figure 4.3.

Percent

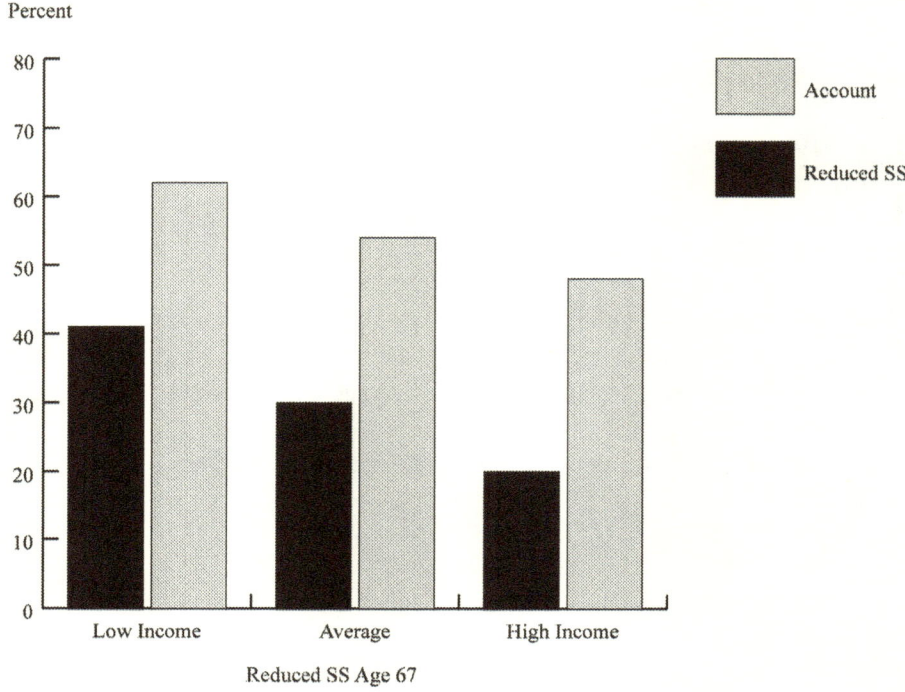

Reduced SS Age 67

Figure 4.3 Regular Retirement Compared to Reduced Social Security

The Most Important Case: Early Retirement with Reduced Social Security

Early retirement is again the primary case for comparing Social Security with reduced benefits to a system of personal retirement accounts. Retirees with a regular retirement age of 67 in 2047 who elect to receive Social Security benefits 5 years earlier in 2042 at age 62 will receive a 30% reduction for early retirement. Coupled with a 30% reduction needed to keep benefits in line with income, early retirees can expect to receive about $(.7)(.7) = .49 = 49\%$ of the Social Security benefits calculated with the current Social Security benefit formula. Since low income, average income, and high income retirees receive about 55%, 40%, and 27% of their pre-retirement income with the current Social Security benefit formula, retirees retiring at age 62 in 2042 can expect that

- low income retirees will receive about .49(55%) = 27% of their pre-retirement income

- average income retirees will receive about .49(40%) = 20% of their pre-retirement income

- high income retirees will receive about .49(27%) = 13% of their pre-retirement income.

If we move to a Social Security system with a large part of FICA contributed to personal retirement accounts coupled with cuts of about ½ in Social Security benefits, reducing Social Security benefits will not become necessary. Our calculation of the replacement income for early retirees from ½ of Social Security and a 5.3% of employee wage income contribution to personal retirement accounts presented above showed:

- 46% of pre-retirement income for low income workers

- 40% of pre-retirement income for average income workers

- 35% of pre-retirement income for high income workers.

Thus

- the 46% of pre-retirement income low income workers could expect for early retirement represents a 70% greater retirement income with a half and half system than they can expect if Social Security is not soon reformed

- the 40% of pre-retirement income average income workers could expect for early retirement represents a 100% greater retirement income with a half and half system than they can expect if Social Security is not soon reformed

- the 35% of pre-retirement income high income workers could expect for early retirement represents a 169% greater retirement income with a half and half system than they can expect if Social Security is not soon reformed.

The comparison of the half and half system with necessary reductions in Social Security benefits for early retirement at age 62 in 2042 is shown in Figure 4.4.

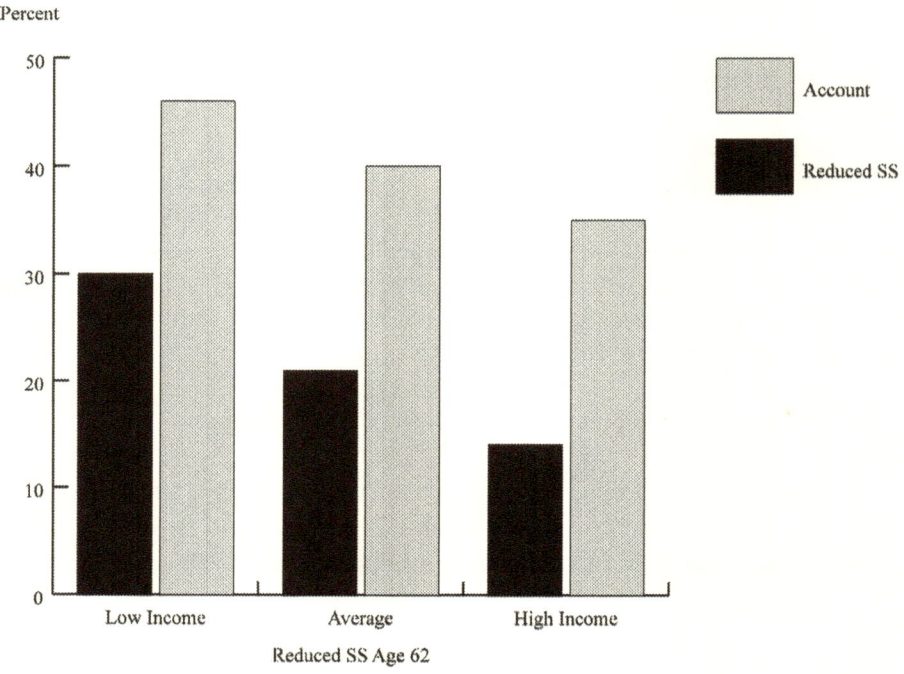

Figure 4.4 Early Retirement and Reduced Social Security

What If a Person's Personal Account gets a Better Return?

Thus far we have presented estimates of replacement income at retirement based on returns from personal retirement accounts realizing a 6.5% return. But what happens if returns are better or worse? It is simplest for purposes of understanding to return to the case analyzed in the previous chapter which used 10.6% of covered wage income as the contribution to the personal retirement accounts. With a basically unreformed Social Security system retirees will do no better than receive the income dictated by the current Social Security benefit formula. In fact a reduction must occur so they will do worse.

However, for a reformed Social Security system with personal retirement accounts it is possible for retirees to do better than we have represented in this chapter and the previous chapter. A few simple calculations can give us an idea of the possibilities. Let us begin by considering the extent to which retirees might do better if their returns exceed 6.5%.

The 68% replacement of pre-retirement income estimate was based on a 6.5% return used by Social Security actuaries for expected long-term returns on equity investments. Higher returns are quite possible given the fact that over the long term the stock market increases over 8% per year. If we consider the case, as in Chapter 3, of 10.6% of covered payroll deposited in personal retirement accounts, a 7% return would accumulate $1.55 million in cash and provide 77% of pre-retirement income (see appendix Table A1.3). The historic total returns in the U.S. stock market from 1790 to 1985 have averaged 8.2% per year, so it is very likely that if people were allowed to invest their entire 10.6% FICA OASI funds in equities excluding very risky investments, they might approach realizing nearly 100% of their pre-retirement income if they invested all the money they currently pay for Social Security retirement. This would be a much better deal than the current average Social Security replacement of 40% of pre-retirement income and certainly much better than replacement of about 28% of pre-retirement income our young people will face if Senators Reid, Baucus, Schumer and the AARP have their way.

Democrats want to preserve Social Security with its pay-as-you-go financing scheme at all costs because it is so wonderful. Socialist transfer schemes take part of the rewards for producing from more productive workers and give them to many who are not producing. Consequently the incentives to produce are reduced and less is produced. The pie of goods and services becomes smaller. When divided more equally, although shares may be more equal, most of the members have less because rewards for producing were undermined. Socialists depend on the principle:

Voodoo Economics Principle #3: It is preferable for everybody to have equal shares of a very small pie than shares that are not exactly equal from a much larger pie.

The socialist ideal to make everyone equal with equal material possessions tends to make everyone equally poor. The underlying belief must be that equality of material possessions is so important that it is worth having the great majority of people get smaller shares of material possessions than they might otherwise have obtained. This is voodoo economics.

What If a Person's Personal Account gets a Poor Return?

It is possible that returns on personal retirement accounts could be very poor although this is highly unlikely for an extended period of time like 40 years. It is hard to imagine that returns could be worse than 4%. Returns of 4% for 42 years, if 10.6% of covered payroll is deposited in personal retirement accounts, would produce 41% of pre-retirement income when retiring at age 67. Since reductions of at least 25% in Social Security benefits will be unavoidable, the following bar charts indicate the relative returns. The results are shown in Figure 4.5. Even 4% returns in a half and half system would produce better retirement income for everyone than Social Security will.

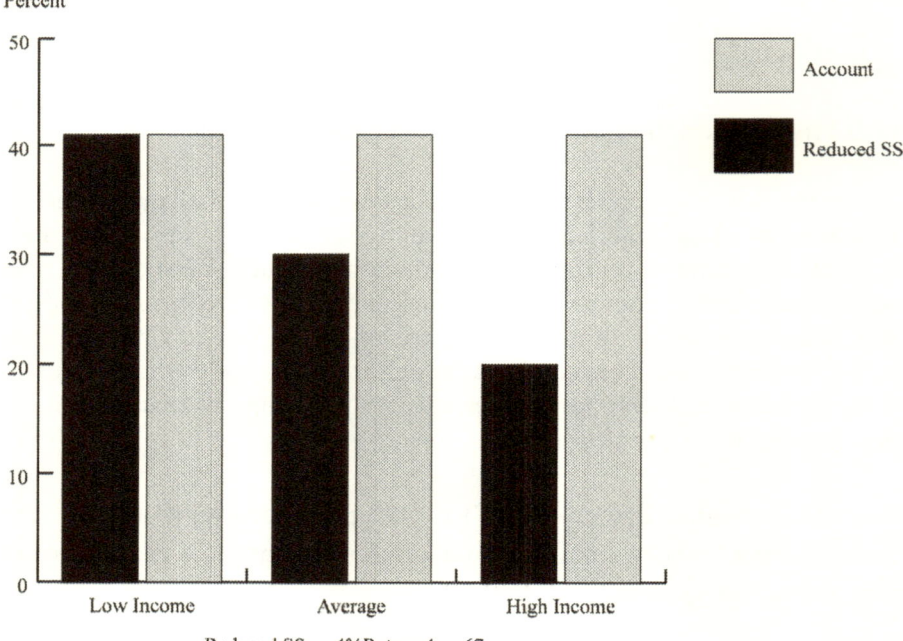

Reduced SS vs 4%Return Age 67

Figure 4.5 Comparison with Very Poor Returns

Returns of 4% for 37 years would produce 32% of pre-retirement income when retiring at age 62. When we make the same comparison with 4% returns for early retirement at age 62 we obtain Figure 4.6:

Percent

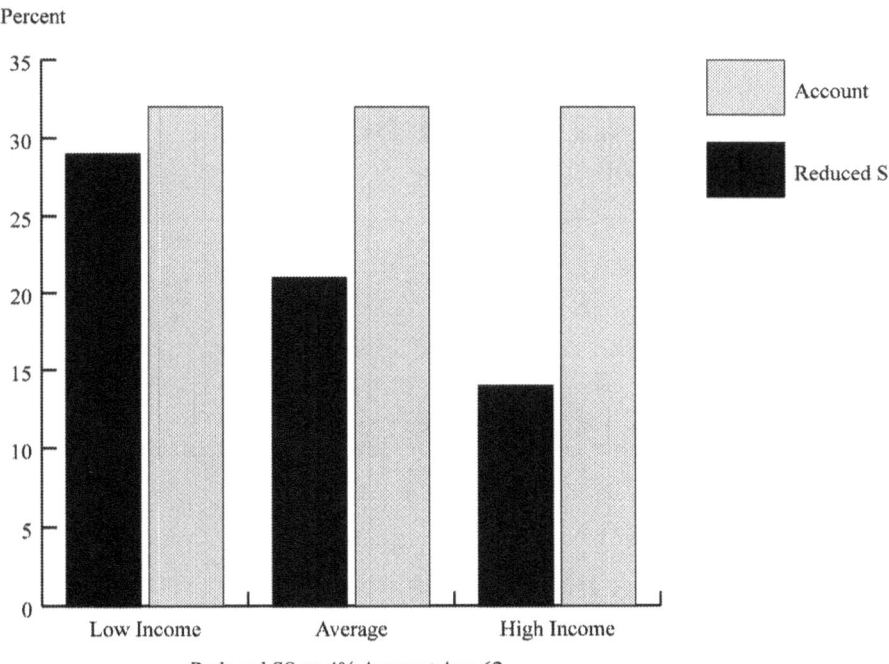

Reduced SS vs 4% Account Age 62

Figure 4.6 Early Retirement Comparison with Very Poor Returns

Conclusion

The results all show that even with returns of only 4% Social Security recipients can expect to have greater income with saving and investment of FICA than with the Social Security benefits they can expect to receive in the 2030's and 2040's. With returns of 6.5% as estimated by the Social Security Administration the results are better for personal retirement accounts than Social Security could provide even if one could maintain benefits at current levels. Retirees may very well do much better even with limitations on allowed investments.

CHAPTER 5

The Marvelous Social Security "Trust Fund"

In Chapter 2 we examined current Social Security from a theoretical stand-point showing why for the long term foreseeable future we can expect to replace no more than 25 to 30 percent of pre-retirement income. In this chapter we will reach the same conclusions by developing the analysis of Social Security actuaries.

Everything is Fine until 2044

Democrats are claiming that the Social Security Trust Funds guarantee that Social Security is "solvent" until 2044. They imply that it will not be necessary to cut benefits before 2044. They also imply that no significant funding changes are necessary. The AARP has TV ads claiming only minor adjustments are necessary. In this chapter we shall see how minor the adjustments are. Presumably, according to Democrats nothing really needs to be done until 2044. So let us look at the best estimates of the future behavior of the Social Security system as provided by Social Security actuaries.

Every year the Trustees of Social Security publish a report indicating the status of the Social Security system.[1] We will use the analysis of the current and future state of Social Security in the 2004 Trustees Report produced by the actuaries of Social Security.[2] Short term projections for ten years are made as well as projections 75 years into the future. The projections are based on three sets of economic and demographic parameters. The three projections are believed to be pessimistic, intermediate, and optimistic. Unfortunately, the long term projections do not show values in terms of dollars, but as percentages of covered payroll. By analyzing the status in terms of percentage of covered payroll instead of dollars, the Social Security Administration, the AARP, and Democratic Senators are able to keep the public confused about Social Security. In order to clarify matters I have taken the numbers from the 2004 Trustees Report for the intermediate assumptions and converted them from covered payroll to dollars.

> *By projecting annual wage increases at the annual 3.9% rate used for the Social Security actuaries' intermediate assumptions and by making some minor adjustments for growth in the labor force based on the intermediate assumption projections, I was able to compute projected covered payroll in dollars. My computations must be very close to the numbers obtained by the Social Security Administration actuaries, because my figures show the so-called OASI "Trust Fund" being exhausted in 2044 the same year the actuaries computed (see Table IVB3).[3] The 2005 Trustees Report did not show sufficient difference from the numbers calculated to warrant recalculating them.*

Table 5.1 shows the key results for the years 2017 to 2045 (the years 2005 to 2016 are covered in Appendix 2). The table is based on the Social Security system continuing as is until the year 2045 *with all benefit shortfalls being paid by borrowing from the public.* After all, Democrats have been claiming the system is "solvent" until then. For the years up to 2017 we will assume the Social Security system remains as is with income exceeding benefit payments by a good margin. We will assume the annual surplus will continue to be spent on non-retirement related government programs. Consequently an amount corresponding to the surplus must be added with interest to the treasury bonds in the "Trust Fund." Based on the actuaries' projections, the "Trust Fund" will accumulate about $4.7 trillion in special Treasury bonds by 2017.

> *The key features to note in Table 5.1 are found in Columns 4, 6, and 7. Column 4 shows the increasing deficits which exceed $500 billion annually by 2032 and $1 trillion by 2045. Column 6 shows "Trust Fund" values which increase to $6.6 trillion in 2028 and then decrease to zero by 2044. Column 7 is the most significant because it shows the national debt caused solely by Social Security deficits that will accumulate. If not reduced by cutting benefits or increasing taxes the national debt from Social Security payments will accumulate to $14 trillion by 2045.*

Year (1)	Benefits Paid $Billion (2)	FICA (OASI) +SS Taxes $Billion (3)	Surplus/ Deficit[a] $Billion (4)	Trust Fund Interest[b] $Billion (5)	SS Trust Fund Bonds[c] $Billion (6)	National Debt for SS[d] $Billion (7)	Total SS Debt[e] $Billion (8)
2017	894	913	19	258	4723	0	4723
2018	960	955	-5	274	4992	5	4997
2019	1030	999	-31	290	5250	36	5287
2020	1105	1043	-62	305	5493	98	5591
2021	1179	1089	-90	319	5721	188	5910
2022	1258	1137	-121	332	5932	310	6241
2023	1341	1186	-155	344	6121	465	6585
2024	1429	1238	-191	355	6285	656	6940
2025	1522	1291	-231	365	6418	887	7305
2026	1614	1347	-267	372	6523	1154	7677
2027	1712	1405	-307	378	6595	1461	8056
2028	1814	1466	-348	382	6629	1809	8438
2029	1922	1528	-394	384	6620	2203	8823
2030	2037	1593	-444	384	6560	2646	9207
2031	2143	1662	-481	381	6460	3127	9587
2032	2254	1733	-521	375	6313	3649	9962
2033	2371	1808	-564	366	6115	4213	10328
2034	2494	1885	-609	355	5861	4822	10683
2035	2625	1966	-659	340	5542	5480	11022
2036	2741	2049	-692	321	5171	6173	11344
2037	2865	2138	-727	300	4744	6899	11644
2038	2994	2228	-766	275	4254	7665	11919
2039	3128	2324	-804	247	3697	8469	12166
2040	3267	2423	-844	214	3067	9313	12380
2041	3403	2525	-878	178	2367	10191	12558
2042	3546	2632	-915	137	1589	11106	12695
2043	3694	2743	-951	92	731	12057	12787
2044	3850	2858	-991	42	0	13048	13048
2045	4010	2979	-1030	0	0	14079	14079

[a] Column 2 shows the projected benefits that must be paid if the benefit payments continue to be calculated as they are currently with no reductions. Column 3 shows the projected income under the intermediate assumptions with nearly all the income coming from FICA OASI collections and a small part coming from IRS collections of taxes on SS benefits. Column 4 represents the surplus or deficit calculated by subtracting the second column benefits paid entry from the third column income entry.

[b] Column 6 shows the amount of money in the Social Security "Trust Fund." So the entries in Column 5 are 5.8% of the amount in the "Trust Fund" in column 6 for the previous year. The interest is added to the entry in Column 6 for the previous year.

[c] The Column 6 entry for the current year must include the deficit in Column 4 as well as the interest in Column 5. When "Trust Funds" are turned in to cover benefits the amount of the bonds cashed in must be subtracted from Column 6.

[d] Column 7 represents the debt owed to the public due to Social Security. The Treasury's Office of Public Debt divides Federal Debt into two main categories: the National Debt owed to the public (now about $4.5 trillion) and interagency debt owed by federal agencies to other agencies (currently about $2.8 trillion of which $1.5 trillion represents the Social Security "Trust Fund"). The total Federal Debt is about $7.3 trillion. Currently none of the official National Debt of $4.5 trillion is due to Social Security. This condition will continue until 2018 (with a "Trust Fund" over $4.7 trillion) when the U.S. Treasury will have to borrow an amount equal to the deficit in Column 4 to cover "Trust Fund" bonds turned by the Social Security Administration to pay benefits. This cancels an equal amount of "Trust Funds." We are assuming that the "Trust Fund" bonds are paid from funds borrowed from the public, so Column 7 indicates the accumulated National Debt owed to the public that results from Social Security.

[e] Since the "Trust Funds" are not assets but debt and part of the total Federal debt, Column 8 adds the "Trust Fund" debt to the Column 7 debt owed to the public for the total Federal debt due to Social Security.

Table 5.1 Social Security Debt Accumulation 2017 to 2045

The table entries begin with the year 2017 since that is the last year that Social Security OASI runs a surplus and ends with entries for the year 2045 the year after the "Trust Funds" are exhausted. Democrats and the AARP claim that only minor adjustments are needed and that the system is solvent until 2044 so we will assume that no reductions in benefits will occur. It is evident that the annual deficits begin small and increase to $444 billion in 2030 and $991 billion by 2044. The values in Figure 5.1 come from Columns 4 and 7 of Table 5.1. Figure 5.1 shows the annual deficit at five year intervals and the cumulative national debt from Social Security owed to the public at the same intervals.

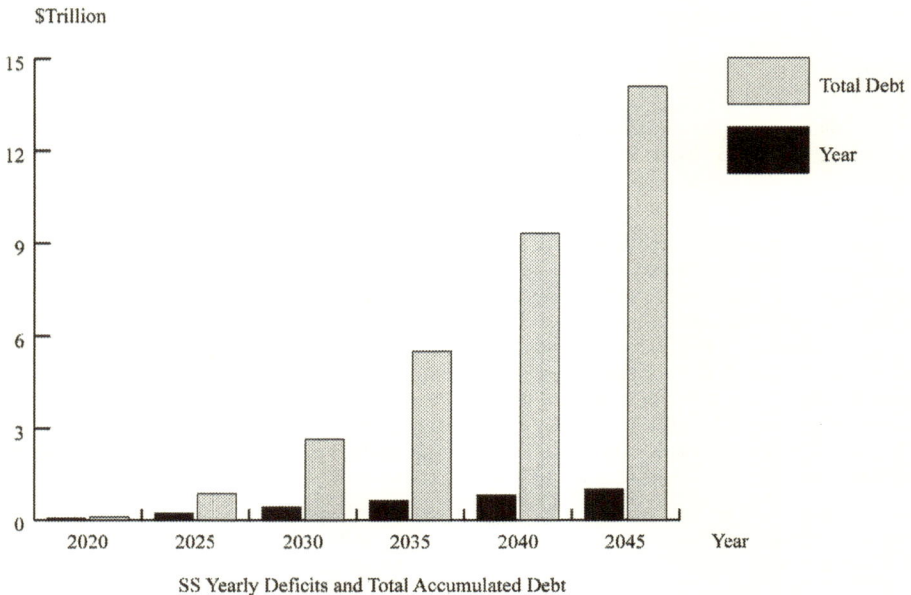

SS Yearly Deficits and Total Accumulated Debt

Figure 5.1 Portion of Federal Deficits and National Debt from Social Security

In 2045 the annual deficit exceeds $1 trillion and by 2060 exceeds $2 trillion (see Table 5.2 below). These are the estimates of the Social Security actuaries. Democrats claim that current Social Security is solvent until the 2044 period when Social Security deficits approach $1 trillion. We see also that if the money to cover the deficits is borrowed from the public instead of raising taxes or reducing benefits, the national debt owed to the public will increase by $13 trillion from 2018 to 2044. We obviously have encountered voodoo economics again. Our fourth principle of voodoo economics is:

Voodoo Principle #4: Pension systems running annual deficits approaching $1 trillion (and increasing the National Debt by that amount) are "solvent."

Senators Reid, Baucus, and Schumer claim nothing need be done before 2044 but a few minor adjustments. Perhaps "solvency" is another "Washington speak" term like 'budget cuts' where increasing a $100 billion department budget to $103 billion instead of $104 billion the next year is a "budget cut." However claiming Social Security is "solvent" until 2044 is far more egregious and deceitful than other "Washington speak."

How the "Trust Fund" Actually Works

During the years from 1983 to 2004 less than $1 trillion in surplus FICA OASI contributions were received. With interest the "Trust Fund" has accumulated to $1.5 trillion in 2005. The surplus contributions and income from 2005 to 2017 will amount to over $1 trillion. Adding interest will bring the "Trust Fund" to about $4.72 trillion in 2017. The Intermediate assumptions peg interest rates for the "Trust Fund" at 5.8%.[4] But some of the "Trust Fund" bonds must be turned in to cover the deficit.

> *This is a very important point to understand. The "Trust Fund" bonds are IOU's. Extra monies collected by FICA taxes not needed to pay current retirement benefits were spent by the government on non-retirement consumption.*

We see that the "Trust Fund" continues to accumulate until it reaches $6.63 trillion in 2028. After this the deficit for each year begins to exceed the interest earned for the year and the "Trust Fund" begins to decline. With deficits increasing and interest declining, the "Trust Fund" declines slowly and then very quickly, disappearing entirely in 2044.

Here is some real economic voodoo. Everything is fine until 2044 because the Social Security deficits can be covered by Trust Fund "assets." From what has been said it seems that Democrats would have everyone believe that the "Trust Fund" is some kind of asset. Here we have a fifth principle of Voodoo Economics:

Voodoo Economics Principle #5: Money borrowed from another Federal Agency and spent is an asset.

This is a peculiar "asset" because every bond cashed in must be replaced by increases in national debt or new taxes. Of course, from the standpoint of the actuaries and administrators of the Social Security Administration the special Treasury bonds they hold in the Social Security Trust Fund are an asset. The U.S. Constitution requires that Treasury Bonds be repaid. *When the Social Security Administration finds that FICA OASI taxes are insufficient to fund retirement benefits, then they will cover the shortfall by presenting bonds in the "Trust Fund" to the U.S. Treasury for payment.* They then conclude that Social Security OASI is "solvent" until 2044 because the projected FICA OASI taxes plus accumulated "Trust Funds" will be sufficient to pay projected benefits until 2044.

What Happens when the U.S. Treasury Department Covers Cashed "Trust Fund" Bonds?

Beginning in 2018 Social Security OASI retirement will begin running deficits and the Social Security Administration will have to begin cashing in "Trust Fund" bonds to pay all the benefits.

> *At that time, that is in 2018, and not in 2044, the Treasury Department will have to find funds from which to pay for the cashed in bonds. At that time, not in 2044, Congress will be forced to pass legislation that will provide a way to provide the money for paying off the "Trust Fund" bonds.*

There are only three options to provide the necessary funds: reduce the benefits paid to retirees, raise taxes, or borrow the money again from the public increasing the official national debt. Let us consider the three options.

Option #1: Reduce Benefits

Initially in 2018 and the first few years of deficits the deficits will be small, so it is unlikely that Congress will reduce benefits for a while. But by 2031 the deficits will approach $500 billion per year and there will be about 70 million Social Security retirees. Using very rough calculations, on average about $7000 per year per retiree or about $600 per month per retiree produces an average deficit of $500 billion. Cutting benefits for retirees by about $600 per month on average would solve the problem. Taxes would not have to be raised nor would any money have to be borrowed from the public. We might note that average Social Security benefit payments for people currently retiring run about $1200 to $1300 per month. After 25 years of cost of living adjustments assumed to be about 2.8% per year (the Social Security Administration's intermediate assumptions), average benefit payments for workers retiring now would be about $2500 in 2030.[5] An average $600 reduction would be a cut of about 25%.

Cutting benefits is actually the most likely action Congress will be forced to take by about 2025 by the time most baby boomers will have retired. It will certainly be long before 2044. The reason is simple. By then there will be about 2 workers for every retired worker.[6] Borrowing and passing the costs on to future generations will be politically difficult and surely immoral.

But of course Senators Harry Reid, Max Baucus, and Charles Schumer assure us that everything is fine. Social Security is solvent until 2044. The AARP's ads claim only minor adjustments are needed. So following Voodoo Economics Principle #4 indicating Social Security is solvent even though it is running annual deficits of nearly a trillion dollars, we have assumed for the time being that option #1 will not be taken.

Option #2: Raise Revenues by Taxation

The Social Security shortfall in income could be solved by raising FICA or general income taxes. Why raise taxes to raise benefits? Overall nothing is really accomplished by so doing. The burden of taxation could be levied on the upper income taxpayers which would reduce investment and economic growth. Taxation represents money that would be available for investment by companies. The potential investment money is diverted for payment of retirement benefits and therefore mostly consumed, causing reduced investment and economic growth. It makes more sense to cut benefits which would not do this. But Senators Harry Reid, Max Baucus, and Charles Schumer assure us that everything is fine. Social Security is solvent until 2044 and the AARP's ads claim only minor adjustments are needed. Presumably we will not need to raise taxes.

Option #3: Borrow the Money

So if we are not to reduce benefits or raise taxes we must borrow the money. The interest on the "Trust Fund" is shown in Column 5. It is paid by adding bonds to "Trust Funds." When the debt to the public accumulates as shown in Column 7, additional interest payments to the public must be made. Thus when the national debt due to Social Security reaches $2.65 trillion in 2030 interest payments on that debt (at an assumed 5.8% interest rate) will be about $150 billion per year and by 2045 the interest payments due to Social Security borrowing of over $14 trillion would run over $800 billion per year. (Of course, because of inflation, $14 trillion in 2045 is equivalent to about $4 trillion in current 2005 dollars. Nevertheless, Democrats complain about the harm done by comparable increases in national debt during the Reagan years.) The $150 billion in interest and later $800 billion represent extra costs that must be covered by increased taxation or increases in deficits of the Federal Government.

It is evident from observing Columns 7 and 8 that if Social Security benefits are not cut nor taxes raised, the Social Security debt represented by the "Trust

Fund" from 2018 to 2044 will be converted to National Debt held by the public reaching $14 trillion by 2045. Moreover, if the shortfall continues to be borrowed, it would rapidly reach $37 trillion by 2060. See Table 5.2.

The Years 2046 to 2060

The main conclusion is that the current system will require significant cuts on the order of 30% or borrowing or taxation of $14 trillion by 2045. But if Social Security is reformed and most people elect to take the retirement accounts, those who elect to remain under regular Social Security and those who elect the personal retirement accounts will do as well or better than if Social Security were able to maintain its current benefits. We shall see this in Chapter 6. Moreover, if the current system were retained and benefits were not cut, the increased borrowing or burden of taxes would accumulate to $14 trillion by 2045. The annual deficits reach $1 trillion by 2045 and then the costs of Social Security explode. By 2060 the borrowing or increased taxes would total $37 trillion.

Year	Benefit %Cov Pay[a]	Benefits[b] $Billion	Income %Cov Pay[c]	Income[d] $Billion	Deficit[e]	Nat Debt from SS[f]
2045	15.37	4010	11.42	2979	-1030	14079
2046	15.38	4180	11.42	3104	-1076	15155
2047	15.38	4354	11.42	3233	-1121	16276
2048	15.39	4539	11.43	3371	-1168	17444
2049	15.39	4729	11.43	3512	-1217	18661
2050	15.40	4930	11.43	3659	-1271	19931
2051	15.44	5148	11.43	3811	-1337	21268
2052	15.48	5375	11.43	3969	-1406	22675
2053	15.52	5613	11.44	4137	-1476	24150
2054	15.56	5861	11.44	4309	-1552	25702
2055	15.59	6116	11.44	4488	-1628	27330
2056	15.64	6390	11.44	4674	-1716	29046
2057	15.69	6676	11.45	4872	-1804	30850
2058	15.75	6978	11.45	5073	-1905	32756
2059	15.81	7295	11.46	5288	-2007	34763
2060	15.87	7625	11.46	5506	-2119	36882

[a]"Cov Pay" represents the total covered payroll, that is the portion of wages and salaries that is subject to FICA deductions for paying retirement benefits. Column 2 indicates the amount of benefits that will need to be paid for a given year relative to the total covered payroll.

[b]The Benefits projected to be paid out is the Column 2 percentage of covered payroll times estimated covered payroll. Estimated covered payroll is given in Table A.1 in Appendix 1.

[c]"Cov Pay" represents the total covered payroll, that is wages and salaries subject to FICA deductions for paying retirement benefits. Column 4 indicates the amount of income that is expected for a given year rela-

tive to the total covered payroll. The amount is the 10.6% FICA employee and employer pay plus taxes paid on Social Security benefits.

dThe Income projected to be received is the Column 4 percentage of covered payroll times estimated covered payroll. Estimated covered payroll is given in Table A.1 in Appendix 1.

eThe Deficit is Income – Benefits or Column 5 – Column 3 in Billions of Dollars.

fColumn 7 represents the Debt owed to the Public from Social Security only if the annual deficits are covered by borrowing rather than increased taxes or benefit cuts. The entry in Column 7 is increased from the previous year by the amount of debt in Column 6.

Table 5.2 Unreformed Social Security without Benefit Cuts or Tax Increases

The size of the shortfall of income relative to benefits to be paid is readily estimated by dividing Column 2 by Column 4 or Column 3 by Column 5 of Table 5.2. The projections for 2045 indicate that 11.42/15.37 = .74 or the income in 2045 is expected to cover 74% of benefits in 2045. By 2060 the ratio is expected to fall to 11.46/15.87 = .72 or 72%. The ratio falls below 70% by 2080. Thus, in order to be solvent the current system of Social Security by 2045 requires either benefit cuts on the order of 30% or increases in borrowing and taxes on the order of $14 trillion. If benefits are cut Social Security would not cause net disinvestments. But if full benefits are paid by borrowing or increased taxes, net investment will be reduced by $14 trillion by 2045. In the first case Americans in their twenties and thirties will have benefits cut significantly without compensation.

The National Debt

Currently the national debt owed to the public is about $5 trillion. Another $3 trillion is owed to Federal Agencies including $1.5 trillion for the Social Security "Trust Fund." We do not know how much additional public debt will accumulate in future years. No doubt there will be additional national debt accumulating from government deficits. It is likely deficits for Medicare and other government programs may accumulate. Let us represent by D the amount of Federal public debt that will be incurred in the future other than for Social Security. Let T be the total amount of extra taxes raised to cover Social Security benefit payments and B the total reductions for cutting Social Security benefit payments. Then $A = D - T - B$ represents the additional debt added to the national debt from 2005 to the year indicated in Table 5.3. Let B be additional Federal interagency debt added from 2005 to the year indicated in Table 5.3. Table 5.3 indicates the amounts of Federal debt in alternating columns with the existence of a Social Security "Trust Fund" and the second case without a Social Security "Trust Fund" having existed. 'A' and 'B' do not represent the same amounts if they are in different rows of the table.

Year	Trust Fund	Trust Fund (No Trust Fund Case)	Other Federal Interagency Debt	Other Federal Interagency Debt (No Trust Fund Case)	National Debt to Public[a]	National Debt to Public[a] (No Trust Fund Case)
2005	$1.5 Trillion	0	$1.5 Trillion	$1.5 Trillion	$5 Trillion	$5 Trillion
2017	$4.7 Trillion	0	$1.5 Trillion + B	$1.5 Trillion + B	$5 Trillion + A	$5 Trillion + A
2030	$6.6 Trillion	0	$1.5 Trillion + B	$1.5 Trillion + B	$7.6 Trillion + A	$7.6 Trillion + A
2045	0	0	$1.5 Trillion + B	$1.5 Trillion + B	$19.1 Trillion + A	$19.1 Trillion + A
2060	0	0	$1.5 Trillion + B	$1.5 Trillion + B	$41.9 Trillion + A	$41.9 Trillion + A

[a]The current $5 trillion National Debt plus National Debt incurred from projected Social Security deficits and other borrowing.

Table 5.3 Federal Debt with and without the Existence of a Social Security "Trust Fund"

> *From observation of the last four columns of Table 5.3, we see that the existence of the so-called "Trust Fund" does not make ONE IOTA OF DIFFERENCE. The money to cover the Social Security deficits will have to be borrowed from the public (or raised by taxes) whether a "Trust Fund" exists or not. The National Debt due to Social Security of $14.08 trillion in 2045 will be that amount whether the "Trust Fund" existed or not. The "Trust Fund" is just a device to confuse and fool the public into thinking assets have accumulated when this has not in fact occurred. The "Trust Fund" is composed of IOUs for FICA tax funds borrowed by the Treasury and spent. Congress must cover the "IOUs" by borrowing or taxing or reducing benefits.*

The impending shortfalls represent an unfunded liability. An unfunded liability is the amount of money that a pension type of fund needs to have invested now to cover future benefits that cannot be funded by assets on hand and future expected income. The current unfunded liability for Social Security is estimated at about $12 trillion.[7] As we argue in Chapter 9, the unfunded liability for Social Security should be counted as part of the national debt because benefits have been promised to American workers. As Table 5.3 demonstrates the unfunded liability although not currently represented will show up on the books unless the deficits are covered by increased taxes or benefit cuts.

What Happens If We Postpone Action?

As I have pointed out, by 2018 decisions to deal with funding of Social Security will have to be made. *When the Social Security Administration presents its special Treasury "Trust Fund" bonds for repayment in order to pay retirement benefits, the Treasury Department will either have to borrow money from the public or Congress must raise taxes or cut Social Security retirement benefits.*

I argue that borrowing will not have political support. Although borrowing is a politically expedient approach much of the electorate will agree that we cannot continue to pass costs on to future generations. Nor will raising FICA taxes have much support. *Why raise taxes to maintain benefits rather than just reduce benefits?* Approximately the same gap will occur in either case, but raising taxes will tend to reduce earnings growth. Democrats will no doubt push for raising taxes on higher income workers so that they can redistribute the income earned by upper middle income people to people with low incomes. However, Social Security is already rather unfair to higher income workers who get very little back for the amounts they contribute. A greater burden on them is quite unfair. Moreover raising taxes slows growth in the economy. Perhaps by then enough people will understand this so that they will not cause the economy to tank.

There is actually a fourth possible option. If the money is borrowed eventually there will be pressure on the Federal Reserve to print money and inflate the economy. Inflation is a hidden tax that people often fail to perceive. They do not realize that their assets are disappearing. The Federal Reserve strongly resists inflation. At some point however if debt accumulates there will be pressure to print money. Inflation will reduce the value of the benefits and reduce the value of debt.

These considerations indicate that benefit cuts to bring Social Security income and benefit payments into agreement is the logical approach. The Social Security pay-as-you-go transfer scheme is simply incapable of replacing more than about ¼ of pre-retirement income on average. The choice is between reductions in benefits without compensation and reductions in benefits with compensation. Fairness requires reductions in benefits with compensation that makes up for the reductions. Recognizing reality and making appropriate accommodations is the right approach. This can be accomplished by implementing Social Security with personal retirement accounts.

Democrats have been castigating President Bush for pushing personal retirement accounts because this means cuts in benefits. They then claim that Social Security is solvent until 2044 implying that if we do not do anything, there will not be any cuts in Social Security benefits. However, as we have seen Social Security with its current benefit formula is not sustainable beyond 2018 without beginning to borrow or raise taxes significantly.

The fact is that there are really two basic choices: a) keep pay-as-you-go Social Security in its present form but cut the benefits about 25 to 30 percent before 2030 or b) allow contributions from FICA taxes to personal retirement accounts and cut benefits proportional to the number of years contributing to a personal retirement account. With the first option the bulk of the cuts could be levied on high income workers. One way to do this is to index the benefits of higher income workers to inflation rather than wages. This is not at all fair. The benefit formula is already highly skewed in favor of low income workers. Any benefit cuts should be equal across the board. Higher income workers already get a very poor deal from Social Security.

For the second option those who contributed 35 years or more to personal retirement accounts would probably have their regular Social Security benefits cut in about half in return for having the accounts. This approach is greatly preferable because the first approach cuts benefits without any compensation. The latter approach provides compensation for the cuts. Participants have every reason to expect to accumulate assets in their personal retirement accounts that will cover the entire cuts, not just part of them. Thus a Social Security system with personal retirement accounts should provide Social Security retirees with greater income after retirement than they would receive if Social Security could be maintained in its present form without any cuts at all.

It seems that Democrats for the pure pleasure of maintaining socialist discipline and socialist programs would deprive our young people in their twenties and thirties from having the same kind of retirement in terms of replacement income that their parents and grandparents have enjoyed or will enjoy.

If personal retirement accounts are implemented belatedly 15 or 20 years from now, our young workers will receive retirement income significantly inferior to what they will realize if we begin to implement it now.

Conclusions

What are we to conclude from the foregoing analysis?

1) The so-called "Trust Fund" does not make ONE IOTA OF DIFFERENCE. The money to cover the Social Security deficits will have to be borrowed from the public (or raised by taxes) whether a "Trust Fund" exists or not. The National Debt due to Social Security of $14.08 trillion in 2045 (assuming borrowing to pay the shortfall) will be that amount whether the "Trust Fund" existed or not. The "Trust Fund" is just a device to confuse and fool the public into thinking assets have accumulated when this has not in fact occurred.

2) It is doubtful that workers comprising two-thirds of the electorate will allow borrowing shortfalls for paying retirees and pass the costs on to their children. It is also unlikely that a large part of the $14.08 trillion shortfall from 2018 to 2044 will be funded by increasing taxes. Most of the reductions are likely to come in the form of benefit cuts which will have to start many years prior to 2044. Our Democrat Voodoo economists are either ignorant or being disingenuous in suggesting that maintaining Social Security benefit levels without change is possible with no more than minor adjustments before 2044.

3) If nothing is done as the Democrats desire (they do not want Republicans to get any credit) and nothing is done for another 20 years, Americans now in their twenties (along with many older retirees) can expect their benefits to be cut on the order of 25% without compensation.

CHAPTER 6

Transition Cost Debt

President Bush has emphasized the impending problems with Social Security financing and has proposed reforming it by introducing personal retirement accounts, allowing everyone to put his or her FICA contributions for OASI into their own personal accounts in return for cuts in the amounts they would receive from regular Social Security. This chapter will analyze the debt and investment for a reformed Social Security with an average of about 4% of wages and salaries invested through personal retirement accounts.

Democrats in Congress have opposed the plan. They oppose combining Social Security reforms with personal retirement accounts. One of their main arguments claims that moving to a system with personal retirement accounts imposes transition costs and incurs large increases in U.S. Government deficits and borrowing. This argument requires a premise like: All borrowing is bad, or Deficits are bad. In fact what Democrats really seem to believe is not that every deficit is bad, but that Republican deficits caused by tax cuts are bad (but Democrat deficits caused by extra spending are not bad). Thus there are various possible variants of our

Voodoo Economics Principle #6: All deficits are bad.

Of course incurring debt and running deficits is often bad and avoiding debt is generally desirable.

But borrowing and running deficits often may be useful or necessary. It all depends on how the money is spent. Spending money for investment or for a war will often justify deficits. Denying the usefulness of all debt and deficit spending is quite foolish.

Is Debt Always Bad?

While it is undeniable that moving to a system with personal retirement accounts will incur some transition costs and extra borrowing and debt, there are further questions to ask. It is very possible that incurring debt can be positive if the borrowed money is used for investment. When debt is incurred to finance consumption it is bad because interest is paid on the debt incurred. If it takes time to pay off the debt, one is likely to pay much more for the consumed items than if one had saved the money and bought them without borrowing.

On the other hand debt and borrowing can be good. Consider two examples.

Jim and Mary Jones rent a house. They have $10,000 in savings and $5,000 in credit card and other debt. So they have $5,000 in net worth. They use the $10,000 for a down payment for a $100,000 home and obtain a mortgage for the other $90,000. They now still have $5,000 in net worth—$95,000 in debt and $100,000 in investment in the house. The house appreciates at 4% per year and is worth $120,000 after 5 years. After 5 years they have paid off $5,000 of their debt including a small part of the principal and now have $90,000 in debt and $120,000 in assets for a net worth of $30,000. If they had not bought the house they would have managed to pay off the $5,000 in debt and would have about $12,000 in savings with interest earned for a net worth of $12,000. If they had remained renters they would be debt free instead of $90,000 in debt. By buying the house they end up $90,000 more in debt, but have $108,000 more in assets. By borrowing they have gained an extra $18,000 in net worth after 5 years.

A second example also shows the fallaciousness of declaring all debt to be bad. Company X has $10 million in assets and $5 million of debt. The officers of the company see a business opportunity which, if exploited, will require borrowing another $5 million to build a small manufacturing plant that will wear out at 4% per year. Twenty five years later the plant and its equipment must be replaced. However, over the 25 years the plant enables Company X to earn an extra $200,000 per year in profits after payments for the additional $5 million in debt. After 25 years the plant will have to be replaced and Company X will again have $10 million in assets and $5 million in debt. Yet when it incurred the extra debt it had $15 million in assets and $10 million in debt. By incurring the extra debt it earned an extra $5 million over 25 years. The increased profits doubled the value of the stock and doubled dividends to shareholders. The extra profits also gave Company X an extra $2 million over the 25 year period to invest and produced some additional profits. Here again carrying twice as much debt was a positive attribute. As we shall see the same considerations apply to the process of transitioning to a Social Security system with personal retirement accounts. But to see this, let us examine an example of a possible transition scenario.

An Example of a Personal Retirement Account System

There are many different options for structuring a Social Security system with personal retirement accounts. The amount of contributions to accounts from FICA taxes allowed can cover a range. Reductions in Social Security benefits would be determined by the percentages of payroll contributed to the accounts and the number of years contributions are made. Workers could have options to change the amounts of FICA deductions contributed every five years, for example.

In general the greater the amount allowed for the personal retirement accounts, the greater the reductions in benefits that are reasonable and fair, and the more quickly the unfunded liability can be eliminated and the system brought into balance. Moreover the greater the contributions allowed to personal retirement accounts the better off the participants in Social Security will be. As is evident from the analysis in Chapter 3 the best option for young workers would be to transition over to a system that permitted contributing the entire 10.6% employer and employee shares to the accounts. However Social Security is popular and the maximum amount of contribution that will be politically feasible is probably about 6% (the 5.3% employee contribution to OASI and .7% of the employer contribution). Perhaps the limit is the 5.3% employee contribution.

President Bush has indicated that Social Security will not change for people born after 1950. Consequently the approach analyzed here will assume there are no personal retirement accounts for workers born after 1950. They will remain under present Social Security. The author believes that it would be fairer to allow personal retirement accounts for those born after 1950 as well. They would have very small reductions in regular Social Security benefits.

One of the proposed options is to levy most of the reductions on the higher income workers by indexing their incomes to inflation rather than wages. The author believes that the current Social Security formulas are skewed sufficiently against higher income workers (as shown in Chapters 3 and 4) as to be rather unfair. To levy the bulk of future reductions almost entirely on them shows even greater unfairness. Thus the system of personal retirement accounts analyzed here will assume the part of the benefits received that are based on the current Social Security benefit formulas are indexed to wages. Additional protections might be put in place. For example a higher floor for reductions for lower income workers could be imposed, so their benefits could not be cut more than 40%, for example. Reductions could be limited to a maximum of 35 years for workers who work more than 35 years—this would be an incentive to work and produce for more years than otherwise.

It is desirable to offer at least four options to those who are under 55, that is those who were born in 1950 or later. Beginning with the time they enter the work force and every year in which they have a birthday ending with a 5 or 0, they could choose or change the option for the next 5 years (the choice could be limited to every 10 years). Years during which they were not in the workforce would not be counted. There would be four options. They could have 0%, 2%, 4%, or 6% of their payroll set aside in a personal Social Security account. For each year up to 35 that they elected a 6% deduction they would have their Social Security benefits reduced by 2%. For each year that they elected a 4% deduction they would have their Social Security benefits reduced by 1.6%, and for each year that they elected a 2% deduction they would have their Social Security benefits reduced .8%. So if a worker worked 35 years and elected the 6% deduction for all 35 years, his Social Security benefits would be calculated by the benefit formula as it currently is, but then would receive a 70% reduction. If a worker worked 35 years and elected the 4% deduction for all 35 years his Social Security benefits would be calculated by the Social Security benefit formula, but then would receive a 56% reduction. If someone else worked 30 years and elected to take the 2% deduction for 20 of those years and the 4% deduction for the other 10 years, the reduction applied to the benefit computation would be reduced $20(.8) + 10(1.6) = 32\%$. People could elect not to have any deduction, that is, take the 0% option for all their working years. They would have no reduction in their benefits. For them the Social Security system would function just as it has for every one heretofore. For our analysis we will assume the reductions would average 56% and the analysis would correspond to the analysis for a case with everyone electing 4% withdrawals.

System Maturity

In order to understand a system with personal accounts we need to understand how and when a system with personal accounts will reach system maturity. It is only after nearly all retirees have been in the personal accounts system their entire working lives that full system maturity can occur. This means that persons retiring around 2040 will have had 35 years in the system and have close to the maximum reduction possible. With a life expectancy at age 65 of about 18 years, by about 2060 nearly everyone will have had close to the maximum reduction. Even by 2050 after 10 years of retirements by people at the maximum or very close to the maximum, the system should be close to full maturity. The 2004 Trustees Report projects the benefits level in 2050 to be 15.4% of covered payroll. With the average contribution of 4% of payroll the contributions for OASI will be about 7.4% of covered payroll (10.6 − 4.0 +.8 income from taxes on Social Security). An income level of 7.4% will pay 48% of full benefits in 2050. If the average number of years with 4% personal account contributions is 35, a reduction of 1.6% per year would be sufficient. *Undoubtedly after twenty or so years of experience with the system some minor adjustments may be necessary.*

> *In order to analyze the transition to a Social Security system with personal accounts, an assumption that an average of 4% will be placed in personal accounts was made. This represents 75% of their 5.3% employee OASI contribution. The results of the analysis are summarized in Table 6.1 showing values at 5 year intervals.*

The transition was assumed to start immediately in 2005. Social Security benefit payments for each year were estimated on the basis that the average worker would work 35 years and have the maximum deduction. Those retiring in 2015 would have had 10 years and have an average reduction in Social Security benefits of 16%. 2016 retirees would get a 17.6% average reduction. An analysis of the relative weight to give each cohort was based on the relative sizes of the cohorts and differences in average retirement income. Average income at retirement was estimated based on average wages at retirement. Current average income for a cohort was then estimated by giving an average 2.8% cost of living adjustment for the years from retirement. From these an estimate was made for the overall reduction in benefits paid for each year from 2015 to 2060.

Table 6.1 has several important features that are noteworthy:

1) Column 7 shows the annual amounts contributed to personal retirement accounts increasing to nearly 2 trillion by 2060.
2) Column 10 shows annual deficits increasing until 2030 and then decreasing to a negligible amount by 2050 before producing surpluses.
3) Column 13 shows the national debt for Social Security reaches a maximum of $14.7 trillion in 2050 and then begins declining.
4) Column 15 show that the money invested in personal retirement accounts exceeds the debt incurred and does so by a very large amount after 2040.

Year[a] (1)	CP[b] (2)	Ben[c] % (3)	Schd Ben[d] (4)	Red Ratio[e] (5)	Red Ben[f] (6)	4% CP[g] (7)	Con+ Tx%[h] (8)	Net Con[j] (9)	Surp/ Def[k] (10)	TrF Int[l] (11)	SSTF Debt[m] (12)	ExtSS Debt[n] (13)	TotSS Debt[o] (14)	Savd no Int[p] (15)
2005	4757	9.11	434	1	434	162	7.49	356	-78	85	1503	78	1581	162
2010	6030	9.16	554	1	554	226	7.22	435	-119	87	1469	550	2019	1156
2013	6884	9.76	674	1	674	271	7.13	491	-183	78	1239	1025	2264	1924
2015	7524	10.29	774	0.995	770	301	7.10	534	-236	64	928	1472	2400	2513
2020	9323	11.85	1105	0.942	1041	373	7.19	670	-370	0	0	3041	3041	4227
2025	11446	13.30	1522	0.867	1320	458	7.28	833	-487	0	0	5237	5237	6340
2030	14039	14.51	2037	0.780	1589	562	7.35	1032	-557	0	0	7886	7886	8932
2035	17246	15.22	2625	0.690	1811	690	7.40	1276	-535	0	0	10623	10623	12114
2040	21215	15.40	3267	0.600	1960	849	7.42	1574	-386	0	0	12886	12886	16026
2045	26087	15.37	4010	0.530	2125	1043	7.42	1936	-189	0	0	14264	14264	20838
2050	32010	15.40	4930	0.485	2391	1280	7.43	2378	-12	0	0	14711	14711	26746
2055	39233	15.59	6116	0.460	2814	1569	7.44	2919	105	0	0	14443	14443	33992
2060	48048	15.87	7625	0.444	3386	1922	7.46	3584	199	0	0	13658	13658	42868

[a]The table shows estimates for a system averaging 4% deposits into personal retirement accounts. The table shows every fifth year only. The numbers for intermediate years can be found in Appendix 2 and appear in the tables in Chapters 7 and 8. Several columns have been added to tables in previous chapters covering the existing Social Security system.

[b]Column 2 is the estimate of covered payroll subject to FICA taxes in billions of dollars.

[c]Column 3 is the 2004 Trustees Report estimate of OASI retirement benefits to be paid for a year.

[d]Column 4 gives the benefits to be paid in billions of dollars based on multiplying Columns 2 and 3.

[e]Column 5 gives the estimated ratio of benefits paid as a proportion of the projected benefits.

[f]Column 5 is multiplied times the estimated scheduled benefits in Column 4 to compute the reduced level of retirement benefits to be paid shown in Column 6. The reductions eventually reach an average 56% reduction or a factor of .44.

[g]Column 7 shows the estimated 4% of covered payroll in billions of dollars contributed to personal accounts.

hColumn 8 shows the estimated percentage of covered payroll that is Social Security income for retirement. From 2015 on it shows an exact 4% reduction from estimates of income in the 2004 Trustees Report(Table IVB3).

jColumn 9 is then the net income for Social Security retirement computed by multiplying Columns 2 and 8.

kColumn 10 is the surplus or deficit computed by subtracting Column 6 from Column 9.

lColumn 11 is the interest (5.8%) on the "Trust Fund" debt applied to the entry in Column 12 for the previous year.

mColumn 12 gives the size of the "Trust Fund" in billions of dollars. Column 12 adds entries in Columns 10 and 11 to the entry in Column 12 for the previous year.

nColumn 13 sums the negative numbers in Column 10 for the current and previous years to compute the total amount of debt owed to the public. We assume as we did for the current Social Security system that the deficits are covered by borrowing.

oColumn 14 sums the entries in Columns 12 and 13 for the total Social Security retirement debt.

pColumn 15 sums the contributions to personal accounts from 2005 on entered in Column 7 excluding any interest earned. Most of the money would probably be invested for about 40 years on average before being spent. If annuities are purchased, insurance companies would invest the money. This extra investment will be a great boon to the economy and will improve wages.

Table 6.1 Social Security with Personal Accounts (Average 4% contributed) In billions of dollars.

The numbers in Table 6.1 are based on all economic trends being the same as for current Social Security. They do not take into account that a reformed Social Security system with personal retirement accounts increases saving and investment while an unreformed Social Security system would just reduce saving and investment. The numbers should actually turn out considerably better from the increased investment.

> *It is very important to see that debt accumulates but that debt is exceeded by the extra investment.*

Table 6.2 shows the amount of debt (National Debt from Social Security) that may be necessary to implement a Social Security system with personal retirement accounts. It is evident that the investment amount exceeds the debt incurred to provide for the personal retirement accounts.

Year	Nat Debt from SS[a]	Savd No Int[b]	Year	Nat Debt from SS	Savd No Int
2005	78	162	2033	9545	10762
2006	156	335	2034	10088	11424
2007	239	520	2035	10623	12114
2008	328	718	2036	11135	12833
2009	431	930	2037	11620	13582
2010	550	1156	2038	12077	14363
2011	685	1397	2039	12500	15178
2012	842	1653	2040	12886	16026
2013	1025	1924	2041	13240	16911
2014	1236	2212	2042	13559	17832
2015	1472	2513	2043	13838	18793
2016	1733	2827	2044	14075	19794
2017	2019	3155	2045	14264	20838
2018	2331	3497	2046	14425	21925
2019	2671	3854	2047	14554	23057
2020	3041	4227	2048	14646	24237
2021	3434	4616	2049	14699	25466
2022	3849	5021	2050	14711	26746
2023	4288	5443	2051	14705	28080
2024	4750	5882	2052	14678	29469
2025	5237	6340	2053	14626	30916
2026	5738	6817	2054	14548	32422
2027	6256	7314	2055	14443	33992
2028	6786	7831	2056	14324	35626
2029	7329	8370	2057	14185	37328
2030	7886	8932	2058	14031	39100
2031	8442	9517	2059	13857	40946
2032	8996	10127	2060	13658	42868

[a]Columns 2 and 5 show the National Debt resulting solely from borrowing to cover benefit payments for Social Security.

[b]The third and sixth columns labeled "Savd No Int" indicate the cumulative amount of money excluding interest that will have been saved in the personal retirement accounts.

Table 6.2 Social Security Debt and Investment

Columns 2 and 5 of Table 6.2 correspond to Column 13 of Table 6.1 and indicate the total national debt incurred to pay Social Security benefits. They are plotted for every 5 years in Figure 6.1 as 'Public Debt.' The third and sixth columns of Table 6.2 correspond to Column 15 of Table 6.1 and indicate the total invested in the personal retirement accounts. They are plotted for every 5 years in Figure 6.1 as 'Invested.' The difference (Invested – Public Debt) is represented by the 'Net Investment' bars in Figure 6.1.

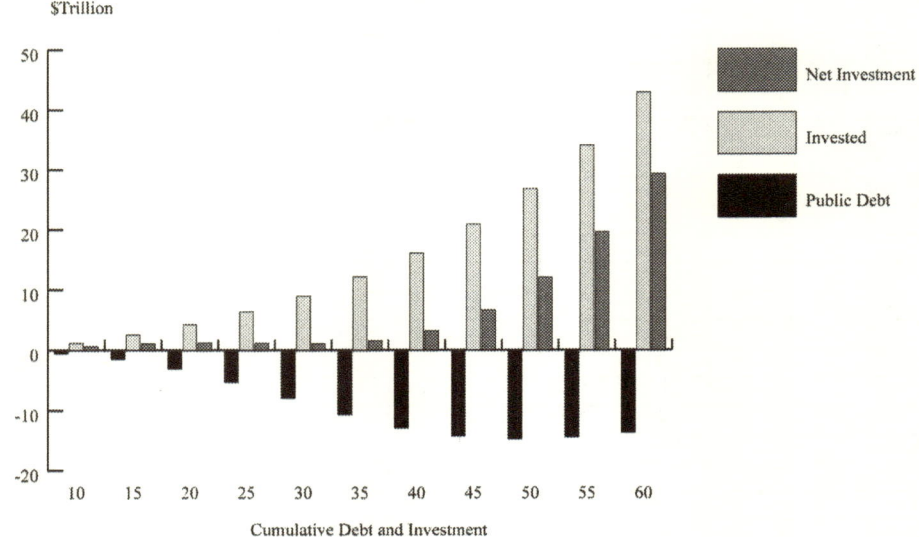

Figure 6.1 Debt and Investment in Current dollars

Converting the numbers in Figure 6.1 to constant 2005 dollars gives a better conception of the effects of the debt and investment on the economy. This is shown by Figure 6.2.

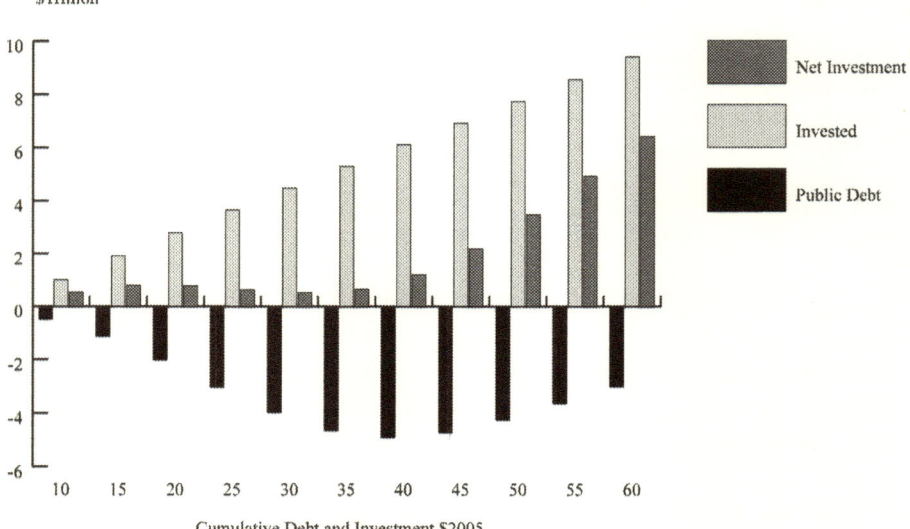

Figure 6.2 Debt and Investment in Constant Dollars

> *The figure shows that a reformed system with personal retirement accounts has positive net investment. This contrasts with an unreformed Social Security that has no investment, just debt.*

The figures do not include earnings or capital gains realized from the investments, nor do they take into account withdrawals for spending.

Participants in a reformed Social Security system with personal retirement accounts, including those who elect not to have personal retirement accounts as well as those who elect to have personal retirement accounts, can expect to do as well or better than they would if they received all the benefits promised under the current Social Security benefit formulas. *But in addition a net of over $29 trillion ($42.9 trillion in savings—$13.7 trillion in increased debt) by 2060 would be invested in the economy which would improve productivity and yield workers higher incomes at retirement and additional increases in the amount of money in their personal retirement accounts at retirement.* This would be a win-win situation with everyone better off. How could anyone claim to be seeking the welfare of the people and yet make them worse off simply to maintain the status quo with a pure pay-as-you-go socialist scheme?

The pay-as-you-go scheme requires borrowing and taxes to the tune of $14 trillion by 2045. This is almost as much borrowing as required by a transition to Social Security with personal retirement accounts.

> *All reasoning has been based on the intermediate assumptions. However, there are very reasonable probabilities that the demographic trends might be worse and that costs and benefit cuts etc will be greater than estimated with the intermediate assumptions. All the more reason to reform the Social Security system to be able to attain true solvency.*

It seems that Democrats for the pure pleasure of maintaining socialist discipline and socialist programs would deprive our young people in their twenties and thirties from having the same kind of retirement in terms of replacement income that their parents and grandparents have enjoyed or will enjoy. If personal retirement accounts are implemented belatedly 15 or 20 years from now, our young workers will receive retirement income significantly inferior to what they will realize if we begin to implement it now.

There are two very important advantages to reforming Social Security to include personal retirement accounts. First, the personal retirement accounts will belong to retirees and can be passed on to children when they die. This is not true for pay-as-you-go Social Security benefits which are lost at death. Second, *all the money that goes into the personal retirement accounts is money invested in the economy.* The current pay-as-you-go Social Security transfers 10.6% FICA contributions for retirements to retirees who consume (spend) nearly all of it. With a system allowing 4% or 6% to go to personal retirement accounts, a reduced amount would go to retirees to consume. Much more would go to investment, which would help grow the economy. This would produce an economy that would grow perhaps one percent per year greater and after a number of years workers would have the additional benefit of earning much higher wages and salaries. Democrats do not seem to grasp the value of this extra net investment for long-term prosperity.

The point of introducing personal retirement accounts is that, unless the economy really tanks for decades on end, investing money where it can grow over time does better than just transferring it from one person to another. Consequently when a pay-as-you-go transfer scheme cannot produce an average 40% replacement of pre-retirement income, a mixture of pay-as-you-go and investment can achieve it and do much better.

The combination of our existing Social Security and personal retirement accounts will be voluntary. Participants will have the option to remain under the current system and continue to pay 5.3% FICA taxes and receive full retirement benefits calculated by the current Social Security methods and benefit formula, or if they so elect, can have their OASI FICA contributions or part of them deposited in a personal retirement account which they own. They control investment of the money and can draw from their investments when they retire. In return for depositing their OASI FICA taxes in their personal retirement accounts they would have their regular Social Security benefits reduced proportionally to the number of years they deposited the taxes.

Summary

Implementation of a Social Security system with personal retirement accounts allowing deposit of large portions of their FICA to their personal retirement accounts, would permit participants who did not elect to have the accounts to receive their full benefits under the current Social Security benefit formulas. Those who elected to have the accounts should do even better with the combination of regular Social Security and the personal retirement accounts.

> *With a system having personal retirement accounts those who do not elect to have the accounts can expect to retain the full benefits promised by current Social Security. They will not experience 25% to 30% reductions that nearly everyone will receive if personal retirement accounts are not instituted.*

Further, the borrowing or extra taxes over the next 40 years to 2045 would be $14 trillion, the same amount current Social Security would need to borrow or increase taxes to pay full benefits. However, the new system with personal retirement accounts would reach solvency in 2051 with no additional borrowing necessary. Although borrowing $14 trillion over the course of 40 years the money deposited in the personal retirement accounts and made available for investing is over $42 trillion or a net investment of $29 trillion.

CHAPTER 7

Comparison of Transition Costs for 2005 to 2060

Democrats have a passion for spending money on current consumption rather than saving and investing some of it in the future and for longer term growth and higher standards of living. This is clear from their resistance to changing Social Security to include investment. They prefer to depend entirely on transfers of earnings of current workers to current retirees for consumption. It would seem that the Democrats believe that if there is any choice, consumption is preferable to investment. This gives us our seventh principle of voodoo economics:

Voodoo Economics Principle #7: Do not Save and Invest. Consume!

The discussion of Keynesian economics in Chapter 9 takes note of additional reasons why Democrats may like consumption so much. The tradeoff between consumption and investment is at the crux of the assessment of the transition costs for installing a system of Social Security with personal retirement accounts. Of course we will probably always consume 75% of income. But the more investment, the better the prospects for future prosperity.

Consequences for the Years 2005 to 2018

In this chapter we will examine transition costs in greater detail focusing on several different periods. Let us begin by examining the implications of the system of personal retirement accounts outlined and analyzed in Chapter 6 for the years 2005 to 2018.

> *During the years up to 2018 FICA taxes will exceed benefits paid to retirees generally by about 100 to 120 billion dollars per year. This provides a wonderful opportunity to transition to a system that redirects these contributions into personal retirement accounts. Rather than being wasted on government spending and consumption as Democrats prefer, the excess contributions should be invested to provide for current workers retirement.*

As was shown in Chapter 5 the "Trust Fund" does not represent assets, but U.S. Treasury Bonds that must be backed up by further borrowing or taxes, when the bonds are cashed in by the Social Security Administration. There is about $1.5 trillion in the Social Security "Trust Fund" which is receiving on average of about 5.8% interest. This money was accumulated by baby boomer contributions, which were borrowed to fund government operations. Democrats want to continue the charade by using up another $1 trillion by 2018. They will then add another $11 trillion interest to the $2 trillion "borrowed" from extra FICA contributions before the so-called "OASI Trust Funds" are exhausted in 2044. What is bizarre is that the money is first taken as taxes, presumably to pay for retirement, but the money is spent on non-retirement government consumption. Further, instead of using present surpluses to cover future deficits, additional borrowing or taxes from the public will be necessary to pay for future income shortfalls. This is a kind of double borrowing or taxation.

Excess FICA contributions past 2005 should be used to help transition to a system with personal accounts. If the "Trust Fund" bonds continue to yield about 5.8%, the $1.5 trillion Social Security "Trust Fund" will be exhausted by 2018. Perhaps some might believe that using the "Trust Fund" bonds involves additional borrowing. The total Federal debt does not change. The internal debt owed to agencies of the Federal Government including the $1.5 trillion "Trust Fund" is now $3.0 trillion and the debt owed to outside entities is $4.4 trillion totaling $7.4 trillion. If the Social Security Administration cashes the $1.5 trillion in "Trust Funds" during the years 2005 to 2018 to pay benefits, and the Treasury borrows $1.5 trillion from the public to cover them, the $1.5 trillion will be added to the $4.4 trillion of debt to the public. At the same time the debt owed to Federal agencies is reduced by $1.5 trillion. So the "Trust Fund" Federal Interagency debt is converted to debt owed to the public.

Table 7.1 provides a comparison of current Social Security with a transition plan for personal accounts spelled out in Chapter 6. Columns 2 to 9 represent existing Social Security with borrowing as covered in Chapter 5. Columns 10 to 17 give the same values for 4% contributed to personal accounts as presented in Table 6.1 of Chapter 6. The Columns dealing with "Trust Fund" debt and interest (3, 4, 11, and 12) are really absolutely meaningless since they make no difference whatsoever to the resulting debt in later years (after 2044) or to the annual interest that must be paid, that is, to Columns 5, 6, 13, and 14. Although the monies in the "Trust Fund" are really meaningless, we track them here because the Democrats and the AARP make much of them and seem to believe that they are some kind of assets rather than government bonds that are nothing but IOU's.

In viewing Table 7.1 there are four important comparisons and trends to observe:

1) *Column 2 shows current unreformed Social Security will run surpluses during this period while Column 10 shows the personal retirement accounts system running deficits that increase during the period.*

2) *Column 5 shows our current Social Security system will not add to national debt until 2018, because it runs surpluses during the period. Column 13 shows the personal retirement accounts system accumulating additional debt owed to the public due to the deficits. By 2018 it accumulates to $2.33 trillion.*

3) *Column 6 shows no interest for public debt due to Social Security because no such debt occurs until 2018. Column 14 indicates that the personal retirement accounts system will require interest payments on the public debt that would exist as indicated in Column 13.*

4) *Column 9 shows the savings and investment produced by existing Social Security, namely none. Column 17 shows that the personal retirement accounts system produces considerable extra saving and investment. In fact the amount more than offsets the extra borrowing in Column 13. The earnings on the investment dollar amounts shown in Column 17 will be considerable, offsetting the need for interest payments as shown in Column 14.*

Year (1)	Surp/ Def[a] (2)	TrustF Int[b] (3)	SS Trust Dbt (4)	Ext SS Debt[c] (5)	Ann Int Pay[d] (6)	Tot SS Debt (7)	Tot Ann Int[e] (8)	Save[f] (9)	Surp/ Def[a] (10)	TrF Int[b] (11)	TF Debt (12)	Ext SS Debt[c] (13)	Ann Int Pay[d] (14)	Tot SS Dbt (15)	Tot Ann Int[e] (16)	Savd No Int[f] (17)
2005	85	85	1666	0	0	1666	85	0	-78	85	1503	78	5	1581	90	162
2006	94	93	1854	0	0	1854	93	0	-78	87	1512	156	9	1668	96	335
2007	103	103	2060	0	0	2060	103	0	-83	88	1517	239	14	1756	102	520
2008	109	116	2385	0	0	2385	116	0	-89	88	1516	328	19	1844	107	718
2009	109	130	2524	0	0	2524	130	0	-103	88	1501	431	25	1932	113	930
2010	107	144	2775	0	0	2775	144	0	-119	87	1469	550	32	2019	119	1156
2011	106	160	3041	0	0	3041	160	0	-135	85	1419	685	40	2104	125	1397
2012	99	176	3316	0	0	3316	176	0	-157	82	1344	842	49	2186	131	1653
2013	88	191	3596	0	0	3596	191	0	-183	78	1239	1025	59	2264	137	1924
2014	77	207	3880	0	0	3880	207	0	-211	72	1100	1236	72	2336	144	2212
2015	61	223	4164	0	0	4164	223	0	-236	64	928	1472	85	2400	149	2513
2016	41	242	4446	0	0	4446	242	0	-261	54	721	1733	101	2454	154	2827
2017	19	258	4723	0	0	4723	258	0	-286	42	477	2019	117	2496	159	3155
2018	-5	274	4992	5	0	4997	274	0	-312	28	193	2331	135	2523	163	3497

[a]Columns 2 and 10 show the surplus or deficit (Social Security Income – Social Security Retirement Benefits Paid) for the two systems.

[b]"Trust Fund" interest in Column 3 and Column 11 is not paid out of taxes but deferred by issuing "Trust Fund" bonds.

[c]Columns 5 and 13 show the debt to the public incurred for Social Security. They sum the deficits from columns 2 and 10.

[d]Columns 6 and 14 represent annual interest payments that must be paid on U.S. Treasury bonds issued to the public. They represent 5.8% of the previous column—the total Social Security debt issued to the public.

[e]Column 8 is the total annual interest accruing on debt owed by the U.S. Treasury for Social Security. It sums the interest on the trust funds in Column 3 and the interest paid on debt to the public in Column 6. Column 16 does the same for the transition to personal accounts adding trust fund interest in Column 11 to interest paid on debt to the public in Column 14.

ᶠColumn 9 reminds us that Social Security as currently constituted produces no savings and in fact undoubtedly reduces personal saving. Column 17 shows the amount of saving placed in personal accounts from 2005 onward in billions of dollars without counting interest.

Table 7.1 Comparison for 2005 to 2018.

The table shows that the transition to personal retirement accounts with an average of 4% of covered payroll deposited in the accounts will produce deficits that, if covered by borrowing, will accumulate to $2.33 trillion by 2018 compared to a total increase in national debt of $5 billion for current Social Security. The total interest paid for 2005 to 2018 would be $762 billion. The interest that must be paid represents the transition costs through 2018.

Figure 7.1 shows the cumulative investment for a system with personal accounts at three year intervals. During this same period our current Social Security system has no net investment. It neither borrows from the public nor invests.

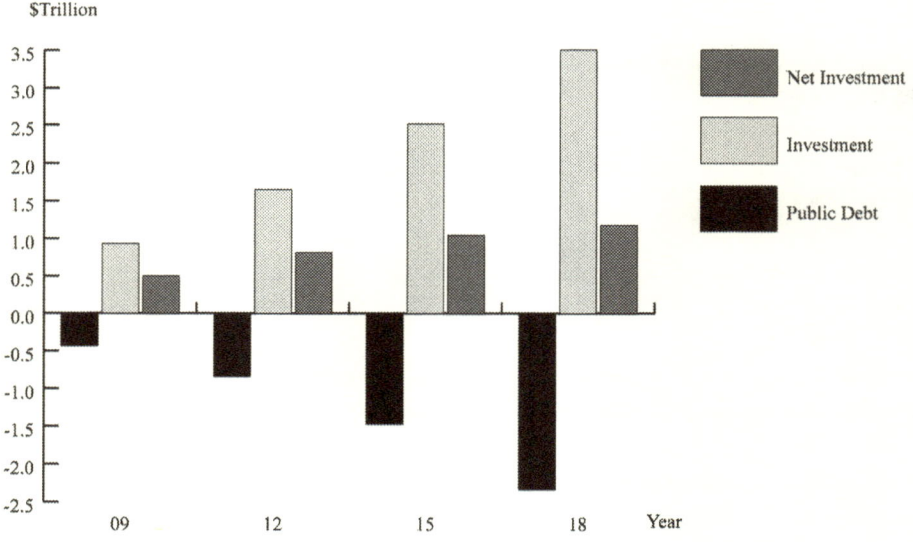

Personal Accounts Cumulative Public Debt and Investment

Figure 7.1 Cumulative Debt and Investment for Selected Years

What about the impact on investment? It might seem that the $2.33 trillion borrowed through 2018 will reduce investment. However it is used to fund personal retirement accounts, which put all of the money in approved less risky investments. Notice that during this period the workers contributing to personal retirement accounts have contributed $3.5 trillion. So $2.33 trillion has been borrowed to put $3.5 trillion in savings and investment, a net saving of $1.17 trillion illustrated by Figure 7.1(contrasted with a net dissaving of $.005 trillion for our current Social Security in the year 2018). If we figured the returns on the investments, the returns would exceed the $760 billion in interest payments. Of course a small fraction of the $3.5 trillion saved would be cashed in and spent by retirees.

> *So for the system with personal retirement accounts, part of the money borrowed is recycled to investment. It does not reduce or "crowd out" the money available for investment as does borrowing under our current Social Security system.*

The U.S. financial markets are very flexible and efficient so that it is doubtful that any negative impact on investment from having personal retirement accounts will occur. Moreover, the excess FICA contributions over receipts occurring from 2005 until 2018 total $1.1 trillion without interest. Under present plans this $1.1 trillion will be borrowed and spent by Congress with virtually all going toward consumption on questionable programs that will waste it. Instead with a system of personal retirement accounts the $1.1 trillion will be additional money allocated to investment in the private sector, which will contribute toward greater economic growth. This is a net positive because it should cause improved productivity and greater economic growth than otherwise.

Years 2019 to 2035

Now what happens with a Social Security plan with personal retirement accounts compared to current Social Security, if as advocated by Democrats there are no changes and deficits increase to over $650 billion by 2035? We have shown that by 2018 the personal retirement accounts accumulate a net of $1.17 investment and therefore have a positive effect on the economy compared to current Social Security. Prior to 2018 the so-called "transition costs" do not have any negative impact on the economy. Earnings exceed interest paid. Table 7.2 shows the trends from 2019 to 2035.

1) *Column 2 shows current unreformed Social Security will run deficits during this period while Column 10 shows in the year 2019 the deficits in the proposed savings plan amount to about $310 billion. The deficits increase to nearly $500 billion in 2025 when the deficit for Social Security as it currently is would be $230 billion. By 2035 the deficits increase to nearly $535 billion compared to $660 billion under the current Social Security plan. After this a Social Security system with personal accounts will experience decreasing deficits as it begins to move significantly toward maturity. We see that up to the year 2033 a Social Security system with personal accounts will run deficits exceeding the deficits under current Social Security.*

2) *Column 5 shows our current Social Security system will add $5.5 trillion to national debt until 2035. Column 13 shows the personal retirement accounts system adding $8.8 trillion in debt owed to the public during the period. The national debt for the personal retirement accounts system reaches $10.6 trillion compared to $5.5 trillion for our existing Social Security system by 2035.*

3) *Column 6 shows increasing interest payments for public debt due to Social Security reaching over $300 billion by 2035. Column 14 indicates that the personal retirement accounts system will also increase interest payments reaching $600 billion by 2035.*

4) *Column 9 shows the savings and investment produced by existing Social Security, namely none. Column 17 shows that the personal retirement accounts system produces saving and investment that more than offsets the borrowing shown in Column 13. The earnings on the investment dollar amounts in Column 17 will greatly exceed interest payments shown in Column 14.*

Year	Surp/	TrustF	SS	Ext	Ann	Tot	Tot	Save^f	Surp/	TrF^f	TF	Ext	Ann	Tot	Tot	Savd
(1)	Def^a	Int^b	Trust	SS	Int	SS	Ann	(9)	Def^a	Int^b	Debt	SS	Int	SS	Ann	No
	(2)	(3)	Dbt	Debt^c	Pay^d	Debt	Int^e		(10)	(11)	(12)	Debt^c	Pay^d	Dbt	Int^e	Int^f
			(4)	(5)	(6)	(7)	(8)					(13)	(14)	(15)	(16)	(17)
2018	-5	274	4992	5	0	4997	274	0	-312	28	193	2331	135	2623	163	3497
2019	-31	290	5250	36	2	5287	292	0	-340	11	0	2671	155	2671	166	3854
2020	-62	305	5493	98	6	5591	310	0	-370	0	0	3041	176	3041	176	4227
2021	-90	319	5721	188	11	5910	330	0	-393	0	0	3434	199	3434	199	4616
2022	-121	332	5932	310	18	6241	350	0	-416	0	0	3849	223	3849	223	5021
2023	-155	344	6121	465	27	6585	371	0	-439	0	0	4288	249	4288	249	5443
2024	-191	355	6285	656	38	6940	393	0	-462	0	0	4750	276	4750	276	5882
2025	-231	365	6418	887	51	7305	416	0	-487	0	0	5237	304	5237	304	6340
2026	-267	372	6523	1154	67	7677	439	0	-502	0	0	5738	333	5738	333	6817
2027	-307	378	6595	1461	85	8056	463	0	-518	0	0	6256	363	6256	363	7314
2028	-348	382	6629	1809	105	8438	487	0	-530	0	0	6786	394	6786	394	7831
2029	-394	384	6620	2203	128	8823	512	0	-542	0	0	7329	425	7329	425	8370
2030	-444	384	6560	2646	153	9207	537	0	-557	0	0	7886	457	7886	457	8932
2031	-481	381	6460	3127	181	9587	562	0	-556	0	0	8442	490	8442	490	9517
2032	-521	375	6313	3649	212	9962	586	0	-554	0	0	8996	522	8996	522	10127
2033	-564	366	6115	4213	244	10328	610	0	-549	0	0	9545	554	9545	554	10762
2034	-609	355	5861	4822	280	10683	634	0	-543	0	0	10088	585	10088	585	11424
2035	-659	340	5542	5480	318	11022	658	0	-535	0	0	10623	616	10623	616	12114

^aColumns 2 and 10 show the surplus or deficit (Social Security Income – Social Security Retirement Benefits Paid) for the two systems.

^b"Trust Fund" interest in Column 3 and Column 11 is not paid out of taxes but deferred by issuing "Trust Fund" bonds.

^cColumns 5 and 13 show the debt to the public incurred for Social Security. They sum the deficits from columns 2 and 10.

^dColumns 6 and 14 represent annual interest payments that must be paid on U.S. Treasury bonds issued to the public. They represent 5.8% of the previous column—the total Social Security debt issued to the public.

^eColumn 8 is the total annual interest accruing on debt owed by the U.S. Treasury for Social Security. It sums the interest on the trust funds in Column 3 and the interest paid on debt to the public in Column 6. Column

16 does the same for the transition to personal accounts adding trust fund interest in Column 11 to interest paid on debt to the public in Column 14.

fColumn 9 reminds us that Social Security as currently constituted produces no savings and in fact undoubtedly reduces personal saving. Column 17 shows the amount of saving placed in personal accounts from 2005 onward in billions of dollars without counting interest.

Table 7.2 Comparison for the Years 2018 to 2035

> *Because pay-as-you-go transfer systems produce no investment, the $5.5 trillion current Social Security borrows is net dissaving. However the personal retirement accounts system will save $12.1 trillion for a net saving of $1.5 trillion from 2005 to 2035.*

The investment figure does not include earnings or withdrawals to fund retirement. The earlier period produced $1.17 trillion of net saving by 2018. The 2019 to 2035 period produces a net saving of $ 330 billion. This is much better for economic growth than stealing $5.5 trillion in potential investment money for growing the economy and diverting it to Social Security benefit payments that are mostly consumed. Figure 7.2 compares cumulative net investment for Social Security with its current benefit formula and no benefit reductions with the system of personal retirement accounts that we have analyzed. There are two evident trends:

> *1) The system with personal retirement accounts analyzed shows a roughly constant net investment of about $1 trillion throughout the period.*
> *2) Unreformed Social Security shows increasing borrowing and net dissaving reaching $5.5 trillion by 2035.*

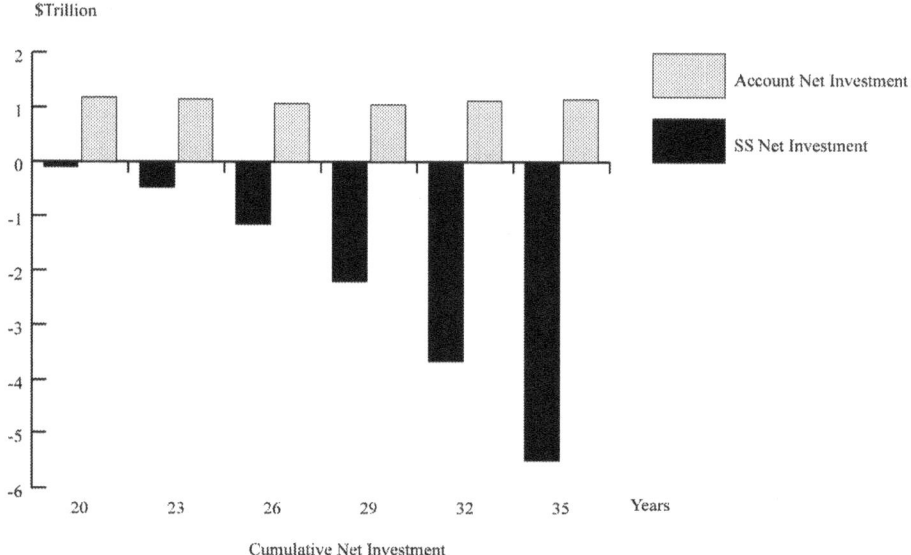

Figure 7.2 Net Investment for Selected Years 2018 to 2035

The interest payments on Social Security debt will be $6.32 trillion for this period compared to $1.93 trillion for our existing Social Security system. Here again the amounts earned on the money invested should be comparable, if not exceeding the interest which must be paid. In contrast there are no earnings in the existing Social Security system to offset the $1.9 trillion in interest paid over the 17 years. We see that although there are "transition costs," the net investment has a positive effect on the economy compared to a negative effect for the borrowing, debt, and interest from the existing Social Security system.

> *During this whole period the amount of money being placed in the personal accounts is about equal to the deficits incurred.*

During this period amounts on the order of $400 billion to $900 billion in annual contributions to personal accounts will take place. The amounts will total about $8.6 trillion. This money all goes to investment. It is a lot of investment and will improve economic growth so that all segments of the economy will experience increased income. This contrasts with the current Social Security system which would borrow about $5.5 trillion during the same period none of which would go to investment but to retirees and hence mostly to consumption.

> *A system of personal retirement accounts should not crowd out money that could go to investment whereas current Social Security will cause a considerable amount of crowding out after 2018.*

Years 2035 to 2060

The calculations indicate that by 2033 the deficits for our current Social Security system would equal a system with personal accounts with an average of 4% contributions. In the following years the deficits for current Social Security with no reductions in benefits rapidly expand reaching about $1.6 trillion in 2055 whereas a system with personal accounts goes into the black by about 2051. The trends for this period are shown in Table 7.3.

1) *Column 2 shows current unreformed Social Security will run escalating deficits during this period exceeding $2 trillion annually by 2059. Column 10 shows decreasing deficits in the proposed savings plan becoming surpluses by 2051.*
2) *Column 5 shows our current Social Security system will add $8.6 trillion to national debt from 2035 to 2045. Column 13 shows the personal retirement accounts system adding $3.68 trillion in debt owed to the public during the same ten year period. In 2045 the accumulated national debt for the two systems is about equal at slightly over $14 trillion. From there the debt for unreformed Social Security rapidly expands to over $36 trillion in 2060 while debt for the personal retirement accounts system reaches a maximum of $14.7 trillion in 2050 and then decreases.*
3) *Column 6 shows increasing interest payments for public debt due to Social Security reaching $817 billion by 2045. Column 14 indicates that the personal retirement accounts system will also increase interest payments reaching $827 billion by 2045. After 2045 the personal retirement accounts system maintains annual interest payments around $800 billion while unreformed Social Security interest continue to increase to more than $2 trillion by 2059.*
4) *Column 9 shows the savings and investment produced by existing Social Security, namely none. Column 17 shows that the personal retirement accounts system produces saving and investment that more than offsets the borrowing shown in Column 13. The earnings on the investment dollar amounts in Column 17 will greatly exceed annual interest payments.*

Year (1)	Surp/ Def^a Fund (2)	Trust Fund Int^b (3)	SS Trust Dbt (4)	Ext SS Debt^c (5)	Ann Int Pay^d (6)	Tot SS Debt (7)	Tot Ann Int^e (8)	Save^f (9)	Surp/ Def^a (10)	TF Int^b (11)	TF Debt (12)	Ext SS Debt^c (13)	Ann Int Pay^d (14)	Tot SS Dbt (15)	Tot Ann Int^e (16)	Savd No Int^f (17)
2035	-659	340	5542	5480	318	11022	658	0	-535	0	0	10623	616	10623	616	12114
2036	-692	321	5171	6173	358	11344	679	0	-512	0	0	11135	646	11135	646	12833
2037	-727	300	4744	6899	400	11644	700	0	-485	0	0	11620	674	11620	674	13582
2038	-766	275	4254	7665	445	11919	720	0	-457	0	0	12077	700	12077	700	14363
2039	-804	247	3697	8469	491	12166	738	0	-423	0	0	12500	725	12500	725	15178
2040	-844	214	3067	9313	540	12380	755	0	-386	0	0	12886	747	12886	747	16026
2041	-878	178	2367	10191	591	12558	769	0	-353	0	0	13240	768	13240	768	16911
2042	-915	137	1589	11106	644	12695	781	0	-319	0	0	13559	786	13559	786	17832
2043	-951	92	731	12057	699	12787	791	0	-279	0	0	13838	803	13838	803	18793
2044	-991	42	0	13048	757	13048	799	0	-237	0	0	14075	816	14075	816	19794
2045	-1030	0	0	14079	817	14079	817	0	-189	0	0	14264	827	14264	827	20838
2046	-1076	0	0	15155	879	15155	879	0	-161	0	0	14425	837	14425	837	21925
2047	-1121	0	0	16276	944	16276	944	0	-129	0	0	14554	844	14554	844	23057
2048	-1168	0	0	17444	1012	17444	1012	0	-92	0	0	14646	849	14646	849	24237
2049	-1217	0	0	18661	1082	18661	1082	0	-53	0	0	14699	853	14699	853	25466
2050	-1271	0	0	19931	1156	19931	1156	0	-12	0	0	14711	853	14711	853	26746
2051	-1337	0	0	21268	1234	21268	1234	0	6	0	0	14705	853	14705	853	28080
2052	-1406	0	0	22675	1315	22675	1315	0	27	0	0	14678	851	14678	851	29469
2053	-1476	0	0	24150	1401	24150	1401	0	53	0	0	14626	848	14626	848	30916
2054	-1552	0	0	25702	1491	25702	1491	0	77	0	0	14548	844	14548	844	32422
2055	-1628	0	0	27330	1585	27330	1585	0	105	0	0	14443	838	14443	838	33992
2056	-1716	0	0	29046	1685	29046	1685	0	120	0	0	14324	831	14324	831	35626
2057	-1804	0	0	30850	1789	30850	1789	0	139	0	0	14185	823	14185	823	37328
2058	-1905	0	0	32756	1900	32756	1900	0	154	0	0	14031	814	14031	814	39100
2059	-2007	0	0	34763	2016	34763	2016	0	174	0	0	13857	804	13857	804	40946
2060	-2119	0	0	36882	2139	36882	2139	0	199	0	0	13658	792	13658	792	42868

aColumns 2 and 10 show the surplus or deficit (Social Security Income – Social Security Retirement Benefits Paid) for the two systems.

b"Trust Fund" interest in Column 3 and Column 11 is not paid out of taxes but deferred by issuing "Trust Fund" bonds.

cColumns 5 and 13 show the debt to the public incurred for Social Security. They sum the deficits from columns 2 and 10.

dColumns 6 and 14 represent annual interest payments that must be paid on U.S. Treasury bonds issued to the public. They represent 5.8% of the previous column—the total Social Security debt issued to the public.

eColumn 8 is the total annual interest accruing on debt owed by the U.S. Treasury for Social Security. It sums the interest on the trust funds in Column 3 and the interest paid on debt to the public in Column 6. Column 16 does the same for the transition to personal accounts adding trust fund interest in Column 11 to interest paid on debt to the public in Column 14.

fColumn 9 reminds us that Social Security as currently constituted produces no savings and in fact undoubtedly reduces personal saving. Column 17 shows the amount of saving placed in personal accounts from 2005 onward in billions of dollars without counting interest.

Table 7.3 Comparison for Years 2035 to 2060 (In billions of dollars)

In the years following the crossover point at which deficits from an unchanged Social Security system exceed falling deficits from a personal accounts system, the personal accounts system may accumulate deficits on the order of $4.1 trillion (from 2035 to 2050). Then the deficit is reduced by $1.1 trillion by 2060. Thus from 2035 to 2060 national debt increases by $3 trillion. During the same 25 year period $30.7 trillion is saved in the personal retirement accounts for a net increase of $27.7 trillion in investment. In the years beyond 2055 the current Social Security system continues to increase annual deficits, borrowing money that should go to investment, and then transferring it to retirees for consumption. Since 4 percent of covered payroll in a system with personal accounts channels increasing amounts of money to saving and investment for real producing assets, significantly greater growth will occur and nearly everyone will benefit from increasing productivity and real income growth. Figure 7.3 compares cumulative net investment for current Social Security with the analyzed system of personal retirement accounts.

1) The system with personal retirement accounts analyzed shows increasing net investment reaching $29 trillion by 2060.

2) Unreformed Social Security shows increasing borrowing and net dissaving reaching $36 trillion by 2060.

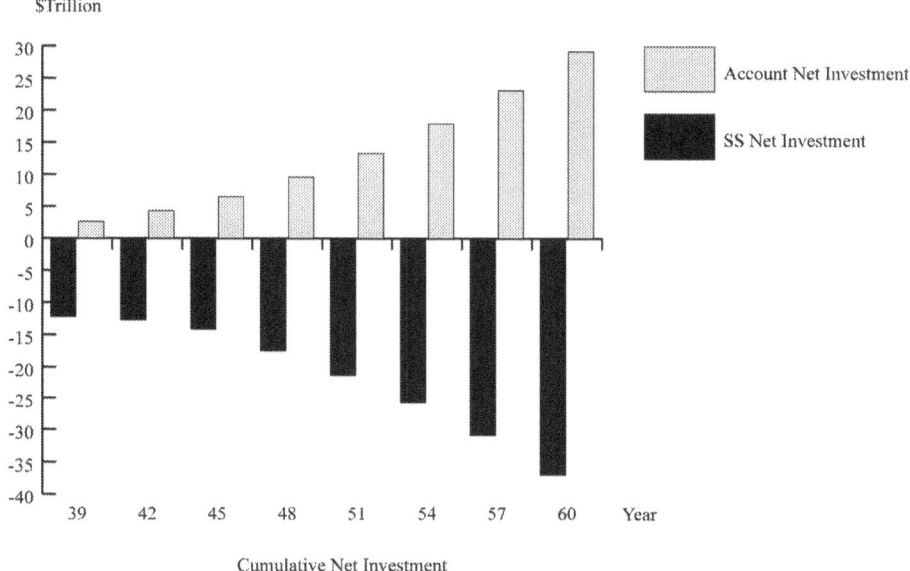

$Trillion

Cumulative Net Investment

Figure 7.3 Net Investment for Selected Years from 2035 to 2060

Contrast an unchanged Social Security system which must borrow (or tax) an additional $31.3 trillion without any investment for a net $31.3 disinvestment during the 25 years. The fundamental fact is that the net $27.7 trillion investment for a system with personal retirement accounts will cause significant increase in economic growth in the economy raising the incomes of all, whereas an unchanged Social Security system would do major damage to the economy. So I believe that we can be assured that before 2035 Social Security retirement benefits will be reduced by nearly 30%. But if the shortfall is eliminated by benefit reductions so that pay-as-you-go Social Security does not need additional borrowing or taxes, the Social Security system is still quite inferior to a personal retirement accounts system which adds about $1 trillion a year in net investment promoting economic growth and provides much better retirement for Social Security participants.

> *The clear conclusion is that only reform of Social Security that provides personal retirement accounts will reduce the shortfall between what is paid in and paid out for Social Security over the long term. A system with personal retirement accounts will increase saving and investment and grow the economy instead of reducing saving and reducing economic growth which the current Social Security system without benefit reductions will increasingly do after 2018.*

CHAPTER 8

Summary of Transition Costs

As was noted in Chapter 7 Democrats want to spend money on current consumption. They put a lower priority on saving and investing in the future for longer term growth and higher standards of living. Their resistance to changing Social Security is another example of this tendency. Rather than fund retirement by savings they want to transfer earnings of current workers to retirees for consumption. Thus the seventh principle of voodoo economics:

Voodoo Economics Principle #7: Do not Save and Invest. Consume!

As noted in Chapter 7 the tradeoff between consumption and investment is central for assessment of the transition costs for installing a system of Social Security with personal retirement accounts. When an economy experiences annual increases of ½ or 1 percent in economic growth over many years, the increases compound and produce very large improvements in average wages and salaries in the long run. If there is a choice between using available funds for consumption or for investment, it is generally preferable to use it for investment, provided the investment is for assets that promise to produce adequate returns. Since investment will generally pay off in greater wealth both corporately and individually over the long run, it is generally preferable to forego some consumption in return for investment. Of course, most income is spent on consumption. But the extra funds that can go to investment generally should be allocated to it.

Comparison of the Existing Social Security System and a System with Personal Accounts

Table 8.1 shows the numbers presented in Chapter 7 in Tables 7.1 to 7.3 but at 5 year intervals to offer an overview and reminder of the trends.

Year (1)	Surpl/ Def (2)	Trst Fnd Int (3)	TF Dbt (4)	ExtSS Debt (5)	Ann Int Pay (6)	TotSS Debt (7)	Tot Ann Int (8)	S a v (9)	Surp/ Def (10)	TF Int (11)	TF Dbt (12)	ExtSS Debt (13)	Ann Int Pay (14)	TotSS Debt (15)	Tot Ann Int (16)	Savd no Int (17)
2005	85	85	1666	0	0	1666	85	0	-78	85	1503	78	5	1581	90	162
2010	107	144	2775	0	0	2775	144	0	-119	87	1469	550	32	2019	119	1156
2013	88	191	3596	0	0	3596	191	0	-183	78	1239	1025	59	2264	137	1924
2015	61	223	4164	0	0	4164	223	0	-236	64	928	1472	85	2400	149	2513
2020	-62	305	5493	98	6	5591	311	0	-370	0	0	3041	176	3041	176	4227
2025	-231	365	6418	887	51	7305	416	0	-487	0	0	5237	304	5237	304	6340
2030	-444	384	6560	2646	153	9207	537	0	-557	0	0	7886	457	7886	457	8932
2035	-659	340	5542	5480	318	11022	658	0	-535	0	0	10623	616	10623	616	12114
2040	-844	214	3067	9313	540	12380	754	0	-386	0	0	12886	747	12886	747	16026
2045	-1030	0	0	14079	817	14079	817	0	-189	0	0	14264	827	14264	827	20838
2050	-1271	0	0	19931	1156	19931	1156	0	-12	0	0	14711	853	14711	853	26746
2055	-1628	0	0	27330	1585	27330	1585	0	105	0	0	14443	838	14443	838	33992
2060	-2119	0	0	36882	2139	36882	2139	0	199	0	0	13658	792	13658	792	42868

Table 8.1 Summary of Costs, Debt, and Interest for Social Security and a Personal Accounts System

Columns 2 to 9 represent existing retirement portion of Social Security (OASI) without reform with borrowing to cover deficits. Columns 10 to 17 provide the same information for a reformed system with personal retirement accounts receiving an average of 4% of covered payroll.

The comparison of calculations for OASI shows several interesting things:

1) Despite all the claims about increasing debt and spending and transition costs, the total Federal Government debt over the long term for Social Security is greater for the current system than for adopting a system with personal accounts and transitioning over to it.

2) A properly designed system with personal accounts will no longer be running deficits and the debt will no longer increase but reach a maximum point around $14 trillion by about 2045. At that time the economy will be 5 times its current size and the debt will represent the same drain on the economy that a $2.7 trillion debt does today.

3) The deficits of an unreformed system will be running in excess of $1 trillion per year by 2045 and will increase to over $2 trillion per year by 2060 reaching a debt of about $37 trillion by 2060.

4) It should be obvious that attempts to maintain the status quo for Social Security will require major cuts in benefits for all workers and retirees to minimize deficits long before 2045. On the other hand a personal accounts system will not require cuts for those who do not elect to have accounts nor for retirees. It will make everyone much better off.

5) Since the economy will be about 10 times the size of our current economy by 2060 the Federal debt for Social Security alone may be comparable to $4 trillion today if benefits are not reduced and the money is borrowed. But it is likely that the non-Social Security debt (currently about $5.9 trillion + $1.5 trillion in the "Trust Funds" = $7.4 total debt listed by the Office of Public Debt in the Treasury department) will increase as well.

For a period of time the deficits for transitioning to a plan with personal accounts will be higher than the deficits for the existing system. The personal accounts system will reach annual deficits no greater than $550 billion after 2030. In that same time frame deficits from the current system rapidly escalate exceeding the deficits from the personal accounts system before 2035, $1 trillion by 2045 and $2 trillion by 2060. Figure 8.1 shows net investment for current Social Security and for a reformed system with personal retirement accounts. The figure shows the debt and investment for three 15 year periods and a ten year period beginning in 2005 and ending in 2060. For each period the first three bars show the accumulated public debt, the accumulated investment and the net investment for the analyzed system with personal retirement accounts. The fourth bar shows the borrowing and net investment for Social Security if its current benefits were sustained through borrowing.

It is the third and fourth bars for each period, namely net investment, that should form the primary basis for comparison of the unreformed and reformed systems.

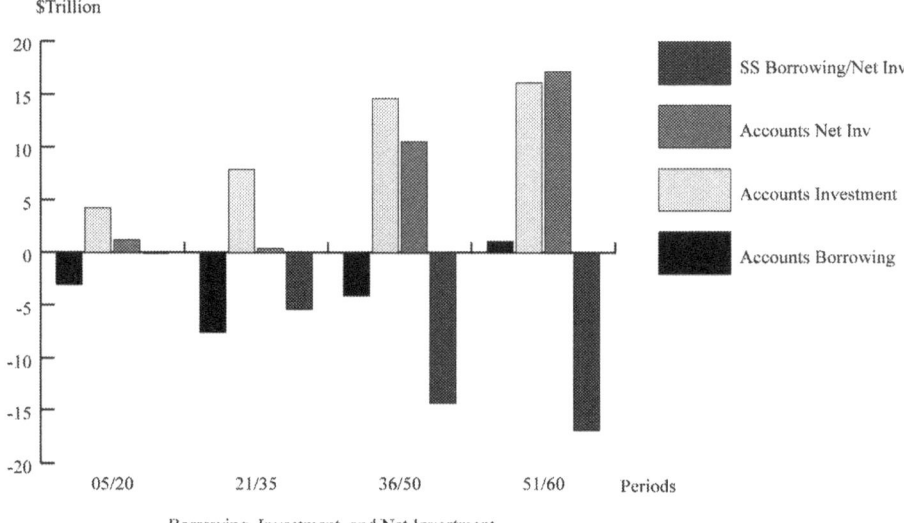

Figure 8.1 Comparison of Unreformed Social Security and a Personal Accounts System for Four Periods

Perhaps it is more illuminating to look at the borrowing and investment in real terms, that is, in constant dollars with no inflation since a considerable amount of inflation and devaluation of the dollar (2.8% per year) is projected to occur and makes the borrowing and investment in outlying years seem greater than it really is relative to today. Figure 8.2 gives the same information as Figure 8.1 in 2005 dollars.

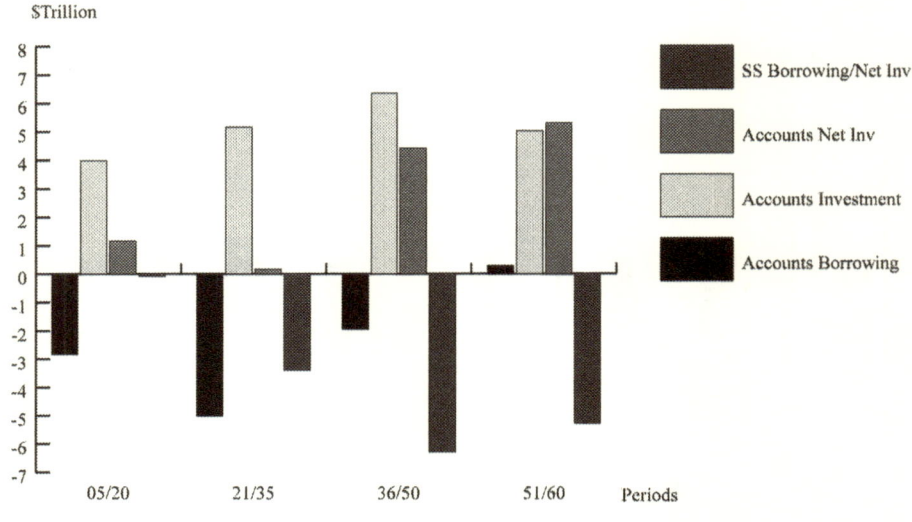

Borrowing, Investment, and Net Investment(In 2005 Dollars)

Figure 8.2 Constant Dollar Comparison of Unreformed Social Security and a Personal Accounts System

There is an exceedingly important point to understand.

The "Trust Funds" are liabilities not assets.

Most of the confusion and demagoguery surrounding the proposed reforms of Social Security depend on pretending that the Treasury bonds in the "Trust Fund" are assets and not liabilities. But the Office of Public Debt in the Treasury Department recognizes them as debt and liabilities. It lists $4.4 trillion in external debt, that is to persons and entities that are not a part of the U.S. Federal Government and $3.0 trillion in debt owed to other Federal agencies of which $1.5 trillion represents the Social Security "Trust Funds." It is Federal debt because after 2018 payroll contributions will be insufficient to pay existing benefits, the Social Security Administration will cash in "Trust Fund" bonds to pay all the benefits, if the AARP's minor adjustments are the order of the day. When it cashes in the bonds, the money will either have to come from extra tax revenues or from borrowing. So the process of using the "Trust Funds" is the process of replacing Federal Interagency debt with Federal debt to the public. The debt is transferred from the internal "Trust Fund" debt to the category of external official debt.

Interest and Earnings

Thus far the amount of money invested in personal retirement accounts in a reformed system with an average contribution of 4% of covered payroll has been estimated as the sum of the money deposited each year (Column 17 in Table 8.1). *The cumulative totals were not modified to take into account earnings on the accounts and withdrawals and spending from the accounts.* It is a difficult matter to estimate the level of investment in the accounts at any one time and the amount of earnings. A number of assumptions are necessary. Nevertheless some estimates are useful for comparison with the extra interest that must be paid on money borrowed in the early years of transition to a system with personal retirement accounts. Two figures, Figure 8.3 and 8.4, compare interest that must be paid on debt to fund the Social Security system as it currently is (assuming borrowing to cover shortfalls in income) with interest paid to fund the account system. Showing the results in nominal and real dollars is helpful because the real dollars give us a better picture of costs relative to our current economy. Earnings on the accounts were estimated. A 6% rate of return was assumed. A small percentage of the total account values was subtracted to represent money withdrawn from the accounts to fund retirement consumption. It may be that earnings are overestimated. Nevertheless a key point is that the earnings on account money invested exceed the extra interest paid to have a system with the accounts.

> *The need to pay extra interest for the personal accounts system during the transition period is more than compensated by the earnings on the accounts.*

Secondly, when we go past the year 2030, the interest on an unreformed Social Security begins to exceed the transitioning system. Of course the borrowing and paying of interest by current Social Security can be avoided by cutting benefits by the 2020's. However then the benefits provided by an accounts system are far better than our current Social Security system.

Figure 8.3 shows the amount of interest that must be paid on borrowing from the public needed to pay Social Security benefits for an unreformed system. The amounts are separated into three 15 year and one 10 year period. The figure also shows the amount of interest that must be paid on borrowing from the public to pay some of the Social Security benefits for the analyzed reformed Social Security system with personal retirement accounts. It also shows estimated earnings on the money invested in the accounts if they earn

6%. Some of the money invested was assumed to have been withdrawn and spent for retirement.

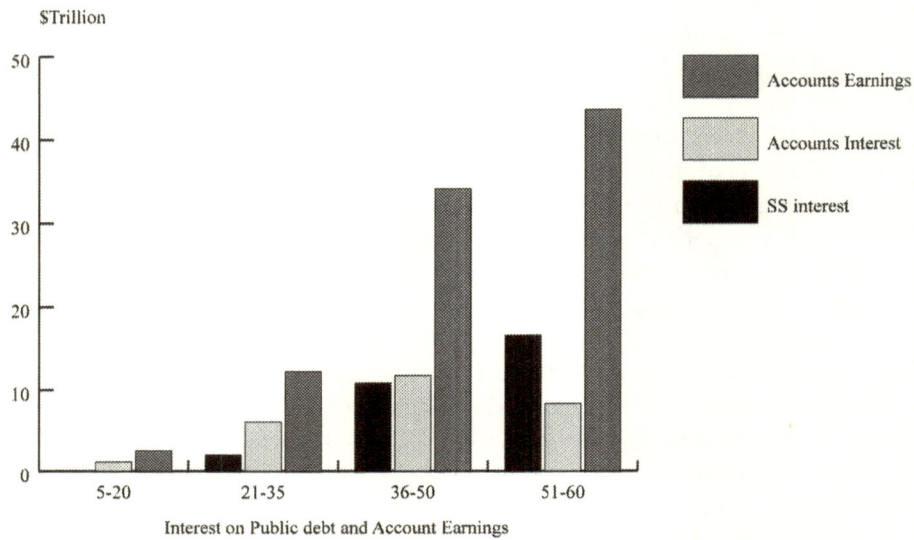

Figure 8.3 Interest on Public Debt for Social Security and Earnings on Accounts in Current Dollars

Figure 8.4 shows the same information as in Figure 8.3 except that the amounts are not in current dollars but in constant 2005 dollars.

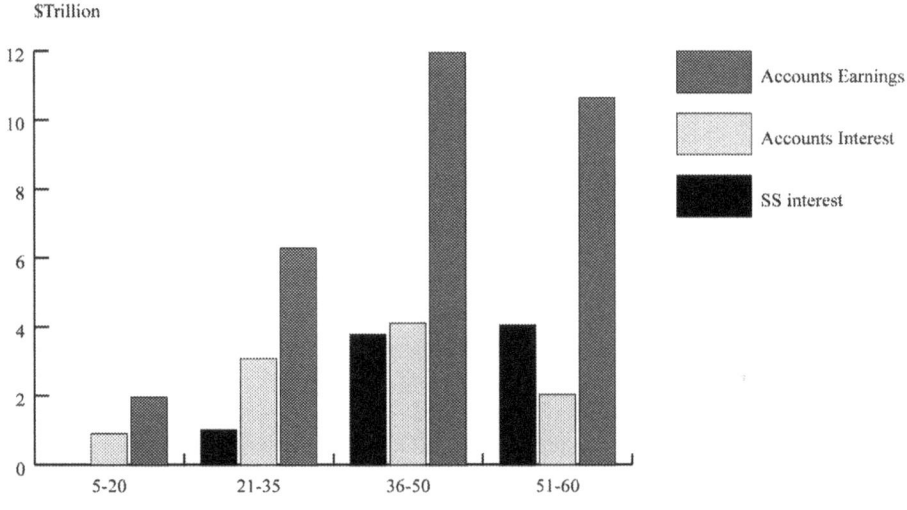

Figure 8.4 Interest on Public Debt for Social Security and Earnings on Accounts in Constant Dollars

We see that in its beginning years the accounts system must pay considerably more interest, although earnings on the accounts are greater yet. After 2035 the interest paid is about equal and then beyond 2050 greatly in the favor of an accounts system.

> *The earnings on the accounts more than double the interest that must be paid to transition to an accounts system. Politicians arguing against reforming Social Security to add personal retirement accounts entirely ignore the fact that a system with personal retirement accounts produces positive net investment and more earnings than extra interest paid.*

Comparison of Transition Costs

A first point of comparison is that after 2045 the *annual interest paid* under the current system will greatly exceed annual interest costs in a personal accounts system which by then will be close to eliminating deficits.

Second, by 2030 the economy will be about 3 times its current size so paying an extra $300 billion in interest on the National Debt will be like $100 billion in our 2005 economy. Consequently, the interest payments needed in a transition to personal accounts will not be as onerous as one might think.

Third, when considering possible transition costs it is highly important to consider savings under each plan. The existing system has no savings and discourages saving. Without a Social Security system people would save for retirement. At this time they expect Social Security payments and do less saving. Poor saving rates reduce investment and economic growth rates and yield slower rates of growth in wages and standards of living. On the other hand a personal retirement plan with an average of 4% of covered payroll placed in personal investment accounts will greatly improve saving rates, increase investment and economic growth rates and yield improved rates of growth in wages and standards of living.

Fourth, *the comparisons between the two systems have not taken into account that greater growth and higher average wages will accrue with a personal accounts system.* A system of personal accounts would produce $8.9 trillion in new saving and investment by 2030. For every year through 2030 the amount of money placed in the personal accounts will exceed the amount of deficits and the interest payments. We might expect that money would remain in personal accounts for about 40 years on average. A large percentage of the $8.9 trillion would still be in private accounts in 2030. This extra investment would more than offset the borrowing. *Remember that the purpose of the borrowing and extra interest payments is made to enable the personal accounts. So whatever extra borrowing or "transitional costs" occur, there is still considerable net investment, which does not occur at all under the current Social Security system which causes borrowing and net dissaving.*

The conclusion to be drawn is that although there are transition costs from additional borrowing and interest costs for the personal accounts system, the extra costs are more than offset by the extra investment. We find also that throughout the period from 2005 to 2042 and beyond, the system with personal accounts has positive net investment and is to be preferred to our current "pay-as-you-go" system.

What is ignored by the argument that transition costs will be very burdensome to the economy is that the transition costs are incurred just to make very large amounts of money available for investment. In most years the amount of money borrowed from the public to offset deposits in personal retirement accounts, is less than the amount transferred to the accounts and made available for investment by the private sector. If the amount of increased debt is offset by a yet greater amount of investment, the development is positive.

In contrast our current Social Security system after 2018, unless benefits are cut significantly, will have to borrow or tax to cover the shortfall. This borrowing or taxation will take funds that were available to the private sector for investment and will give them to Social Security retirees to spend. Nearly all will go to consumption. So any borrowing and taxation to cover the income shortfall will have negative consequences on the economy. Investment provides the equipment and resources necessary for creating new jobs and hiring new workers. Reducing investment money reduces the new equipment and resources put to use and reduces the number of new jobs and new workers hired. Under current Social Security, if benefits are not reduced, then the borrowing and taxation will reduce productivity, economic growth, and will increase unemployment.

Conclusions

The analysis and comparison of our current system of Social Security maintained intact with no benefit cuts to a reformed system with private accounts shows several things:

1) *There are extra transitioning costs in terms of extra borrowing that must occur in the transition to a reformed system with personal retirement accounts.*
2) *While the transition to a system with personal retirement accounts temporarily increases national debt, the increase is only temporary. By 2044 the level of borrowing by our current system would be just as great as for a reformed system with personal retirement accounts.*
3) *The current Social Security system would reduce net investment by absorbing money available for investment through borrowing it or taking it through taxes.*
4) *In contrast, a Social Security system with personal retirement accounts will increase net investment far beyond any extra borrowing.*

CHAPTER 9

The Reagan Years: Tax Changes and Deficits

Until the introduction of Keynesian economics in the 1930's, classical economics generally was "supply side." "Supply side" economics emphasizes the need for investment to improve productivity and produce greater supply of goods and services. With greater available supply, demand can increase and there is greater wealth and economic growth. In the 1930's Keynesian economics changed the thinking of many economists. Keynes emphasized the importance of demand driving supply and the usefulness of government spending to increase demand and economic growth. A percentage of spending (about 20%) goes toward investment because there is depreciation and necessary replacement of capital goods required to produce consumer goods and services. The Keynesian theory was developed to imply that investment from extra government spending for consumption had a multiplier effect that multiplied the impact on the economy. This viewpoint basically holds that the general welfare is promoted best by government control through increasing or decreasing consumption. So from the mid-1930s to 1981 when the Reagan administration took over, significant Federal deficits occurred virtually every year. They were readily justified by Keynesian economics.

In the first years of the Reagan Administration President Reagan succeeded in reducing tax rates, but could not get comparable reductions in spending. As a consequence the Federal Government ran large deficits for several years. The official national debt increased from about $1 trillion to over $4 trillion during his Presidency. The purpose of the tax cuts was to increase investment and supply. The economy improved. Tax revenues increased significantly even though rates had been reduced. This behavior fit the "Laffer Curve" which predicted that if tax rates were too high, decreasing tax rates would increase revenues. So it would seem that supply side economics explains the economic improvement. However, the "demand-side" Keynesians could explain the improvement also because the tax cuts caused deficits which meant the government spent considerably more than its revenues and so presumably increased demand.

Although Democrats could make a case for the economic growth being explained by Keynesian economics, they switched to criticizing Reagan for running large deficits. Left leaning pundits still regularly make this criticism. It is clear that their argument entirely depends on the official national debt being the true national debt and the official deficits being the true and real deficits.

However, considerable monkey business has occurred in defining the official national debt. Many items that are debt owed to Federal agencies have been placed "off-budget" so that they are not included in the official debt. In fact the true debt must be far greater than the official national debt. We must convert the official debt to a realistic amount of debt.

> *In order to estimate the debt we must realize that the unfunded liability of the Social Security system is really a part of the national debt. The unfunded liability is the money we would need to have invested right now in the stock market or other investments in order that it would grow to be a sufficient sum to fund all the promised benefits that will not be funded by FICA payroll taxes.*

Social Security retirees have been promised a level of benefits based on their earnings during their working years that for average workers replaces about 40% of their pre-retirement income. A considerable part of the benefits to be paid will be paid from the FICA OASI contributions of current workers. However, there will be a shortfall beginning in 2018. The Democrats under FDR in the 1930's created Social Security as a pay-as-you-go transfer system. Because the funding method has never invested any of the money to provide for later retirement needs, an unfunded liability was created that grew over time. Unfortunately an exact figure in terms of dollars cannot be placed on the unfunded liability because the amounts that will be paid in benefits depend on future events. Estimating the unfunded liability requires making various assumptions about wage rate increases, interest rates, immigration, birth rates, life expectancy and the like into the distant future. This unfunded liability is a part of the national debt because it results from benefits promised to current workers. After having spent their working lives paying FICA taxes, Americans expect the benefits to be paid. Savvy bond traders who determine long term interest rates know this and demand interest rates 1 or 2 percent higher to cover the risks of future inflation to reduce the debt. Government has an obligation to pay.

The unfunded liability for OASI is now about $11 trillion.[1] The reason that Social Security benefits will have to be cut or taxes raised within 20 years is to eliminate the unfunded liability. Reborrowing the money would just kick dealing with the unfunded liability down the road to be solved later. Borrowing would convert the liability to a concrete amount of debt.

If those who criticized Reagan for increasing national debt from $1 trillion to $4 trillion and running large deficits are correct, they are depending on the principle:

Voodoo Economics Principle #8: The official deficits are the true deficits and the official national debt is the true debt.

We may also recall that Chapter 6 contradicts Voodoo Economics Principle #6:

Voodoo Economics Principle #6: Deficits are always bad.

But the actual Democratic Party position on deficits and debt is probably that they are objectionable only if Republicans run them up:

Voodoo Economics Principle #6A: Deficits are good if Democrats cause them by overspending, but bad if Republicans cause them by cutting taxes.

We should not forget that the source of all spending bills, the House of Representatives during the entire Reagan Presidency, was controlled by Democrats. Democrats blame Ronald Reagan for various perceived problems and especially for greatly increasing the national debt. However, the economy Reagan inherited had very high interest rates and high unemployment. Within three years the interest rates and unemployment had been conquered. The economy experienced strong economic growth.

There are several points to make about the U.S. economy during the Reagan Administration. First, the rationale for criticizing high government deficits and increasing debt is that these conditions supposedly increase interest rates. Economic theory seems to require that large Federal deficits will cause interest rates to rise and yet study of historical data does not demonstrate any correlation between official deficits and interest rates.[2] High deficits have not shown high interest rates as Keynesian demand oriented theory would lead one to expect.

There are important reasons why the correlation between interest rates and deficits has not been observed to hold. First, the comparisons are made between the official national debt now at about $4.4 trillion and fundamental interest rates. However, the official debt is not the true debt. Various Federal agencies have borrowed money and spent it. With off-budget debt included, the Federal debt is now about $7.5 trillion. In addition there is the unfunded liability for Social Security.

The Unfunded Liability of Social Security

I estimated a 90 year unfunded liability of Social Security for 1980 and 1988 based on future deficits projected by Social Security actuaries in the 2004 Trustee Report. Because Democrats doubt that earnings for personal retirement accounts can be 6% over the long term, I used 4% as a conservative interest rate.

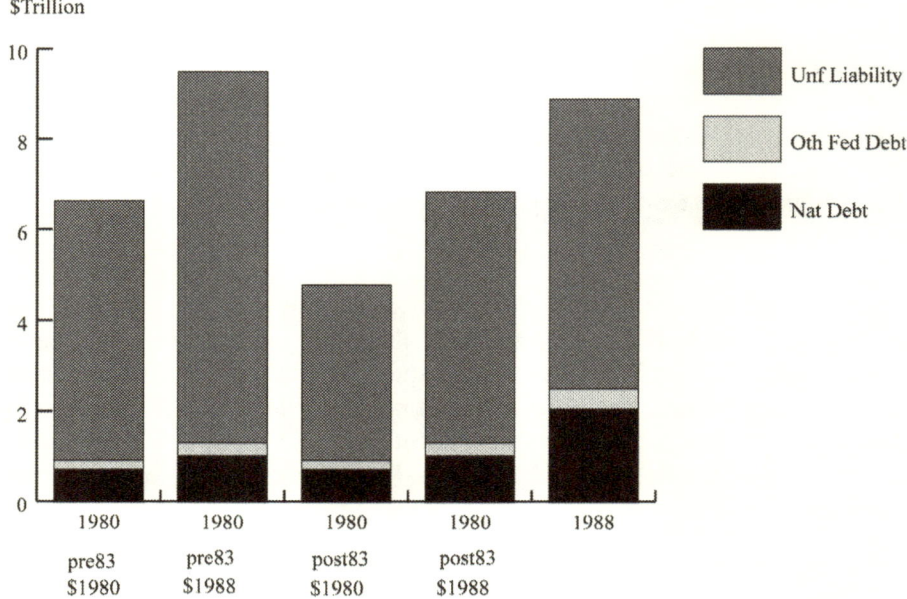

Figure 9.1 National Debt with Unfunded Liability for Social Security 1980 and 1988

Figure 9.1 shows four different representations of the national debt for 1980 which includes unfunded liabilities. The first two bars show estimates of the total debt in nominal ($1980 dollars) and $1988 dollars if the unfunded liability is calculated for Social Security as it was before the 1983 changes. The third and fourth bars give the debt in nominal and $1988 dollars as if the 1983 changes were projected back to 1980.

If we include the unfunded liability for Social Security in the national debt, we get a more realistic assessment of the level of debt during the Reagan Administration. In 1980 the unfunded liability was probably about $5.7 trillion and with a $.7 trillion national debt to the public and $.2 trillion other Federal debt, the true national debt was on the order of $6.6 trillion represented by the first bar of Figure 9.1.[3] In 1983 during the Reagan Administration the retirement age was extended modestly and the FICA OASI deduction was increased nearly 2%. These actions produced a reduction of about $1.8 trillion in liability. So if we figure the debt as if the changes made in 1983 were in place in 1980, the unfunded liability would have been $3.9 trillion with a total Federal debt of $4.8 trillion represented by the third bar of Figure 9.1.

If we want to make a true comparison between debt in 1980 and 1988 we must take inflation into account. When we put $6.6 trillion and $4.8 trillion in 1988 dollars, the Federal debt comes to $9.5 trillion and $6.8 trillion respectively as indicated by the second and fourth bars of the figure. The unfunded liabilities are $8.2 trillion and $5.5 trillion. The unfunded liability for 1988 at the end of Reagan's Presidency in 1988 dollars is about $6.4 trillion with a total Federal debt of about $8.9 trillion excluding the "Trust Funds."

> *Comparing the 1980 debt of $9.5 trillion in 1988 dollars to $8.9 trillion in debt actually shows a 6% decrease in debt during the 8 years of the Reagan presidency. When unfunded liability and inflation are taken into account the huge deficits Democrats assert were run up by Reagan were not real deficits and certainly the criticisms leveled by Democrats against Reagan's tax cutting policies are completely misplaced.*

These numbers are very rough but they show that realistic estimates of the Federal debt do not really show much change during the 8 years of the Reagan Administration. We see that the increases in the true size of the debt are not real. This explains why interest rates could fall despite the large deficits in the first Reagan term and why the Democrats' complaints about the deficits and debts do not really hold water.

The bond traders are among the most savvy groups in Wall Street. They know that the true debt includes the unfunded liability and know that with a large debt politicians are likely to procrastinate until inflation is unavoidable. Consequently, they demand a reasonable premium in higher interest rates for the risk they are taking when they buy long term Treasury bonds. Including the unfunded liability in the debt also shows why the interest rates have remained relatively stable. So if we include the unfunded liability of Social Security as part of the true deficit, the proper valuation of the Reagan years is far more positive than Democrats would allow.

Tax Developments During the Reagan Years

A brief analysis of economic developments in taxation during the Reagan years will prove insightful. First, Reagan succeeded in getting both personal and corporate income tax rates significantly reduced in 1981.[4] However, in 1982 the corporate rate reductions were rescinded in a deal intended to cut spending. This was a mistake. Reagan apparently thought that corporate taxes were passed on to consumers and did not really matter. However, corporate income or profits taxes do matter a great deal. As we shall see below and particularly in Chapter 13, high profits taxes have a number of deleterious consequences. They increase industry concentration by imposing barriers to entry into an industry. Most importantly they discourage investment.

Figure 9.2 indicates the changes in the top marginal rates in the tax code during the 1980's. The top marginal rate has a strong impact on the amount of money invested and how it is invested. It applies to the people with the greatest investment in the stock market. The top rates also give a rough idea of the rates for income brackets below the top level. In the figure the bars for 1980 show the rates that held prior to the Reagan tax legislation in 1981. The 1985 bars show the rates that held for the years 1982 to 1985 and the 1990 bars show the rates that held for 1986 to 1990 from the 1986 tax legislation. We see that over the decade there was relatively little change in corporate profits taxes and capital gains. But there was a very large change in the top personal rates. Lower brackets also received significant reductions.

Percent

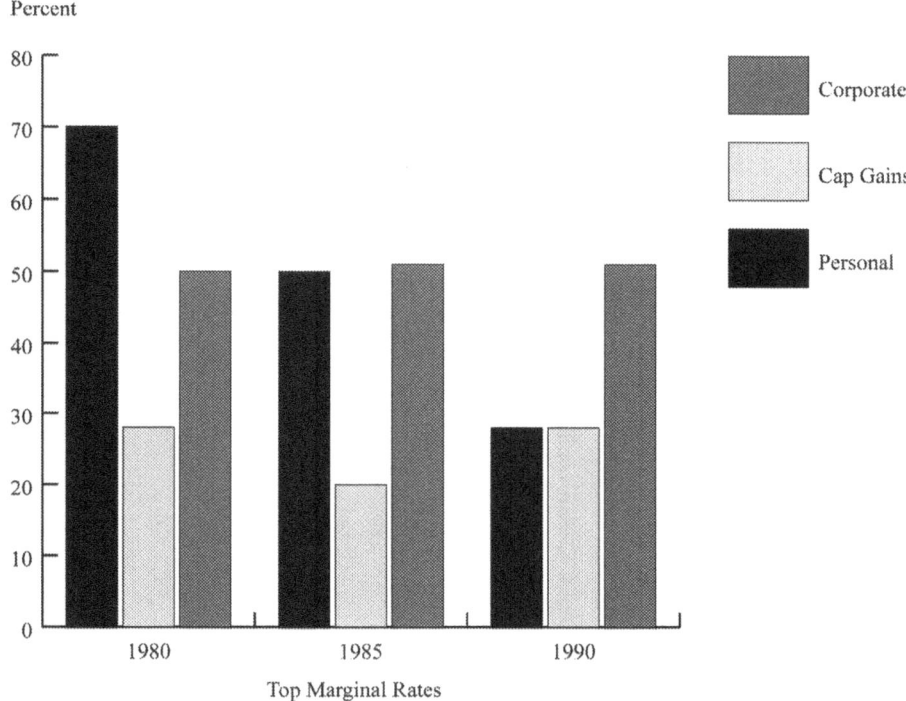

Figure 9.2 Top Income Tax Rates in the 1980's

The figure shows negligible change in corporate rates. However, in 1986 investment tax credits were eliminated increasing effective corporate tax rates significantly. But the main reduction was in personal rates. This of course also reduces the overall effective corporate rates since individuals pay taxes on the dividend part of profits.

Figure 9.3 shows marginal effective tax rates[5]. Marginal rates are most important because the marginal rate tells us what a person can expect to pay in taxes if he or she can earn an extra $1 or $100. If the tax rates are high, that is over 40 or 50 percent, there is a much greater likelihood that a taxpayer will decide not to bother because the return expected does not seem worth the effort. The effective rates are rates estimated for the economy as a whole or for particular groups within the U.S. economy. The line in Figure 9.3 for personal rates gives the average marginal rate for personal income. The line in Figure 9.3 for corporations shows the marginal effective rate for all corporations.

There are also lines for manufacturing business and for retained earnings (profits less dividends paid).

> *We see that profits are taxed quite highly and the manufacturing sector higher than the corporate sector in general.*

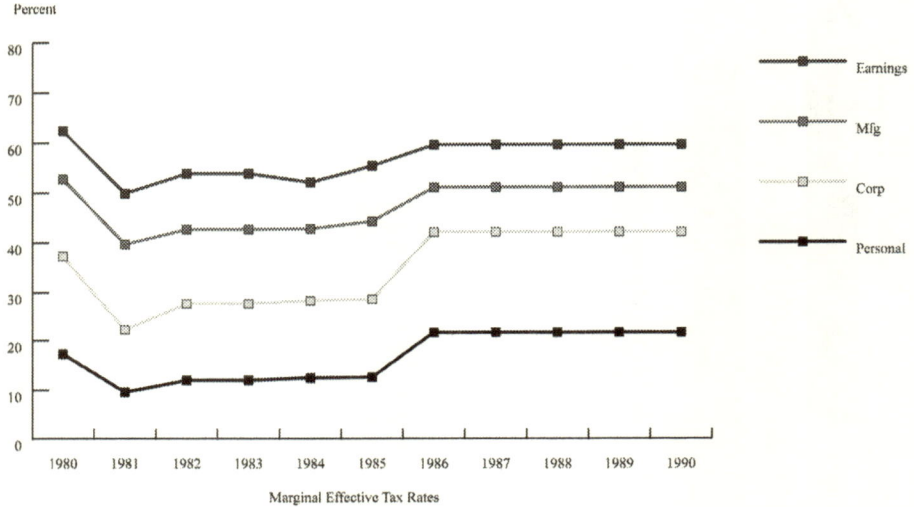

Figure 9.3 Effective Tax Rates in the 1980's for Four Categories of Taxes

The Pernicious Effects of the Corporate Income Tax

> Over the long run it is actually more beneficial to cut corporate taxes than personal income taxes. After-tax profits largely go to investment. Corporations are responsible for the great majority of investment, especially in manufacturing.

Cuts in personal income taxes give consumers more money to spend and the bulk of the money is spent on consumption rather than saved and invested. Cuts in corporate income taxes produce increases in investment and not investment to replace depreciated plants and equipment, but to expand into new areas and new investments. The corporate tax cuts do much more to produce long term economic growth and higher wages and salaries. Consequently, by retaining relatively high corporate tax rates on retained earnings the Reagan Administration, although bringing considerable improvement to the economy, failed to realize higher rates of economic growth that were possible.

Our tax code has caused slower economic growth than we should have experienced. The worst part of the code is its high rate of taxation of capital. If we want to improve economic growth, reducing marginal tax rates across the board is desirable. Eliminating taxation of profits would be more beneficial than reducing personal rates. When personal rates are reduced a considerable part of the income retained by households goes toward consumption, investment in real estate, and to bid up stock prices. On the other hand, when rates on corporate profits are reduced, much more of the retained income will be invested in plant and equipment and for human capital.

When double taxation of dividends (about a third of profits) is considered, the marginal tax rate for corporate investment that is not financed by debt is about 60% (counting taxes on dividends to stockholders). By focusing on the capital gains tax as the tax needing to be fixed, many proponents of change seem to believe that reducing the capital gains tax solves the problem. But reducing or eliminating capital gains does not address the high taxation of profits. Profits taxes remain. Corporate officers must still make investment decisions based on paying the tax.

As globalization increases competition between American and foreign corporations, the relative effective tax rates on profits levied by different countries become more important. The U.S. is among a small group of countries with the highest effective corporate tax rates (see Chapter 13 Figure 13.4). This puts the U.S. at a disadvantage in competition with most other countries. Our corporations usually have to pay higher taxes on profits. If they want to maintain their after tax profits to satisfy their stockholders and keep their stock prices up, they must charge higher prices than most of their foreign competitors. If we wish to eliminate this disadvantage the simplest solution is to abolish corporate income taxes.

When one considers the adverse effects of the corporate profits tax on our economy, it becomes apparent that the benefits of increased investment, better paying jobs, and economic growth from eliminating profits taxes far outweigh the relatively small amount of revenue that profits taxes produce (about 11% of Federal revenue and 8% of all government revenue).[6] To promote the most growth, profits taxes should be eliminated altogether. If profits taxes were eliminated by repeal or by moving to a sales tax, there would be added reason to end corporate subsidies which are also very bad for the economy. Democrats are as responsible, if not more responsible than Republicans for many of the subsidies given to big business. Politicians of both parties use subsidies of various kinds to encourage and reward large corporations for large campaign contributions. The Clinton Administration introduced many new subsidies.[7] Eliminating all subsidies at the same time all profits taxes are eliminated would seem to be fair. Eliminating profits taxes and subsidies would eliminate favoritism given to the very large corporations.

> *Negative effects of profits taxes on investment are very significant because the bulk of saving and investment is done by corporations (77% of gross saving in 2004).[8]*

Corporations employ a majority of the workforce (over 50% of total employed and over 60% of private workers) and can create many well-paying jobs if the economy provides the incentives for them to do so. Profits are the primary source of financing for expansion and new projects. When the government takes most of the profits and spends it on bureaucratic projects, opportunities to improve productivity go to waste as well as many potential well paying jobs.

Allowing companies to keep all their earnings would yield higher returns on invested capital and improve incentives to invest. The most significant impact of the imposition of corporate profits taxes is a direct effect. The profits tax depresses returns by expropriating part of the return. Returns to capital are depressed also by other factors. Burdensome bureaucratic regulations squeeze profits by forcing corporations to invest capital in projects for the sake of compliance without yielding any return on the investment. There are also a number of indirect effects of profits taxes that have a very serious negative impact on capital investment. These effects cause reduced competition in industry and increased perceptions of risk. When competition is reduced there is less incentive for corporations to invest. Other effects cause resources to be misallocated. More detail in support of these contentions about the negative effects of profits taxes is provided in Chapter 13.

Economic Trends During the Reagan Years

Thus far we have concluded that the level of debt during the Reagan Administration did not change much in real terms if we take the unfunded liability for Social Security retirement into account. Corporate income taxes remained relatively high. Personal income tax rates were reduced significantly. So given these changes in the tax environment, what economic trends do we observe during the 1980's?

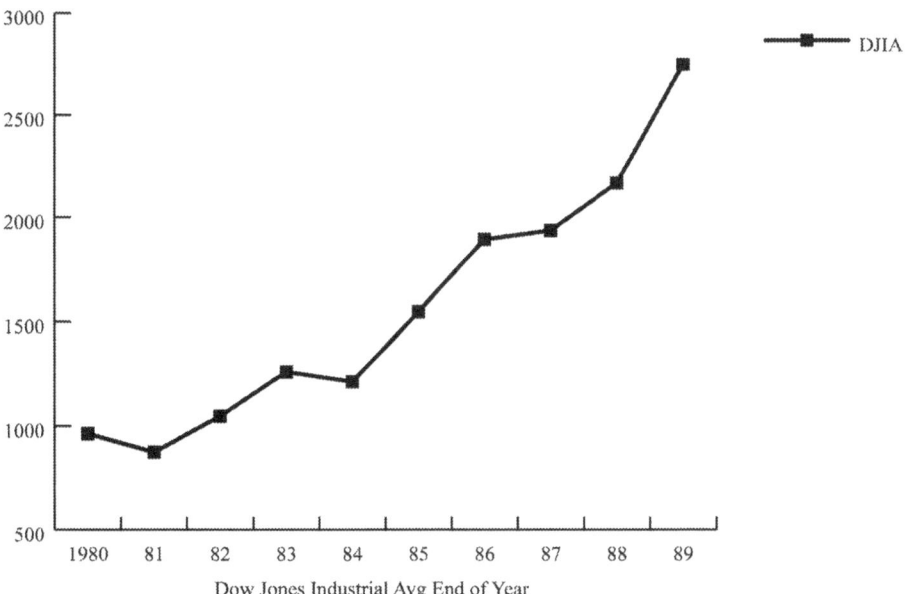

Figure 9.4 Increase in Dow Jones Average during the 1980's

Figure 9.4 shows the end of year levels of the Dow-Jones Industrial Average for the 1980's. We see steady growth during the Reagan years which is an indicator that the economy was doing well. Figure 9.5 shows some additional key rates.[9] The after tax returns or after tax profits stayed around 3 percent of capital invested. A higher rate would have produced more income available for investment. More investment would have meant greater economic growth. Long term interest rates came down from extreme highs to relatively high levels. *High interest rates that are higher than after tax returns on capital discourage capital investment.* Real growth fell during the 1982 recession but did generally improve over the decade, although falling at the end during the George H.W. Bush Presidency.

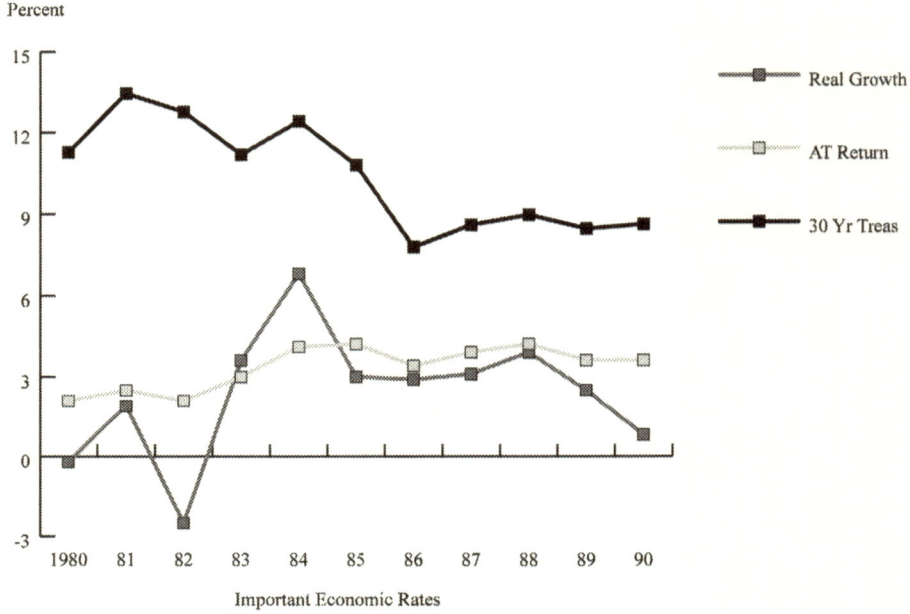

Figure 9.5 Interest, Earnings, and Growth in the 1980's

We can understand what happened during the Reagan Years. Retention of high corporate income taxes has the following effect. The money received from cuts in personal rates that goes into saving and investment can go into one of three kinds of investment: 1) capital investments in plants, equipment or in training, 2) real estate, and 3) financial assets. In the 1980's the high taxation of capital meant that expected returns were much better if devoted to real estate or financial assets. Consequently most of the investment money freed up by the Reagan tax cuts went into real estate and financial assets. The real estate market exploded. Eventually the bubble burst. Many Savings and Loans went bankrupt. The stock market also increased dramatically during the 1980's. The investment in capital was not what it could have been. Economic growth was decent (averaging about 3% per year), but it could have been better and it would have been better had profits taxes been reduced. An additional problematic trend of the 1980's was the abundance of mergers.

When corporate income taxes are high there will be more mergers. The lower returns that result from high profits taxes keep stock prices lower and make mergers easier. Companies are cheaper to buy. High taxes on profits make expanding business empires the old fashioned way through capital investment and internal expansion much more difficult. The entrepreneur who wants to expand his empire finds it easier to expand by buying competitors than by building new plants and investing in new equipment.

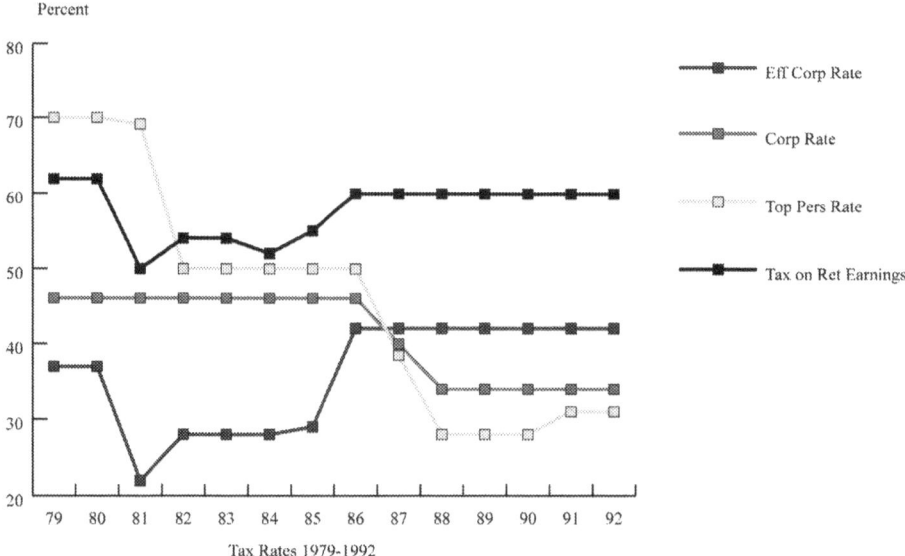

Figure 9.6 Corporation and Personal Marginal Effective Rates

Figure 9.6 shows a number of trends.[10] We see that the top personal rate fell dramatically from 70% to 50% and then 28% over the period. During this time the corporate statutory rate began at 48% and dropped to 34% in 1986. The overall effective marginal corporate income tax rate began the period at about 37%, fell to about 28% or less from 1981 to 1985 and then climbed back over 40% for the rest of the period. A marginal rate is the rate a corporation or individual will pay on one additional dollar of income. It is the best measure of incentives to invest extra dollars. Corporations have three sources of funds for investment: borrowing money, issuing and selling new stock, and retained earnings (earnings after paying taxes and dividends to stockholders). The effective rate of taxation for retained earnings began the period at 62%, dropped about 10% from 1981 to 1985 and ended the period at about 58%. The taxation of new issue of stock is comparable to the taxation of retained earnings, while funding by debt is subsidized.

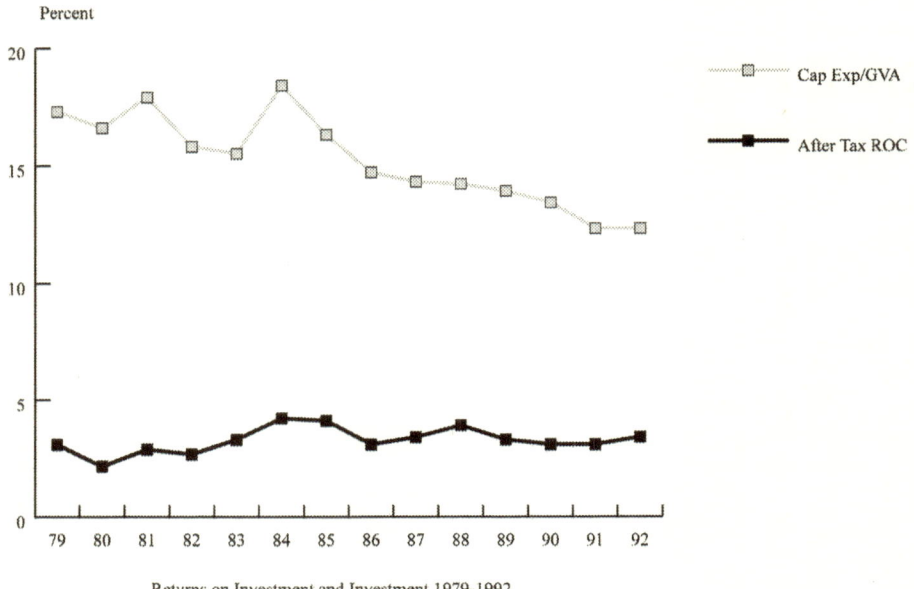

Returns on Investment and Investment 1979-1992

Figure 9.7 Returns to Capital and Capital Invested as a Percentage of Gross Value Added

> *The high taxation of retained earnings causes lackluster returns and discourages capital investment (Cap Exp).*

Figure 9.7 shows the rate of return (ROC) on invested capital by non-financial corporations and the amount of investment relative to gross value added (GVA).[11]

> *The returns on capital after taxes run in the 2 to 4% range for the period. This is not very good. It is below interest rates, and so serves as an incentive to invest in financial assets which brought higher returns during the period.*

We see from Figure 9.7 that non-financial corporate capital expenditures relative to gross value added by non-financial corporations was higher in the earlier part of the period when corporate income taxes were lower. This does support the claim that higher corporate income taxes reduce corporate investment and that lower corporate income taxes increase corporate investment.

These trends show why the 1980's did not have good capital investment, but strong investment in real estate and financial assets leading to booms and then busts in those areas.

Greater tax and spending cuts might have improved matters but were probably not politically feasible. Reagan's legacy makes him a great president by what he accomplished economically despite the opposition of the House of Representatives. This is not an ideal world in which we can expect perfect outcomes.

CHAPTER 10

Static Analysis

When discussing tax matters Democrats always insist on using static analysis. They always calculate the effect of the tax increases and decreases using static analysis, whether it is Ted Kennedy, Al Gore in 2000, or John Kerry in 2004. Perhaps the best example of this is the Clinton Tax increase of 1993, which Democrats still, a dozen years later, tout as having brought about a balanced budget and having led to 7 years of prosperity. The great claim that Democrats have been making ever since 1993 is that the Clinton tax increases of 1993 were the basis for a terrific economy during the Clinton two-term presidency. Based on static analysis the Clinton tax increase was supposedly a $500 billion tax increase over 5 years. One-half of the increase was in the nature of user fees for government services which had previously been free. The other $250 billion was based on static analysis of increases in income tax rates including taxes on Social Security benefits if the recipients' total income exceeded certain amounts. The top personal rate went up by 8% to 39.6%. Corporate tax rates were raised 1% to 35%.

What is Static Analysis?

Static analysis works as follows: if in 2004 $100 billion was subject to a 30% income tax and raised $30 billion in tax revenue, then if we raise the tax rate to 60% we should obtain a proportionate $60 billion, an increase of $30 billion. Correspondingly if we lower the tax rate to 10%, proportionality indicates we will expect to get $10 billion in taxes, a tax cut of $20 billion. Normally an assumption is made that the $100 billion is increased with inflation to $103 billion. Thus static analysis as applied to tax matters asserts:

Voodoo Economics Principle #9: Income tax revenues increase or decrease proportionally to increases or decreases in the income tax rate.

We might replace Voodoo Economics Principle #9 with a principle upon which it depends, namely

Voodoo Economics Principle #9A: Wealthy, greedy, capitalists will gladly submit their earnings to higher tax rates and pay proportionately.

Obviously the principle depends on taxpayers not making changes in investments or their amount of work. Common sense tells us that if taxes are very high taxpayers are likely to try to protect their assets. Common sense tells us the principle is surely false. Let us consider evidence.

Economic Trends during the Clinton Years

During the 8 years of Bill Clinton's presidency Democrats and many in the media crowed about the U.S economy. The stock market increased moderately until November 1994 when the Republicans gained control of both houses of Congress. After the Republicans gained control of Congress in the November 1994 elections, the stock market rose spectacularly until the year 1999. The Dow Jones increased at a rate of about 25% per year reaching a peak in 1999 (see Figure 10.1).

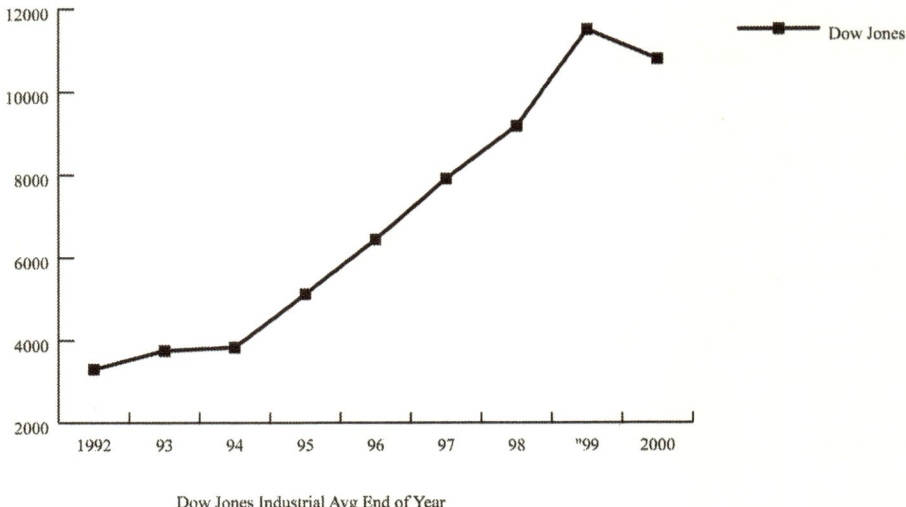

Dow Jones Industrial Avg End of Year

Figure 10.1 Increase in Dow Jones Average during the 1990s

Interest rates increased some during 1994, the second year of the Clinton Administration, when Democrats controlled Congress and the Presidency, until November 1994 when the Republicans gained control of both houses of Congress at which time the interest rates began falling. This is shown by the line in Figure 10.2 representing the rate for 30 year Treasury Bonds.

Percent

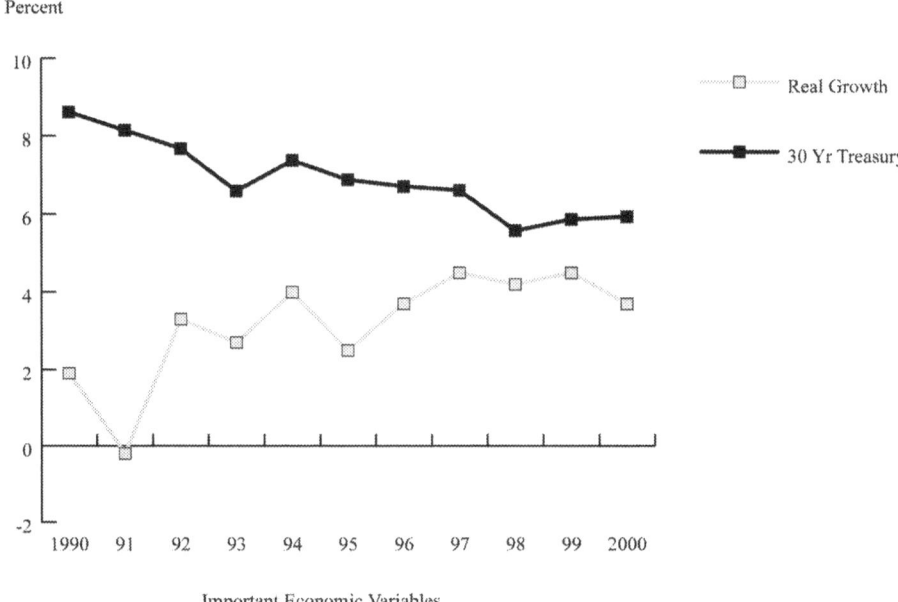

Important Economic Variables

Figure 10.2 Long Term Interest Rates and Economic Growth in the 1990s

The figure also shows annual rates of economic growth for the U.S. economy.[1] Annual growth rates of 4% are good and they improved in the last year of George H.W. Bush's Presidency and were strongest after Republicans had gained control of both houses of Congress. When Wall Street is highly enthusiastic it usually signals that the economy is a little anemic. During the Clinton years economic growth was not spectacular, it could have been significantly better.

Low income workers were struggling just as much as they were prior to Clinton or after Clinton. The main difference was that the media were much more sympathetic to Democrats. They criticized Republican presidents but ignored the problems of the Clinton presidency in order to rave about its apparent accomplishments instead. The economy during the Clinton years was not as robust as the media suggested. There were still many low-income and unemployed workers struggling just as much as during the Bush years before and after Clinton. During the last Clinton years the corporate profit numbers published by the Bureau of Economic Analysis (BEA) were inflated.[2] For 1999, 2000, and 2001 the corporate profits were overstated by

$143 billion. Since the BEA is the agency that is the official source of economic statistics for the U.S. economy, it's numbers are believed. The result was that Wall Street believed corporations were doing better than they really were doing. The economy was credited with being somewhat better than it really was.

So did the Clinton static analysis projected tax increases balance the budget and give the economy the kick in the pants Democrats claim? Let us look first at the initial tests of static analysis on U.S. tax revenues.

The First Test

The first test of the accuracy of static analysis came from 1916 to 1921 when taxes needed to be raised to pay for World War I. In 1915 the top rate for personal income tax was 7% on incomes above $500,000. In 1916 there were 206 millionaires. The net income for those with incomes of $300,000 or more was close to $1 billion yielding $81 million in revenue.[3] World War I had caused considerable government debt which needed to be reduced. Congress using static analyses judged that raising the top rate to 70% would increase revenues proportionally, that is, a tenfold increase in percentage would yield a tenfold increase in revenues. Figure 10.3 shows the yearly changes in the top personal income tax rate.[4] Note the big increase in 1917 when the top rate went from 15% to 67%.

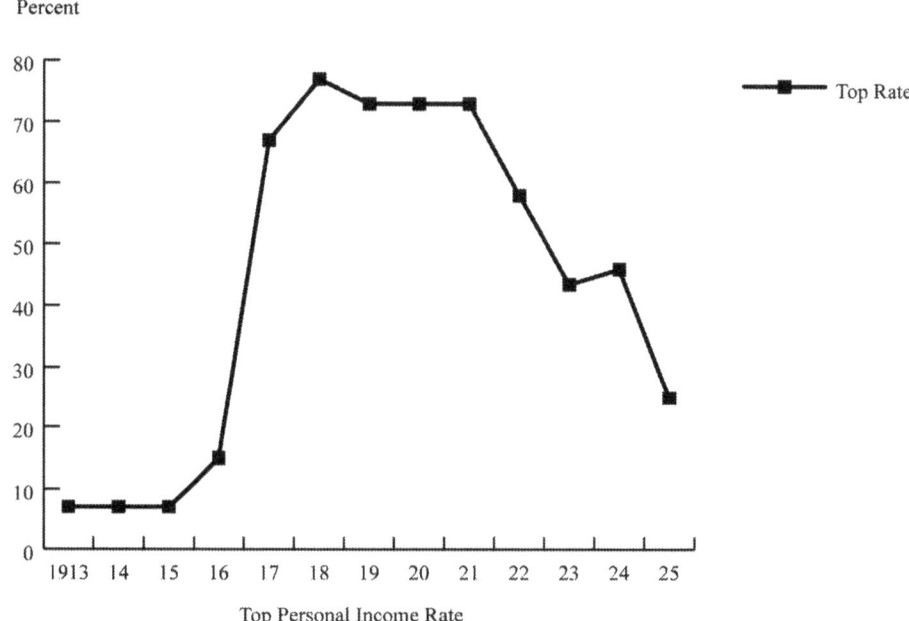

Figure 10.3 Tax Rate for Millionaire Incomes

So according to Voodoo Economics Principle #9 the 70% rate should have yielded the U.S. Treasury about $600 million.

In 1921 as proponents of Voodoo Economics with four years of top rates over 73% or more, we would expect to still find about 200 millionaires. On a net income of about $1 billion for those with incomes greater than $300,000 we would expect to collect about $600 million in revenue. BUT NO!! When we look at the tax statistics we find that in five years the number of millionaires fell from 206 to 21 and the net income for those with incomes greater than $300,000 dropped from $1 billion to $153 million.[5] So the taxpayers in the top brackets produced $84 million in revenue, slightly more than for the year 1916 despite the tenfold increase in tax percentage.

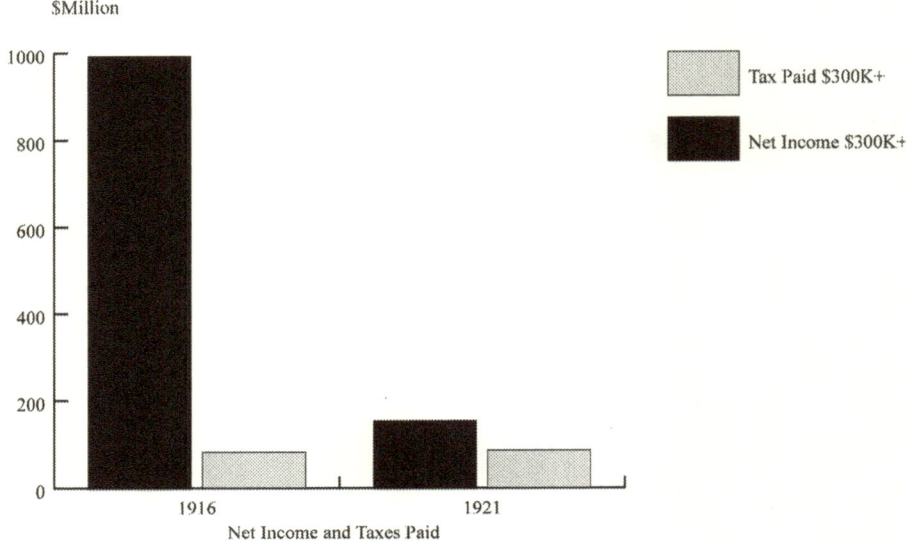

Figure 10.4 Decrease in High Incomes 1916 to 1921

Figure 10.4 shows the decrease in net income subject to income tax for taxpayers with more than $300,000 of net income. The taxpayers paid approximately the same amount of tax even though the top tax rate in 1916 was 15% and 73% in 1921. Figure 10.5 shows the decline in number of million dollar incomes and incomes over $300,000. After 1921 the top tax rates were cut significantly, so for 1924 we see the number of persons in the top brackets beginning to increase again as well as did net income.

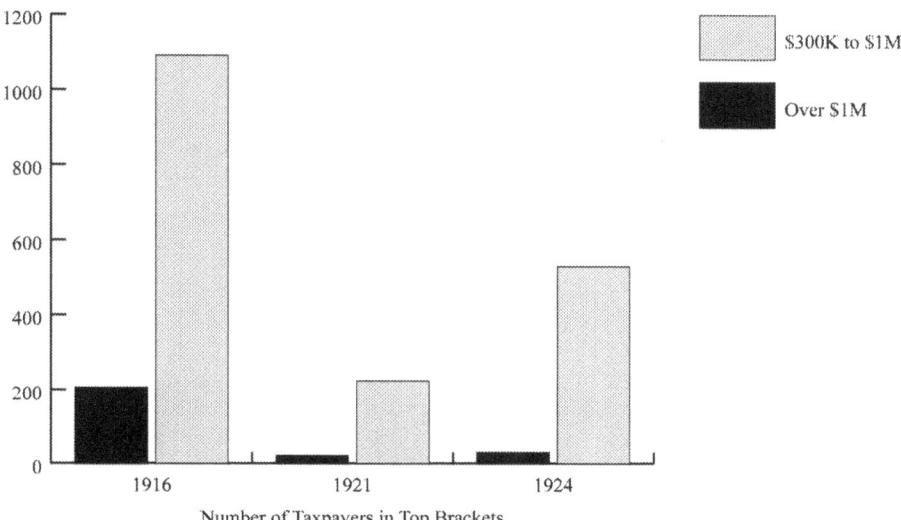

Figure 10.5 Number of Taxpayers in Top Two Brackets

Figure 10.6 shows the decline in incomes over $300,000 for the years. Principle #9A is surely not true. Wealthy people do not passively submit to tax increases if they can avoid them.

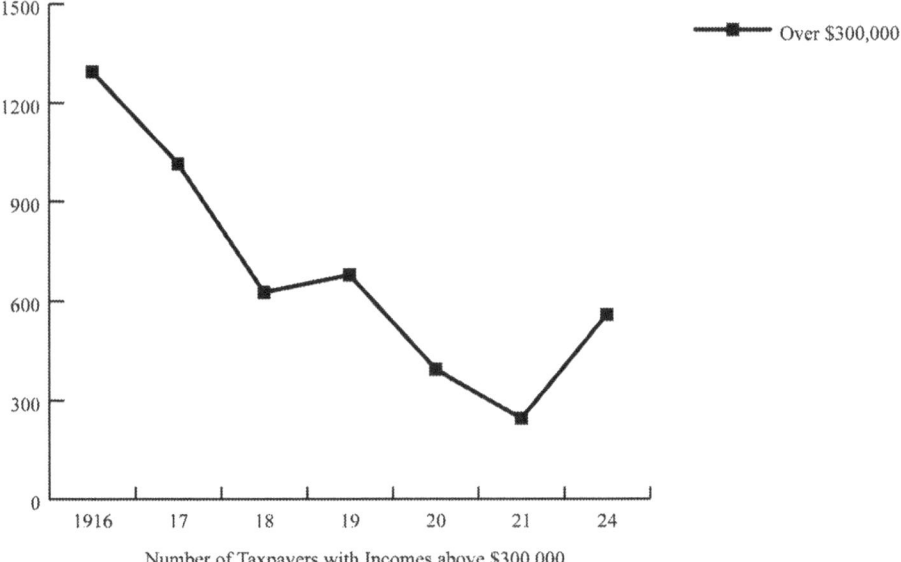

Figure 10.6 Number of Taxpayers with Incomes greater than $300,000 by Year.

Either many high income earners moved to the Bahamas or other countries or sold assets and bought municipal bonds.[6] Perhaps they, like Andrew Mellon, invested heavily in art collections. Figure 10.7 shows the rapid increase in tax-exempt bonds.[7] Note the surge in 1917 when the top rate went from 15% to 67%. Raising the income tax rates was a boon to communities desiring to build office buildings, bridges, roads, sewers and the like and to art collectors. But putting investment into assets of this type is not very beneficial for growing an economy.

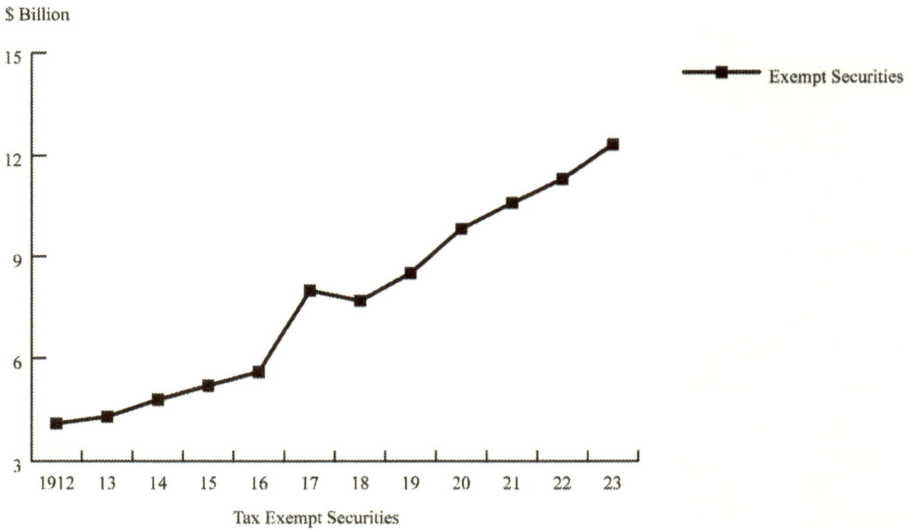

Figure 10.7 Increase in Investment in Tax Exempt Securities

While the large tax rate increases on the wealthiest taxpayers failed to increase the receipts from those taxpayers, the tax base was broadened considerably. In 1916 the taxpayers with more than $300,000 in net income constituted .34% of all taxpayers and had 10.7% of taxable income. The next year there were 7.5 times as many taxpayers as in 1915 and net income more than doubled.[8] The government revenues quadrupled, but only because the tax base increased. Revenues increased by increasing the number of taxpayers subject to tax. In 1921 the number of taxpayers was 10 times the number in 1916. The net income subject to the tax was over 3 times the amount in 1916. Yet the income tax paid increase only from $173 million to $719 million, just over 4 times more than in 1916, despite the much higher tax rates.

Static Analysis and Tax Rate Cuts

Thus far we have examined static analysis of tax rate increases. It is clear that static analysis is not correct—that revenues do not increase proportionally for increased rates. What can we say concerning use of static analysis to project results of tax rate cuts or decreases? It seems that the Laffer curve has clearly been validated by the experience of the 1980's when rates were cut and income tax revenues significantly increased. Above a certain point reduction in income tax rates actually increases revenues. Below that point some reductions in revenues may occur, but not necessarily proportional to the cuts. Yet Democrats insist on static analysis and proportionality for tax cuts as well. What is the reason? No doubt they oppose tax cuts in virtually all cases.

> *Static analysis implies that tax rate cuts cause proportional cuts in revenue and consequently that the dollar amount of the cuts will be much greater than will actually occur. By insisting on static analysis opponents of tax rate cuts can claim that the cuts will cost more revenue than they will in fact cost. They want to frighten voters about the cuts, making the cuts politically more difficult to receive approval.*

It is very clear that static analysis does not work for tax rate cuts any better than for tax rate increases, especially if the tax rate is above the point on the Laffer curve that produces increased revenue from rate cuts. This was shown by the results of the Reagan tax cuts in personal rates in the early 1980's. Personal tax rates were cut significantly and yet the tax revenue *increased* significantly. However, spending increased more and deficits resulted.

Continued Use of Static Analysis

Static analysis for estimating tax revenues is just wildly inaccurate. One would expect Democrats to get it. But have they? It is now 85 years after 1920 and Democrats all continue to use static analysis and insist on using it to evaluate tax bills. When will they ever learn? Are they just stupid or are they disingenuous using static analysis to fool the public by suggesting tax cuts cost the government more in revenue than they really do, so that they can continue to spend?

In the 1970's and 1980's a new school of economics arose called "rational expectations" economics. Rational expectations economics emphasizes the rationality of players in the economy who alter their choices to take into account what is in their best interest. Rational expectations economics requires tax policy to be analyzed in dynamic terms assuming that the taxpayers will alter their behavior if tax rates are changed significantly. Unfortunately most leaders in the Democratic Party learned Keynesian demand side economics and are still operating with it.

The Clinton Tax Increase and Static Analysis

What then happened with the Clinton increases of $500 billion over 5 years that were supposed to reduce the deficit and benefit the economy so much? There were several different kinds of tax increases in the 1993 tax bill. About $125 billion was expected to come from the increases for persons with taxable incomes over $140,000. As anyone with a little common sense who does not believe that everyone is wholly altruistic by nature knows, when wealthy tax-payers are faced with a substantial increase in tax rates they move a lot of their investments into municipal bonds which the Constitution prevents the Federal Government from taxing, or into collectibles like art. Less money is invested in the private sector and economic growth rates drop. People who understood the impact of the Clinton tax increases of 1993 realized that the Federal Government would be lucky to collect even 40% of the $125 billion increase calculated by static analysis. An analysis of the 1993 IRS tax data showed that the upper income persons affected by the tax legislation would have produced an extra $19.3 billion in tax revenue by static analysis from the rate increases. But the taxpayers affected actually produced only an extra $8.4 billion.[9] The study did not estimate some further losses due to shifting income to earlier tax years. Thus the Federal Government collected at least $11 billion less than expected from static analysis for 1993. Over 5 years we can figure that nearly $100 billion of the projected increases were phantom. Some of the other taxes and user fees may not have materialized either. Let's say the 1993 tax bill increased collections by about $70 billion per year. With the U.S. GDP around $7 trillion, this amounted to only about 1% of the economy per year. Peanuts! How could anyone seriously believe that increasing revenue by 1% of GDP make the difference between a lackluster and a flourishing economy? Since Democrats have been crowing about how wonderful the economy was during the Clinton years, it is clear that they believe in the principle:

Voodoo Principle of Economics #10: Miniscule changes in government revenue can transform the economy.

Another example of this principle occurred during the 2004 Presidential election campaign. Sen. John Kerry suggested cutting profits taxes to help U.S. companies compete against their global competitors. This was a useful idea. But the cut was only about 3% and yet this was touted as a change that would make a major improvement.[10]

Most Democrats seem to think that the full tax increases projected by the Clinton Administration were realized, caused the budget to be balanced, and that this explained the good economic growth during the Clinton Years. In fact the impact was so small that the Clinton tax increases cannot be given credit for balancing the budget or for rejuvenating the economy. The fact that the economy did as well as it did is a testimony more to shifting control of Congress from Democrats to Republicans. The so-called "shutdown" of the government and spending discipline from 1995 to 1998 was brought about by the Republicans. Also Bill Clinton's policies were relatively benign once the medical plan was defeated.

> *The fact is that Presidents do very little to improve the economy, unless they succeed as Reagan did in getting significant cuts in tax rates.*

A key event during the Clinton years was the "government shutdown" during the months following the 1994 election when Republicans took over Congress. The Republicans insisted on severe spending reductions. Bills funding government activities did not get passed on time and Clinton was able to cause the media and the general public to place the blame with the Republicans.

> *The "shutdown" of the government and holding up spending legislation slowed the growth of government for four or five years. The growth path in U.S. Government spending was lowered permanently.*

When Clinton took office he was claiming the deficits could not be eliminated in less than about 10 years. In fact from Republican pressure, the U.S. Government began running surpluses by 1998 within 5 years of his taking office.

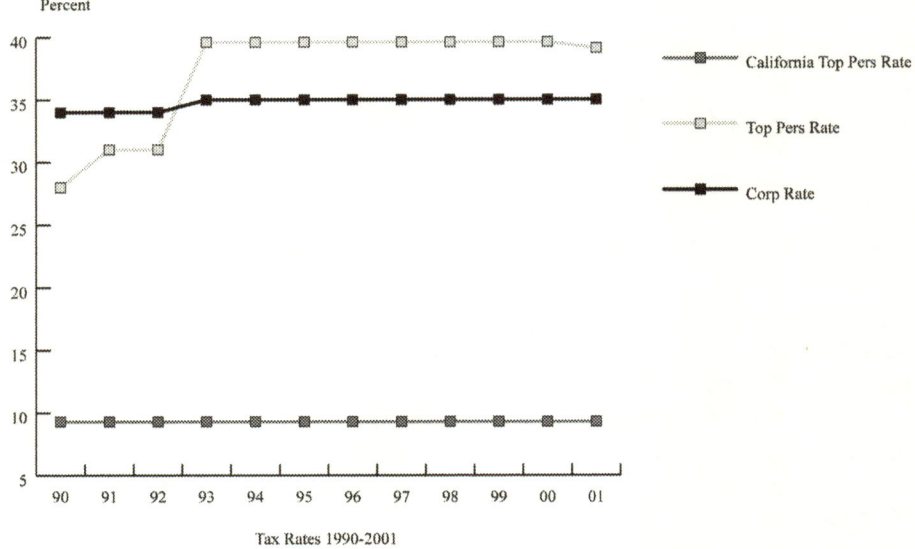

Figure 10.8 Top Personal and Corporate Tax Rates in the 1990s

Figure 10.8 shows top tax rates during the 1990's. Taxes on corporations and personal income increased moderately with the Clinton tax increase in 1993.

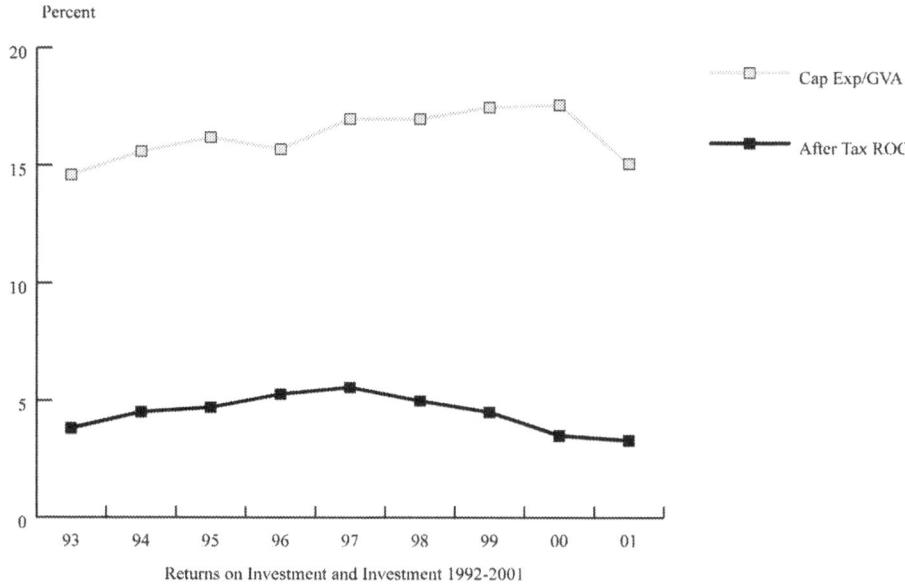

Figure 10.9 Returns to Capital and Capital Invested as a Percentage of Gross Value Added

Figure 10.9 shows returns on capital invested and investment.[11] Returns on investment were best from 1995 to 1998 when the Republican Congress was able to hold the line on government spending. Increases in investment occur after increasing returns with a lag.

So the claims by Democrats that the Clinton policies were the cause of good economic times for 8 years have very little to do with Clinton. Some credit must go to him because he did little harm to the economy. But at the same time it was the Republican controls on spending that delighted Wall Street and did the most to keep the economy growing.

> *The measures taken during the Reagan years were still having a positive effect. Yet corporate profits taxes were still quite high. Consequently, there are reasons to believe that economic growth was lower than it could have been.*

CHAPTER 11

Will Elites Protect the Public?

As pointed out in Chapter 1 there is a principle implicit in the views of socialists and others on the left who desire to put more of the economy under the supervision of bureaucrats:

Voodoo Economic Principle #1: Elites (legislators and bureaucrats) know better than entrepreneurs how money should be invested in an economy.

Socialists apparently believe that it does not matter who spends money earmarked for investment needed to improve productivity, to create jobs, and to provide the services desired by citizens. They are quite willing to tax profits earmarked for investment and have bureaucrats spend it instead. Their incentives are opposite to those affecting entrepreneurs. Bureaucrats want their empires to expand and this will only happen if they waste the investment money on boondoggles and fail in their tasks. They can then claim that more money and a larger empire is needed to do the job.

Capitalists on the other hand use profits as a guide to where money should be invested. Profits will show the goods and services most in demand by the public. If they invest to provide the goods and services most in demand, the demand will quickly be met. Market problems will get fixed. New areas of demand will arise which will be met by shifting investment to new areas. In this way economies have the money invested in the most useful and fruitful ways leading to the best economic growth because it is invested where most needed.

The "Greedy" Capitalists

People on the left tend to believe that people are good, but the poor are victims of society especially of the evil, greedy capitalists who take advantage of them and exploit them. It is necessary for the welfare of the downtrodden that elites must step in to help them. They assume the principle:

Voodoo Economic Principle #11: Only Elites will protect the public from the depredations of greedy capitalists.

The person from the left tends to believe in the goodness of man and to believe people will not try to take advantage of others. Secondly, the only evil people are the entrepreneurs or capitalists who exploit people to gain greater profits. The public apparently is not sufficiently intelligent to recognize that they are being exploited. Elites and bureaucrats are needed to recognize problems and deal with them.

As will be shown by a number of examples in Chapter 12, bureaucrats in fact do NOT protect the public well. Free markets do a better job.

> *The nature of a capitalist economy is not to find ways to exploit but to find ways to serve the needs and desires of the citizens of a society.*

Companies compete to serve the needs. The companies that best fulfill needs are the companies that will be successful. Companies that exploit will send exploited consumers and employees elsewhere and may suffer legal sanctions. If they want to stay in business, it is very advisable to serve rather than exploit. In practice and in fact the public is best served and protected by capitalists not bureaucrats. When laws and bureaucratic regulations intended to protect everyone proliferate and become complex, many opportunities for exploitation are actually created. Lawyers and parasites on society are given opportunities to take advantage of their compatriots and line their pockets from public funds and from meritless lawsuits against private parties.

Increased Government Services and Taxes

Democrats believe that everybody in the U.S. should have equal access to education and health care. The only way to try to ensure equality of treatment is to impose socialistic approaches. Government bureaucrats are to be given oversight and to attempt to provide equal funding for all. In order to provide services for all, the government must increase taxes. Those on the left who demand socialistic approaches point to the Scandinavian countries as examples of countries with higher taxes than the U.S. and more socialism which have a high standard of living and seem to work very well. Even though we already have a high degree of socialism (about 50% of the economy according to Milton Friedman) and a considerable level of taxation to support socialism, the Left wants a lot more. Asking for more taxation indicates belief in

Voodoo Economic Principle #12: High taxes do no harm.

Perhaps a better way to characterize the belief that producers can be heavily taxed without reducing the amount of production is expressed as a corollary principle:

Voodoo Economic Principle #12A: There are Free Lunches.

Specifically the belief in free lunches involves belief that a heavy tax burden can be imposed without doing harm. But even small changes in taxes change incentives enough to cause significant reductions in investment. Another way to state the principle is:

Voodoo Economic Principle #12B: Money grows on trees.

The Left thinks that corporations are rolling in money from exploiting workers and consumers through excessive profits and that taking some of this money away to use for health services and education is beneficial and does little or no harm to the economy. The problem is that increasing taxes is harmful to the economy. Even small increases in taxation change entrepreneurs' incentives to produce a greater supply of goods and services. This reduces long-term economic growth and prosperity. Taxes and regulation will steer investment money away from its most fruitful uses and reduce efficiency. Regulation usually causes wasting of resources. Government intervention often subsidizes activities it wants to encourage. Large companies receiving such largess are likely to waste the money. Government bureaucrats also have a very poor record when trying to promote industries and technological advances.

The Left responds by pointing out that everything works well in the Scandinavian countries which have higher taxes than the U.S. We might take a closer look at this claim. Consider Norway. Norway like all the European countries that have high degrees of socialism has a serious problem trying to find jobs for younger workers. A distant cousin of mine in Norway who is very bright and competent, spent at least 15 years in college studying various subjects before she could find a job in the legal system in her mid-thirties. And she is not atypical. In France and Germany unemployment is running over 10% with 20% unemployment for the young.

The Scandinavian countries and other European countries with considerable socialism are wiser than the U.S. insofar as most have lower effective corporate income tax rates, although they have very high personal income taxes. Nevertheless because their overall tax burden is much higher they have unemployment rates that are double the rates in the U.S. and have great difficulty finding employment for young people. Historically when tax rates have exceeded about 40%, countries and civilizations have begun to go downhill.[1] This has been true for agricultural societies when the rates were applied to farmers and the upper classes avoided taxes. The threshold may be somewhat higher in modern developed economies where the tax burden falls more heavily on the upper classes and is lower on the working classes. For the long term welfare, low taxes are desirable.

The Left does not seem to realize the severity of the long-term consequences of high taxes. Long-term economic growth is highly important. Strong growth provides jobs for the least skilled and least employable, whereas slow growth causes high unemployment for the least skilled and employable. When economic growth slows, the least skilled are the first laid off and the last to be hired when the economy picks back up again. In the U.S. when economic growth is in the 4-5% range, unemployment is quite low. Obtaining an extra 1% growth in any year is very desirable since over a long period an extra 1% per year in growth compounds to double the economy and the standard of living in 80 years.

Many on the left are not bothered by poor economic growth because they believe that economic development and advances are bad because we use more of the earth's resources. Many of them are not particularly bothered by people having lower standards of living. One of the problems with this attitude is that many people in a society might wish to have better living standards, to have various electronic devices etc, whereas those who want socialism and lower standards of living want to deny the opportunity for many of the members of their society to live better lives. They want to take away some of the freedom enjoyed by members of a society to bring greater equality of outcomes. Unfortunately not only do attempts to bring equality of outcomes tend to make everyone poorer, the equality must be engineered by elites. Historically, when elites or any other group try to impose equality of outcomes in society or some sector of society, the groups in charge take advantage and arrogate extra privileges to themselves.

Why Taxes and Regulation should be Kept Minimal

We might call a capitalistic economy that has minimal government and very little regulation of economic markets a "laissez-faire" economy. If the markets are free allowing corporations and private individuals to buy and sell goods and services with little government intervention, there are two main mechanisms that promote the general welfare of human beings and of the environment and minimize exploitation and criminal economic behaviors. These mechanisms are competition and the legal system.

The primary mechanism that keeps a free market economy functioning well is competition. Companies that can provide a better product or service than other competing companies will begin to increase their share of the market. Increased sales will provide increased profits and those profits can be used for investment to produce more efficiently and to improve products further. Competition keeps companies from charging profits that are excessive. If high profits are earned because a product is new and innovative, it will not be long before other firms will make the product or similar products to exploit the high profits. With many companies entering the market competition, the supply will greatly increase to satisfy demand and will force prices down and profits also. With many companies competing there will be new innovations and availability of virtually everything people want to buy.

It is important to have a few laws that protect property and patents from being stolen or defrauded or producing products that expose people to unexpected dangers. Laws that protect property belonging to the public, for example the air, are also necessary. The legal system is sometimes needed, but generally simple competition and the availability of alternative sources from which to buy will keep companies in line. If they do not provide desirable and needed products, some of their competitors will, and they will lose market share and go out of business. If they exploit, many people will recognize this and will seek alternative products so that the exploiting companies will see their sales, market share, and profits fall.

Many have complained that "laissez-faire" allows companies to exploit their workers. This complaint is quite erroneous however. When there is strong competition there will always be dynamic companies looking for hard working people. They will pay a little more to employ productive people. Consequently, if companies try to exploit or abuse their workers and there is strong competition, workers will have the option to switch to companies that will treat them well.

> *It is actually economies that have considerable government meddling by imposition of too much taxation and regulation, that are most likely to have problems with exploitation of workers.*

Economies slow and there is more unemployment. When governments meddle with taxes and regulation, they reduce competition and the lesser skilled are less likely to find other companies prepared to hire them. When employment opportunities are scarce, it is more difficult to escape exploitation, since options are more limited.

Many people view the U.S. economy as a capitalist economy and criticize many of the problems in the economy as problems of capitalism. This is a very erroneous inference. As Milton Friedman likes to point out frequently, the U.S. economy is about one-half socialist and one-half capitalist. A nation's national income is its production of consumer goods and services excluding investment replacing used up capital goods needed to produce goods and services. If the national income of the U.S. is examined, one finds that Federal, State, and Local government entities spend about 40% of that national income. In addition they impose many regulations that dictate spending of another 10% of the national income by private entities to comply with their regulations. The problems that people assign to capitalism invariably are problems that surface as a consequence of bureaucratic meddling in the economy, not from capitalistic business.

Economists who want to justify more government regulation and planning of the economy put forward many arguments claiming that various free capitalist markets are uncompetitive or deficient in some respect. This supposed problem will be considered in Chapter 12. However nearly all inefficiencies and failures result from the socialist half of the economy. Government regulative agencies are dominated by large corporations that use them to restrict competition and prevent smaller competitors from competing with them on an equal basis. The taxes that governments collect in order to spend 40% of the national income reduce the competitiveness of many excellent corporations. If the tax burden were reduced substantially, governments spent less, and corporations had substantially more to spend, they would be able to provide more goods and services that people want, solving many of the problems that people ask governments to solve.

Government agencies are bound to fail because bureaucracies work in an opposite fashion from private enterprises. All incentives for a bureaucracy are to fail, because administrators, if they fail, will need more money and more workers and a larger empire, on the other hand if they successfully solve a problem, their money, workers, and bureaucratic empire will vanish. When taxation is kept to a minimum people are best off. Of course, some taxation is needed to fund necessary government functions like defense, the judicial system, and the police, but should be held to a minimum.

Conservatives and libertarians believe that free markets with plenty of competition work wonderfully well. The markets do nearly all the regulating and policing of the system that is needed. In addition, recourse to the courts and the legal system for theft of property and other basic violations of legal rights is available. People have a wide variety of needs and interests. The free enterprise system works admirably to satisfy those various needs and interests.

When free markets are left to solve problems we expect to have good solutions. When people want something done they are willing to pay for it. If there are adequate rewards available for providing appropriate goods and services, there are incentives for ingenious entrepreneurs to find ingenious solutions. When the problem is handed over to bureaucrats to solve, the bureaucrats do not have an incentive to solve it since they will not benefit financially. It is in their interest to *pretend* that they are trying to solve the problem, but to fall short so that they need additional funds and manpower. They will tend to create a bottomless pit to swallow up investment resources, which if left in the private sector could produce solid economic growth.

When bureaucracies control spending for one-half of the economy, we can be sure that there is great waste of our economic resources, so that economic growth is significantly below what it could and should be. If this is not evident, consider the fact that we have two industries or economic sectors that are riddled with problems of all kinds and are poor at producing the services they are supposed to provide. The industries are primary and secondary education and medicine. Consider also that we have two major industries or economic sectors that are funded primarily by taxes and controlled largely by bureaucrats, namely, primary and secondary education and medicine. The fact that the two sectors that function so very poorly relative to the others are also the sectors controlled and funded primarily by government is not an accident, but eminently predictable. Education receives 90% of its funding from government taxes and government provides more than 90% of elementary and secondary education. When an economic sector is dominated by monopolies, it will not work very well. There is little competition providing parents with better choices of schools available for their children. If education were provided by private schools competing to do the best job of educating children, the competition would provide a wide variety of efficient schools designed to educate children with different needs and interests.

Because Medicare and Medicaid are funded by government from taxpayer's taxes, about 50% of the medical industry is funded by government. As a consequence government controls the treatments available to the elderly and distorts the proper functioning of medical practitioners. The medical field would provide affordable medicine if it were funded by medical savings accounts.[2]

There is little doubt that we would receive the best medical care and best education if it were funded privately and the services provided by private entities. However, the voodoo economists from the left think just the opposite. They believe in socialism—that health care and education should be funded by government and therefore by taxes and controlled by bureaucrats.

Obviously if many services are provided by and through government, taxes must be raised substantially. Because these services will be provided by bureaucracies which have every incentive to fail, many more workers will be needed than when services are provided by private enterprise. The total goods and services provided by the economy must be reduced, since far more workers must be diverted to government sectors than would be needed if most of those services were provided by the private sector. Moreover, equal often means equally bad. More money is spent per pupil in Washington, D.C. than in localities with very fine schools, yet the education provided is very poor. Most Catholic schools are far superior to most public schools on one-third the expenditure per pupil. Yet when proposals are made for school choice to let the market and competition solve the problem, the left just wants more money spent.

The rationale for wanting many goods and services provided by the government sector can only be a socialistic rationale. Democrats want equality and they want, as much as possible, for all people from all income levels to have the same level of treatment in education and health care and some other government services. For them it is apparently better to have equally bad education than to allow school choice which requires schools to perform to stay in business. To them equality of treatment is highly important. They do not want to see the rich getting better medical treatment or health care than the poor. But in the real world things can never be entirely equal.

Charge: Capitalists Waste Resources

Environmentalists and others on the left believe that capitalists will waste resources if given half a chance. They want laws and many regulative agencies to prevent enterprises from polluting the water and the air. The process of extraction or mining may do damage to natural areas and may leave toxic chemicals improperly disposed of.

There is of course some merit to these charges and some need of regulation. The main reason is that the air and rivers and streams are not privately owned. The air cannot be owned by private concerns and the rivers in the U.S. are publicly owned. Also much of the land that is mined is public land. A very large part of the western U.S. consists of public lands. If the lands were privately owned the owners would have an interest in ensuring that users or others leasing the land to extract minerals would not cause damage. Public ownership means that responsible bureaucrats often fail to protect the environment.

Many bureaucrats have laudable intentions, but the land does not belong to them and they will tend to do a superficial job.

What members of the left do not understand is that capitalism encourages corporations and individuals to avoid wasting resources and in fact to use resources as efficiently as possible. The more efficiently resources are used and the less they are wasted, the greater the profits. The classic example is found in John D. Rockefeller and his Standard Oil Company. Rockefeller found ways to process virtually all of the crude oil to produce products that could be sold.[3] There was very little waste. Many of his competitors however processed 70% of the crude oil and dumped the remaining 30% causing considerable damage to the environment. Obviously Rockefeller could sell his products at prices below his competitors cost of production and still obtain a good profit. Not surprisingly he put many of them out of business. His competitors complained that he was competing unfairly by selling below cost. They were wrong. When he bought the operations of those whom he put out of business, those operations were put on a basis of recovering nearly all of the oil and having little environmental adverse impact or they were abandoned. Standard Oil's success was a tremendous victory for the environment. Kerosene and later, gasoline, were sold at very low prices which was good for all consumers. In order to compete with Russia for international sales, Rockefeller had to become very efficient. His wells pumped 4.5 barrels per day and Russia's pumped 280 barrels a day.[4] Had he not found ways to become ultra-efficient, Russian companies might have controlled international sales.

Another apt example of free market incentives to avoid wasting resources is the aluminum soft drink can. Aluminum is expensive to process in terms of the energy required. Over the years the producers of aluminum cans have continually been finding small ways to improve the cans by reducing the amount of aluminum needed per can. Even reduction by a gram per can yields significant savings and increased profits given the volume of cans produced. Less aluminum resources are used. Less energy is used. Capitalism encourages minimizing the resources used.

Air Traffic Control

Bureaucrats and regulators are very wasteful of resources. For example, consider the FAA which was set up to regulate private aircraft. In 1957 a mid-air collision of two aircraft occurred. Congress stepped in and funded an air traffic control system designed to prevent such collisions from occurring. The FAA developed a computerized system with consoles for the air traffic controllers in the early 1970's to track the aircraft they were controlling. The system is designed to maintain control of commercial instrumented aircraft from the time that a plane takes off from a U.S. airport or enters U.S. airspace to the time it lands or leaves U.S. airspace. In the early 1980's the FAA decided the system needed to be replaced. A newer system was installed in the early 1990's.

With the system as it has existed for nearly 50 years, there are 21 regional control centers each with many controllers who handle aircraft after leaving the airspace of an airport or group of airports. A cadre of 10,000 air traffic controllers is required to man the regional control centers. The cost of employing them is at least one billion dollars per year. The cost of maintaining the equipment is several billion dollars per year. The operational budget for 2006 is almost $8 billion. The cost of developing and installing the new system of the 1990's was over $10 billion.

Rather than installing a bureaucratically run system, the government could have left air traffic between airports to the markets to handle. Suppose the system had been left to the airlines (it is strongly in their interest to avoid any mid-air collisions) and free markets. The system would have dispensed with the regional air traffic control centers and air traffic controllers. Instead commercial aircraft would have small radio transmitters that broadcast their GPS position (originally LORAN position), altitude, speed, and direction of flight, for 50 to 100 miles. They would have receivers that would collect the information transmitted by other aircraft, and their computers would have software installed that would compute the predicted flight paths of the other aircraft in the area to determine the potential for collisions. A system like this would have a number of advantages:

1) The flights would be safer. GPS gives position to within a few feet. With our current system, measurements by radar 200 miles away can often be off by hundreds of feet. Air traffic controllers rely primarily on assignments to airways and different altitudes to keep aircraft separated. Air traffic controllers depend on viewing traffic on visual displays with much cluttered information which can sometimes confuse.

2) The current system requires that aircraft follow designated air routes in the sky. The routes usually do not follow the shortest distance between two airports. With a GPS system aircraft could fly direct routes saving airlines millions of dollars per year in flight fuel costs and reducing use of crude oil and the amount of crude oil imported. Flights would be a little shorter and save some passengers a little time.

3) By eliminating salaries of the regional air traffic controllers and computer system maintenance on air traffic control computers, savings of several billion dollars per year would occur.

It is quite unlikely that the FAA will ever implement such a system. The FAA would lose billions in funding and more than ten thousand employees. The FAA empires would shrink dramatically.

The Savings and Loan Debacle

Democrats believe that bureaucrats and regulatory agents protect the public and do so better than a laissez-faire economy with little regulation. They believe in the principle:

Voodoo Economics Principle #12: Only elites will protect the public from the depredations of capitalists.

There is plenty of evidence that this is false, that in fact government bureaucrats are poor at protecting the public.

As an example let us examine the regulation of the Savings and Loans. Federal law guarantees that deposits in Savings and Loans are guaranteed up to $10,000. The Savings and Loans are charged fees for insurance to cover possible bankruptcies and pay off all depositors in a bankruptcy up to $10,000 each. The fees are uniform based on the amount of loans. Periodically auditors from the Federal Deposit Insurance Corporation (FDIC) will examine the books of a Savings and Loan. But bureaucrats do not have any personal resources at risk if the S&L should fail. They do not examine books with any great rigor. They also charge the same premium rates to S&Ls that have portfolios with *many* high risk loans and to S&Ls that have *few* high risk loans. This behavior encourages banks and S&Ls to take on risky loans. They can charge higher fees, the government guarantees their deposits, and there are no adverse consequences.

Consider what would happen if insuring banks and S&Ls were left to the private sector. S&Ls would seek insurance from a private insurer. That insurer would charge different rates depending upon the amount of the risky loans and the riskiness of the loans. The insurer would audit the books much more carefully and accurately. There is obviously a significant difference between the way government bureaucrats handle this matter and a private insurer. The reason for this is simple. The private insurer has much to lose if he must pay back deposits for depositors when an S&L goes bankrupt. Consequently the private insurer must demand premiums for the insurance that accurately reflect the amount of risk. Insurers make careful studies of risks. On the other hand, the government bureaucrat expects the government to back up any losses from tax money and is not particularly concerned about the amount the government will have to pay. If S&Ls were charged different fees depending upon the quality and riskiness of their debt, the information could be made available to the public and the public would be able to know the soundness of the banks and S&Ls they planned to use. S&Ls that had to pay higher premiums would have less ability to give higher interest than their competitors. Consequently the S&Ls with less risky loans would be more competitive than they are when bureaucrats are in charge. Depositors would tend to want to use the S&Ls with fewer risky loans. Market forces would tend to force banks and S&Ls to make fewer risky loans and the banking system would be more sound with no government regulation and oversight necessary.

During the Presidency of George H.W. Bush there was a Savings and Loan crisis that cost taxpayers hundreds of billions of dollars to back up bad loans. Nearly all the risk was born by taxpayers, but not by Savings and Loans. Bad precedents were set by allowing Federal Agencies to seize private S&L assets of entrepreneurs who were merely following market forces and incentives established by lawmakers and bureaucrats. Nothing was done to fix the fundamental problem so we may expect in the future to have more such crises when real estate markets go bust again.

Public versus Private Safety and Security

The public believes that agencies like the FDIC are protecting them when in fact these agencies, by giving equal protection to all the banks and S&Ls including those with many risky loans, actually increase the risk to the public far beyond the risks of protection by private companies in a laissez-faire economy. When government agencies are tasked with the job of protecting the public, citizens are lulled into thinking they are protected when in fact the practices of the bureaucrats actually increase their risk above the risks that would occur had protection been left to the private sector.

Under laissez-faire, consumers ask private companies and individuals to undertake the task of providing services they desire. They desire protection for safe airplane flights or for their bank accounts. In the case of safe airplane flights it is exceedingly important to the survival of an airline that it avoid accidents. An airline has abundant incentives to make every effort to ensure that its planes are safe. It is when an FAA is made responsible that airlines actually become more lax. To protect bank accounts the banks themselves would pay insurers. In short the private sector would do a better job of protecting people. The belief that government elites will do better is quite erroneous.

CHAPTER 12

Market Failure and Externalities

Capitalism with free markets has proven its great superiority over socialism during the past several decades. Rigidly planned socialist economies have failed abysmally. When there is very little regulation of markets, essentially *laissez-faire*, markets are free to solve almost any problem and will do so most efficiently. A business that will produce products and services that people want will reap great rewards. So the free market system provides incentives to provide what is needed. If allowed to do so the free market would solve problems in the education and health care industries. Free markets do not provide free lunches so that some people can live off the productivity of others. Democrats however want the government to provide many services. Those services may be funded by government by taxes, but then government bureaucrats control the markets in certain respects. The bureaucrats do not have all the information about the markets to make pricing decisions. Very often they hold down prices below costs to help the poor. This causes inadequate supply of the goods controlled. Their interferences in markets usually reduce efficiency. The taxes they need to provide inefficient services waste investment resources and reduce productivity and wealth.

People from left of the political center point to the Scandinavian countries as examples of socialism working. They claim market failure in many industries as a rationale for government bureaucrats to step in to regulate or provide services. They are dissatisfied with the way markets distribute goods and services so they want to redistribute wealth. The redistribution of wealth to help the poor is an indicator of belief in socialism. They have succeeded in placing about one-half the U.S. economy under control of bureaucrats. They still advocate more control due to reputed failures of capitalism. But this is bad logic, because the failures almost entirely stem from failures caused by the socialist part of the economy, not the capitalistic part. In this chapter we will point out why claims of market failure are generally bogus.

Socialism and Capitalism

During the Nineteenth Century and three-quarters of the Twentieth Century socialists criticized capitalism for exploitation of workers, bad working conditions, and inequality of incomes. They believed that intervention by government to regulate industry and to redistribute incomes would produce better societies without costing prosperity. States like the Soviet Union tried to implement pure socialism by managing a planned economy. Pure socialism with full government control of an economy failed. It failed for various reasons but the main reason is that the bureaucrats had but a tiny fraction of the amount of knowledge needed to make an economy run well and progress. Free markets and the prices they produce carry a vast amount of knowledge and information about markets. The factors impacting proper prices cannot all be known by a few people. Socialist bureaucrats running a planned economy do not have needed information and they do not have prices to guide them. As a consequence the price decisions and investment decisions they make are very poor and very inferior to what happens in free markets with buyers and sellers who act freely with minimal or no regulation.

Of course in many advanced economies socialists have succeeded in having their ideas melded in with capitalism through redistribution of income and government regulation of significant parts of an economy. Most markets are left partially free, but persons and corporations are heavily taxed and many social services and programs are supported by the taxes. In the Scandinavian countries and France and Germany the taxation has become rather burdensome. Yet the countries cited have high standards of living. The markets set prices, but are heavily influenced by tax rates and bureaucratic rules. Bureaucrats do not entirely control the market decisions, but they do cause less efficient decisions which waste resources.

Socialists apparently believe that it does not matter who spends money earmarked for investment. Investment money is needed for improving productivity and for creating jobs and for providing the services desired by citizens. They are quite willing to tax profits earmarked for investment and have bureaucrats spend it instead. As noted above, bureaucrats want their empires to expand. This will only happen if they waste the investment money on boon-doggles and fail in their tasks. They then can claim that more money is needed to do the job.

Capitalists on the other hand use profits as a guide to where money should be invested. Profits will show the goods and services most in demand by the public. If they invest to provide the goods and services most in demand, the demand will quickly be met. New areas of demand will arise which will be met by shifting investment to new areas. In this way economies have the money invested in the most useful and fruitful ways leading to the best economic growth.

Market Failure

During the last several decades many economists and intellectuals who have a desire to expand government have found various ways in which they claim different markets fail. Markets are said to fail if they have inefficiencies or imperfections or if they have spillover effects or externalities that negatively impact third parties. The mere purported existence of the market failures is implied to require government intervention to fix the problems.

There is a principle implicit in the views of socialists and others on the left desiring to put more of the economy under the supervision of bureaucrats. It is the principle discussed in chapter 1:

Voodoo Economics Principle #1: Elites (legislators and bureaucrats) know how to invest capital better than entrepreneurs.

Generally one of the means advocated to deal with externalities and market failure is to impose special taxes to pay for problems caused by failure. The Left thinks that corporations are rolling in money from exploiting workers and consumers through excessive profits. Hence, taking some of this money away to use for health services and education is beneficial and does little or no harm to the economy. Asking for more taxation indicates belief in

Voodoo Economics Principle #12: High taxes do no harm.

Stated in a more colloquial fashion the principle is:

Voodoo Economics Principle #12A: The economy provides Free Lunches.

or

Voodoo Economics Principle #12B: Money grows on trees.

Levying high taxes indicates an attitude that the money people and corporations earn can be confiscated by government just as one picks fruit off a tree that one has not cultivated. Unfortunately those who levy high taxes fail to see the effects taxes have on incentives to produce goods and services. They apparently think there are economic free lunches. People with common sense know that there are no free lunches and that money does not grow on trees. They also know that high taxes are very harmful and cause all kinds of problems. Increasing taxes is harmful to any economy. Even small increases in taxation change entrepreneurs' incentives to produce a greater supply of goods and services. This reduces long-term economic growth.

Arguments for Market Failure

We need to investigate two issues: are the claims of market failure correct? And if so, is there need for government intervention to correct the problems? We must first examine some of the market failure claims.

One of the main rationales for government intervention has been that markets fail and government needs to move in and make needed corrections. Economists have made efficient markets the measure for evaluating them. Economic theorists have found numerous possible causes of inefficient markets. There may be transaction costs. Laws may interfere. Customs of a society can interfere. Government may interfere. The markets may provide buyers or sellers imperfect or insufficient information to make good decisions.

A wide variety of anecdotal and theoretical arguments have been used to conclude that practically all markets are subject to serious imperfections. Some of the more prominent examples of alleged market failure are the following:

1) The existence of public goods which private entrepreneurs are for some reason unable to provide. A favorite example is the lighthouse, a service needed by mariners.[1] Presumably private entrepreneurs would not build lighthouses because they would not readily be able to collect tolls and if they could collect some tolls they would not be able to collect tolls from many boats that would benefit. Roads offer another example. Private entrepreneurs could build turnpikes but would have trouble collecting from all users. Some free riders would take advantage of the locations of toll booths.[2]

2) The existence of externalities or effects on the public or third parties. There is a tendency for people to pollute the air or water which belongs to the public. Another example is the "tragedy of the commons." In the Eighteenth Century towns and cities had commons which were areas belonging to the public. Everyone could allow their cattle to graze on that land. Consequently the common areas tended to be overgrazed.

3) The phenomenon of technology lock-in by which the nature of a type of product requires that it conform to some standard and an inferior standard becomes accepted. This makes transition to a future superior standard virtually impossible. A favorite lock-in example is the QWERTY keyboard which is supposedly inferior to the Dvorak keyboard.[3] Another example is the success of VHS over the apparently superior Betamax video cassette recorder.[4]

4) Monopolistic practices by companies like Standard Oil in the Nineteenth Century.[5] Standard Oil presumably set prices below cost in markets to force out competitors, then gained a monopoly, and after taking over, raised prices.

5) The phenomenon of adverse selection. Adverse selection is a phenomenon of asymmetrical information whereby the seller or buyer has information which the other party does not. This phenomenon supposedly causes used cars put on the market to be lemons.[6] Sellers know whether a car is in good condition or is a lemon. Since the price for used cars is an average price, presumably the good cars will not bring what they are worth so sellers will not sell them. The phenomenon is also presumed to apply to buying life insurance. Buyers of life

insurance are much more likely to buy if they know that their health is poor and not so likely to buy if their health is excellent. The insurer does not know the state of the buyer. This will tend to cause insurers to insure bad risks at insufficient premiums.[7]

Why Government should Avoid Market Interference

There are many other examples of presumed market failure. During the past 25 years or so economists have brought forward so many examples of alleged market failure that it would seem that all markets fail. The theorists who bring forward the examples want government to step in and make the markets efficient and more perfect. But there are two reasons to leave markets alone rather than meddle or intervene. First, an assumption is made that market failure is readily fixed by government. Proponents of market failure presume that government bureaucrats can step in and fix the problems. However, there is no reason to believe that any bureaucrats would have even a small part of the knowledge needed to find the proper solution to a problem, if a problem exists. Moreover, even if some markets are less than perfect, they have an amazing capacity to fix themselves or to ease the problems. The second reason is that market failures are not nearly so widespread or problematic as the market interventionists would have us believe.

Market Failure Not Widespread

There is little reason to believe that market failure is remotely as widespread as the proponents of government intervention allege. In virtually all examples of alleged market failure, the arguments have been based on purely theoretical arguments or on anecdotal information. When the proponents of market failure have investigated historical and more detailed evidence, they have usually overlooked some important evidence. To see that this is the case let us look at the examples mentioned above.

In the case of alleged public goods like lighthouses, it turns out that many of the early lighthouses in Britain were actually built by private parties.[8] In a number of cases where the organization which had responsibility dragged its feet, private parties petitioned for the right to build a lighthouse and collect the tolls. The rights were granted. Of course, some government involvement was necessary to enable private parties to collect the tolls appropriate for various classes of ships. Since ship owners had requested many of the lighthouses in the first place, they were quite willing to pay reasonably assessed tolls. Organizations representing the mariners were involved in setting the tolls and determining needed maintenance and construction of new lighthouses. Thus in the case of the lighthouses it is not true that they cannot be provided by private parties.

For many other alleged public goods the same situation will hold. Of course, some public goods like national defense and the legal system with law enforcement and the courts must be provided by government. But many services provided by government in the U.S. would be provided much more cheaply and efficiently by private companies. Many cities and states in the U.S. have realized considerable savings by contracting out various services to private enterprises. In the case of roads, early American toll roads were built because of need despite their poor economic performance. Companies that built toll roads could tolerate some free riders.[9] With the advent of new technologies in the form of transponders attached to vehicles, toll roads can collect proper tolls automatically from the owners of vehicles traveling on a toll road.

What about the so-called spillover effects? In the case of externalities and the "tragedy of the commons," laws restricting emissions or assigning portions of the commons to different families can solve the problem. If actions of buyers and sellers impact third parties adversely they have recourse to the courts to obtain a remedy or compensation. Consequently buyers and sellers in a market have incentives to pay attention to how they impact third parties so that any spillover effects are relatively benign. Some special laws may be necessary to protect public air and water. But tasking bureaucrats to fix problems usually only makes them worse, because failure promises to produce more money to expand bureaucratic empires.

The lock-in problem is another example of anecdotal information that did not include all the relevant information. The U.S. Navy study that is universally cited as showing the superiority of the Dvorak keyboard was conducted by none other than Dvorak the inventor of the keyboard himself! A more thorough government study concluded that the QWERTY keyboard was not inferior to the Dvorak keyboard.[10]

In the case of the VHS versus Betamax competition, it was the case that Beta was superior for editing purposes. However, the vast majority of users were not interested in editing, they just preferred the system that enabled them to record for the longest period of time on one cassette. Since VHS provided longer recording times it won out over Beta.[11] Beta is still available and used by editors. It took some time before the true reason VHS won became clear.

The practices of Standard Oil and John D. Rockefeller were vilified by many and led to an antitrust suit which broke the company into parts in 1906. Interestingly Ida Tarbell who fomented much of the opposition to Standard Oil was the daughter of a competitor to Standard Oil. There were over 13,000 pages of testimony in the court record covering all aspects of Standard Oil's actions from the 1860's onward.[12] Nowhere is there any evidence that Standard Oil operated as a predator by pricing at a loss to drive out competitors. It would have been illogical and economically stupid to operate in this fashion. Why undergo losses much greater than the competition one is trying to drive out? Why should not one could just buy them out by paying them an amount greater than the profits they could collect by staying in business? In fact buying out was a typical tactic used by Rockefeller. Moreover because those he bought out received good value for the sale, they often opened new refineries only to sell them later to Rockefeller. His competitors did not behave as if they feared he would take advantage of them. Secondly, intelligent owners of refineries being undercut could have stayed in business. They could have shut down operations until he raised prices again and then resumed operations selling refined products. Further in the testimony on the record it turned out that when price wars occurred it was usually competitors who complained about Standard Oil, that actually started the price wars.[13]

Careful examination of markets supposedly subject to adverse selection also do not bear out the claims. If used car markets were limited to selling "lemons" then comparison of maintenance records for used pickup trucks should show higher costs than the maintenance records for comparable trucks that had never been resold on the used car market. However, studies comparing the two cases showed the same costs.[14]

In the case of insurance markets although buyers of insurance supposedly know more about the state of their health, careful studies have not shown any adverse selection effects. Insurance companies do detailed studies of risks.

Further, middlemen with special relevant knowledge show up to provide the needed information to help insurance companies set their rates.[15]

Thus we find that arguments for market failure typically overlook features of the market or historical evidence that show the market is far less subject to imperfections than the anecdotes suggest. Moreover where there are imperfections, usually new companies will find ways to eliminate or greatly reduce the problem.

> *But the most important point is that if indeed imperfections exist, there is no reason to think government bureaucrats will alleviate the putative problem. In fact they are more likely to exacerbate it. Bureaucracies have incentives to fail to solve problems to continue in business.*

Flawed Rationales

Claims of market failure depend on various assumptions. Neoclassical economics assumes that markets should exhibit perfect competition and should produce a general equilibrium. If markets fail to produce an equilibrium or if the competition is imperfect or there are spillover effects (the exchange between buyer and seller have negative effects on third parties), many people mechanically call for government intervention to fix the failure. Manufacturers may pollute the air or water used by the public. Government intervention is supposedly needed to fix the spillover effects. If competition is imperfect, advocates of government intervention want to even the competition through tax rates and regulation.

There are several fundamental problems with the rationales for government intervention. First, if someone is to be able to produce equilibrium or produce perfect competition, then that person or persons must have complete knowledge of all the market conditions that produce the less than perfect competition or destabilize a potential equilibrium. Fixing the problem then depends on economic omniscience regarding a particular market. But no one is close to having complete knowledge of any market. The complete information about any market is widely defused among the many participants in the market. It includes knowledge of various subjective preferences of buyers and sellers which only God could know. No one but God could have anything but very restricted knowledge of the economic consequences of various actions taken to counteract imperfect competition or disequilibrium conditions. Not only must bureaucrats lack the needed knowledge to fix problems, their incentives push them toward failure. Failure enables them to ask for more money to hire more bureaucrats to build a larger bureaucratic empire. Should they be successful there would no longer be a justification for their intervention and their money and empire would wither away.

Second, the notion by neo-classical economists that markets must reach equilibria is flawed. It depends on markets being static. But markets are dynamic. They are constantly changing over time. The preferences of market participants change with time. Presupposing a market equilibrium is not realistic. Consequently, the rationale that governments should step in to restore equilibria even if they could obtain the requisite knowledge is fundamentally mistaken.

Third, the assumption that markets should be perfectly competitive or government should intervene is also mistaken. Trying to produce perfect competition is likely to disturb the market and waste resources. It is never clear what measures would make a market perfectly competitive. The presence of some imperfections of competition in markets and some inefficiency does not prevent the markets from functioning quite well and doing what we expect them to do: provide adequate supply at good prices. Interference through levying of taxes or regulations raises costs to consumers, discourages investment to increase supply, and restricts freedom of buyers and sellers.

CHAPTER 13

Eliminate the Corporate Income Tax

Most people to the left of the political center believe that Big Business is bad, that the officers of large corporations are greedy and exploit people. Most Democrats believe they are for protecting the little guy against the depredations of the powerful. But it is not what one believes or one's motives, but what one does that counts. As Jesus said, "You shall know them by their fruits."[1] When those on the left point their finger, they should remember the Three Fingers Rule which reminds us that when I point a finger, three fingers are pointing back toward myself. The rule implies that the finger pointers may have the greater responsibility for the great size of the major corporations. I will contend that the corporate income tax is a major cause of increasing concentration in industry. Republican progressives started the corporate income tax in 1909. However, most of the increases incurred during FDR's presidency and during Truman's presidency. Figure 13.1 shows increases in the corporate tax rate during Democratic administrations from 1933 to 1952.

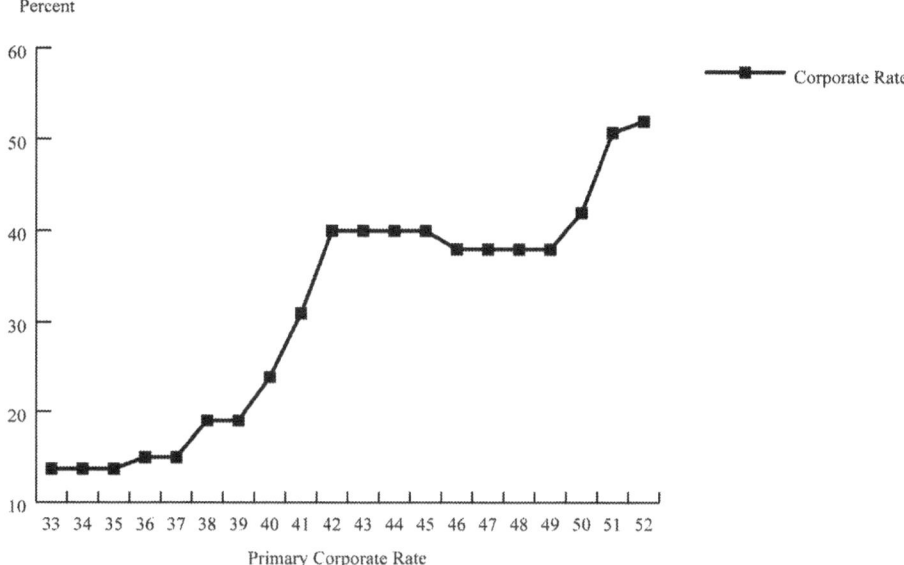

Figure 13.1 Corporate Tax Rate 1933 to 1952

Democrats controlled both houses of Congress and the presidency during the period covered by Figure 13.1 (the Senate was controlled by Republicans in 1947 and 1948). Since World War II was very costly it is understandable that taxes were increased substantially at this time. The rate stayed at 46% or higher until 1987. With the exception of 1953 and 1954, Democrats controlled the House of Representatives (in which all tax bills originated) from 1933 to 1994. Although Reagan was able to reduce tax rates despite a Democratic House of Representatives, his tax cuts were strongly opposed by most Democrats. During Clinton's presidency the corporate rate was increased from 34% to 35%.

Not only have Democrats increased and insisted on maintaining high corporate income tax rates, they have also promoted regulatory agencies to keep corporations in line. Yet the presence of regulatory agencies enables the largest corporations to politically influence the Federal agencies to appoint people favorable to their interests. The boards and agencies actually become tools that benefit the large corporations at the expense of smaller competitors or potential competitors. Competition is reduced. The largest corporations maintain or increase their market share of their industry.

Democrats also have provided subsidies either directly or indirectly in the form of tariffs or trade quotas. Subsidies and tariffs are imposed because large corporations employ many people and unions want the jobs protected. Subsidies do help large corporations become larger at the expense of smaller corporations, but do not usually save very many jobs. Over the last 80 years many subsidies have been granted to large corporations and during most of that time Democrats have controlled Congress.

After considering the effects of profits taxes, I would claim that if any party is the party of Big Business, of the large multinational corporations, it is the Democratic Party. Although Democrats point fingers at Republicans, when we judge the fruit of their efforts, the actual consequences of their actions, we find that they have done most to increase and protect the power of large corporations. This is particularly true of their stance on the corporate income tax which has remained high. They favor concentrating power not only in the Federal government, but also in Big Business. Reduction of competition and concentration of power allows the large corporations to become stodgy and inefficient and get away with it.

Democrats and Profits

The readiness of Democrats to tax profits shows that another principle the left and left leaning economists apparently believe in is

Voodoo Economics Principle #13: Profits don't matter.

Socialists and others who want to raise taxes to provide more health and social services and are willing to place high taxes on profits, either do not believe that profits matter to the viable functioning of the economy or do not care.

The economic theory applied from the 1930's to the 1970's and taught in college economics courses was a demand side or Keynesian economics which was based on using government spending to manipulate the level of demand in the economy. With this understanding of economics, the level of demand in the economy determines the amount of investment and economic growth. For Keynesians profits have little to do with the growth of the economy. Consequently profits matter little for determining economic policy. In fact in college economics textbooks little or no mention of profits was made. Typically there would be a small, short chapter on profits comprising about 1% of the book found toward the end of the book, just before a discussion of socialistic and communistic economies which were thought to be working rather well. Just examine Samuelson's *Economics*, the primary textbook for introductory economics courses in American colleges for many years.[2] So profits do not matter to most Democrats and those on the left. However, profits are the basis for making capitalism work at all. Adequate after tax profits to provide funds for investing in new enterprises and expanding the economy are essential for a healthy economy.

Democrats actually facilitate growth of large behemoth corporations by taxes and regulations that reduce competition. Competition ensures products will satisfy consumers and meet their needs. Lack of competition means less choice and less opportunity to address significant problems. Chapter 12 emphasized the problem of reducing competition through regulation. In this chapter we will see the adverse consequences for strong competition caused by high profits taxes.

> *The most advantageous change in the tax code would abolish income taxes altogether since they tax saving and investment. Income taxes could be replaced with a national sales tax. However short of abolishing income taxes altogether, abolishing the corporate income tax on profits would be very desirable. It would promote stronger economic growth and increase wages and employment.*

Explanation of the Corporate Income Tax

The corporate income tax is the tax paid on profits. A corporation's profits are the monies remaining from sales and other sources of income after deducting all business expenses. Business expenses include the costs of producing and providing goods and services. They include interest payments and depreciation. The profits constitute the return on capital invested before taxes. Many corporations pay dividends to stockholders out of the profit. Dividends usually amount to about one-third of the profit. The corporation must pay corporate income tax to the Federal government and to some states on their reported profits including dividends. Stockholders will also pay personal income taxes on the dividends they receive from corporations. Hence the dividends are doubly taxed. The money remaining after paying taxes is the after tax return on capital (ROC) invested. The profits remaining after payment of dividends are the retained earnings. The remainder of the retained earnings after paying taxes is available to fund capital investment in new plants and equipment or to invest in financial assets or for buying other companies. The kinds of investment decisions made by corporate executives about the way to invest this money has a significant impact on future economic growth and standards of living. Investment decisions are affected by perceived risks and the incentives induced by the tax code and government regulations. It is important to understand how the corporate income tax laws affect those decisions.

To understand tax rates some knowledge of the effect of depreciation rules on taxes is necessary. First, businesses are permitted to depreciate plants and equipment used in the business. Obviously the tax code should allow writing off depreciation as a cost of business. Depreciation of plants and equipment is a cost of business maintenance. It should be charged off at a rate that represents the true depreciation. However, over time the IRS bureaucrats have a tendency to tighten up so that less depreciation is permitted. This forces companies to report greater profits than their true profits. Consequently they pay taxes on a larger amount than they should. This is equivalent to paying a higher tax rate on the true profits. Thus to the extent that they must report more than their true profits, the excessive strictness in depreciation rules represents a higher tax on profits. On the other hand, periodically Congress will liberalize depreciation rules so that companies are allowed to charge off costs for depreciation at a greater rate than is warranted by true depreciation. This means companies report smaller profits than their true profits. The tax rate then applies only to a part of the true profits and thus represents a lower rate on the entire profit. So in effect loose depreciation rates reduce the tax rate on the true profits.

When corporate income rates reached 50% or more during World War II and after, the depreciation rules were very tight and restrictive. Reported profits were significantly larger than true profits. The tax rate then applied to a significantly larger amount than true profits and thus represented a higher rate on the true profit. The rate applied to the true profits was at least 70%. State taxes added about 5%.

People own stock in corporations. A corporation pays taxes on its profits. Then it pays out dividends from part of the remaining profits (after tax profits).

Many corporations pay dividends on their earnings. The dividends paid are part of the income of individuals. Most people receiving dividends must pay taxes on the dividends as part of their income. When individual stockholders pay their taxes, the dividends are then taxed at personal rates which are often fairly high. So there is a double taxation of profits. Since dividends are usually about 1/3 of the profits and during the period after World War II most of the dividends were received by those in the top personal income brackets paying rates over 80%, double taxation of dividends adds at least 25% to the total.

If we add 70% + 5% + 25%, we get 100% indicating that the government was essentially expropriating the entire profits earned from private investment.

All things considered, in recent years the level of U.S. taxation on the corporate sector has been about 40% of the funds available for investment as calculated by Dale Jorgenson and other experts on taxation.[3] The Federal Government charges 39.6% on corporate profits. The average state income tax adds another 5% or so. Dividends are taxed. When all the relevant factors are combined the taxation of U.S. corporation retained earnings is at about the 60% level.

The History of the U.S. Corporate Income Tax

The U.S. corporate income tax began in 1909. Republican progressives instituted the tax to be good citizens. They had the idea that corporations benefited from government and therefore should pay a share. This was a terrible reason, because corporations and business in general are the creators of jobs. By reinvesting their profits they produce technological innovations, improvement in productivity and economic growth They also provide training. Any siphoning off of funds to fund bureaucracies spending money with little benefit, is detrimental to growing the economy or improving salaries and living standards. Although the initial corporate tax rates were low, the taxes were increased. During the 1930's when FDR became President, the Roosevelt Administration raised personal tax rates and corporate rates substantially (Figure 13.2). During World War II the economy operated under the supervision of the government with a considerable amount of rationing. It was felt that companies should not profit from the war effort especially if they were given government contracts for weapons and other war materials. So the corporate profits taxes were raised substantially.

Percent

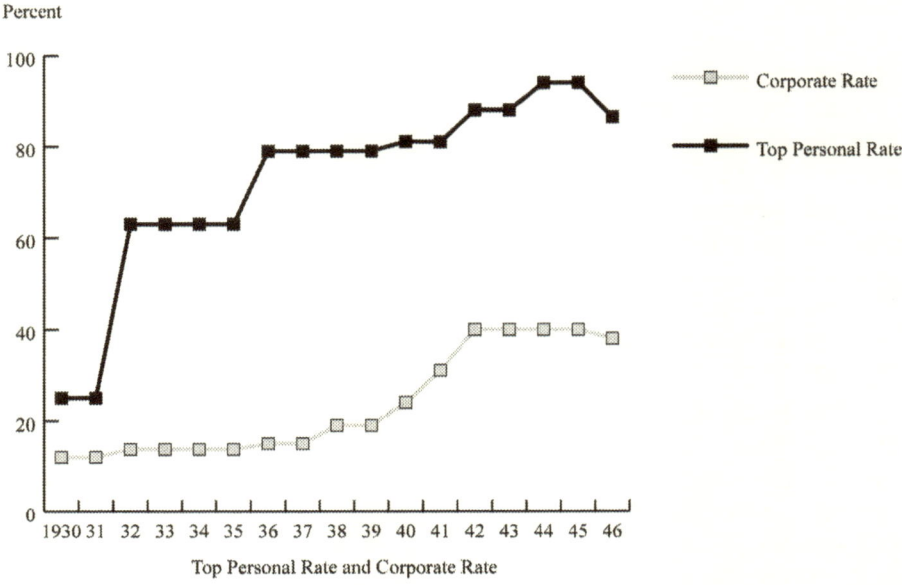

Top Personal Rate and Corporate Rate

Figure 13.2 Top Tax Rates 1930 to 1946

Thus far we see that after World War II the tax rates on corporations became essentially expropriatory. Although 52% was the highest rate for taxing corporate profits, the depreciation rules were too strict, so the true rate was significantly higher. Adding 5% or so for state taxes and high rates for double taxation of dividends made the taxation of profits become essentially expropriatory. The Federal rate alone was 90% for many receiving dividends, so with state taxes and double taxation of dividends, the entire profits were being taxed away. In 1954 Congress loosened the depreciation rules so that true profits were greater than reported.[4] This reduced the tax rates considerably although remaining high.

In 1961 President Kennedy introduced tax cuts in the form of investment tax credits that were targeted and usable primarily by the largest corporations. This stimulated the economy but increased concentration, since it favored the large corporations. During the 1970's the Nixon Administration lowered rates on corporate income taxes. Figure 13.3 shows the tax rates for 1947 to 1970.

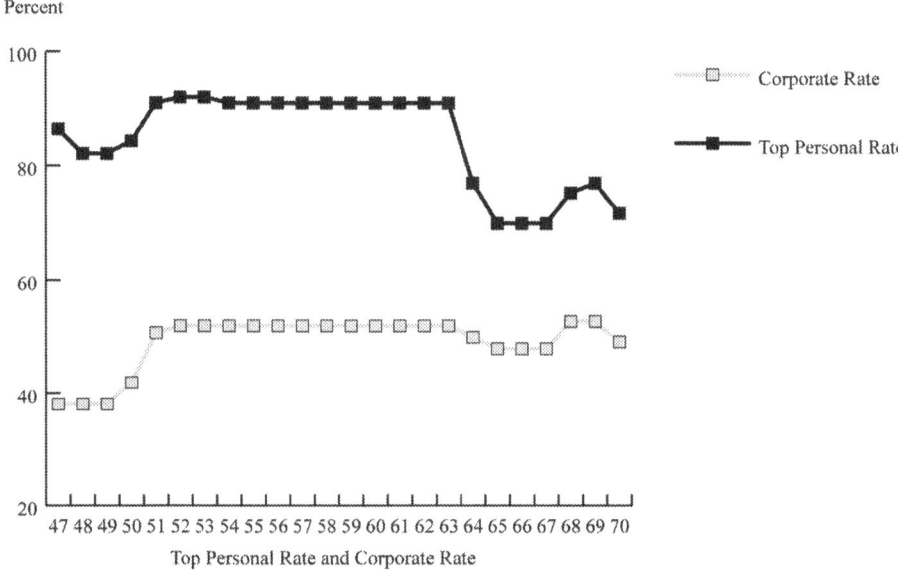

Figure 13.3 Top Tax Rates 1947 to 1970

When Reagan became President major tax cuts were enacted. Graphs showing the rates were provided in Chapter 9 (Figure 9.6). Major reductions in personal rates occurred. In the case of the corporate income tax the rates were reduced for one year, but then in 1982 the corporate rates were raised again. More liberal depreciation rules were enacted that reduced effective profits tax rates. The investment tax credit was removed in 1986 raising the effective rates again. Since that time the corporate income tax rates have remained fairly stable except for a 1% increase that was added by the Clinton Administration in 1993. They were reduced a little in 2002, but the effective corporate income tax rates are still around 40%, and the rate is about 60% on retained earnings when all factors are considered. If the tax were eliminated we would see great expansion in economic growth.

Comparison of Corporate Tax Rates for Five Countries

The U.S. is among countries with the highest profits tax rates in the world which gives corporations in other countries an advantage over U.S corporations.[5] Higher taxes require charging higher prices and being less competitive. The newly formed republics in Eastern Europe and many less developed nations have reduced their profits taxes. Globalization will force the U.S. to cut profits tax rates to remain competitive. Figure 13.4 shows the overall effective tax rates for five major industrialized nations. If France and Italy had been included in the graph, France would have had the highest tax rate at about 60% and Italy a low rate around 20%.

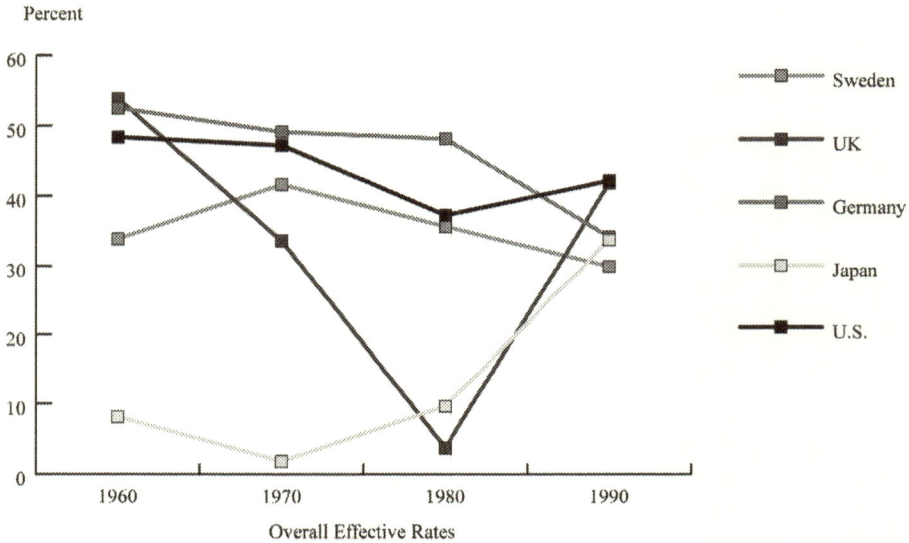

Figure 13.4 Five Country Corporate Tax Rate Comparison

It is essential to understand the meaning of the rates depicted in Figure 13.4. The tax rate includes the tax on earnings corporations have available for investment. Corporations can invest in machinery, buildings, or inventories. The money they have to invest comes from one of three sources: the earnings they retain after paying dividends to stockholders, new issues of corporate stock, and money borrowed either from banks or through issuing corporate bonds. The amount of tax paid will also depend on who owns corporate stock. A considerable part is owned by individuals or households. They must pay personal taxes on dividends received. But insurance companies and tax-exempt institutions also own large amounts of stock and pay lower taxes. The relative proportions of the corporate stock owned by different entities will affect the overall rate of taxation.

The overall effective marginal rates of taxation shown in Figure 13.4 were based on 10 percent rates of profit and the actual rates of inflation. The effective rate takes into account a country's mixture of machinery, buildings, inventories, different kinds of financing, different kinds of non-financial industries, and different proportions of ownership of corporations. The rate gives the percent of an extra dollar invested in the corporate sector that would be paid in Federal, state, and local taxes. The overall effective tax is the total tax on the corporate sector collected from corporate taxes, personal income tax, and property taxes.

Several points related to Figure 13.4 should be noted. First, we see that the *overall rate tends to be somewhat lower than the statutory rate.* Thus for the U.S. for most of the period up to 1986 the corporate tax rate on profits was in the 46 to 52 percent range. In 1986 it dropped to 34%. If we look at Figure 13.5 we see the effective tax rate on retained earnings.[6] It is high exceeding 60%. The decrease from over 70% is positive. However, it is still about 20% higher than the statutory rate. The reason is that in addition to the corporate income tax, personal taxes must be paid on dividends which come out of earnings. The tax on retained earnings is sufficiently high that corporations have a strong incentive to obtain funds by borrowing. Hence the main reason that the effective rates are lower than the statutory rates is that financing by debt is subsidized. Interest payments are deducted before paying tax.

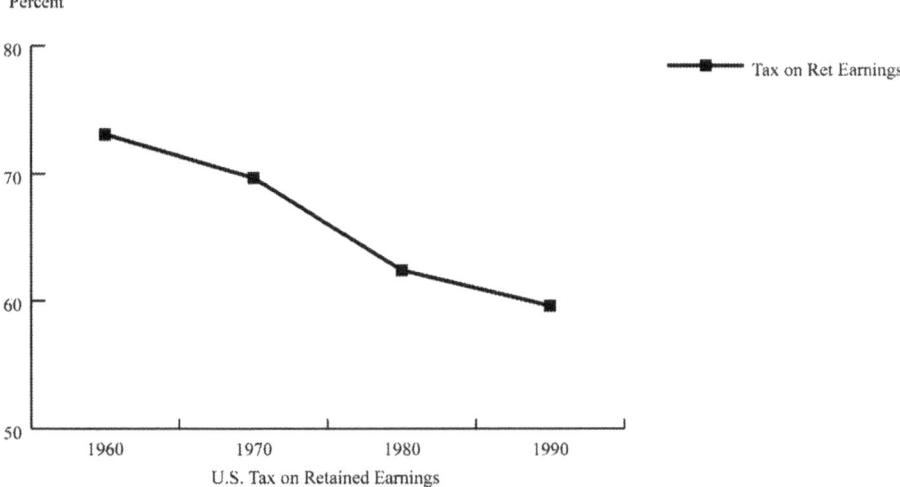

Figure 13.5 U.S. Taxation of Retained Earnings

A second observation is that Figure 13.4 shows U.S. taxation of the corporate sector has been among the highest in the developed countries. Our rates are higher and have generally been higher than countries showing strong economic growth. The rates have been higher than for Sweden.

A third point is that the U.S. had investment tax credits for corporations that together with debt financing lowered the effective rate. These tax credits were eliminated in 1986. This explains why after 1986 when the corporate tax rate decreased to 34%, the effective rate remained relatively steady and became greater than the statutory rate (Chapter 9 Figure 9.6).

A fourth observation is that Japanese economic growth during the postwar period was phenomenal. It is evident that *low taxes on the corporate sector were very beneficial for Japanese growth*. Germany also had strong economic growth, especially during the 1950's, despite fairly high tax rates. The effective tax rates are computed as if there is no tax avoidance. German corporations are mostly privately owned and not required to publish detailed annual reports and accounting statements as in the U.S where tax avoidance by corporations is more difficult. It is quite likely there was a significant amount of corporate tax avoidance by German corporations so that the actual rate paid was lower than the U.S. The U.S. economy grew in the 1950's and 1960's despite much higher taxes on corporations. Japan and Germany were rebuilding after the war as were many other countries. Corporations in many of these countries were not in a position to compete as well with U.S. corporations. But in recent years a high corporate income tax is a more serious problem for global competition.

Negative Effects of the Corporate Income Tax

Allowing companies to keep all their earnings would yield higher returns on invested capital and improve incentives to invest. The most significant impact of the imposition of corporate profits taxes is a direct effect. The profits tax depresses returns by expropriating part of the return. The reduction in the returns to invested capital resulting from expropriation of nearly 60% of retained earnings by corporate income taxes that include double taxation of dividends, reduces the incentives for corporate managers to make capital investments and invest in research and development. Returns to capital are depressed also by other factors. Burdensome bureaucratic regulations squeeze profits by forcing corporations to invest capital in projects for the sake of compliance without yielding any return on the investment.

Figure 13.6 shows the after tax returns to invested capital for non-financial corporations and the capital expenditures by corporations as a percentage of gross value added (GVA) by corporations. The figure tends to suggest there is a correlation between returns on capital (ROC) invested and U.S. corporate investment.[7] If profits taxes were eliminated returns to capital would be about 60% higher. This extra $125 billion or more if spent mostly for capital investment would increase capital investment by 15% or more. The extra investment every year would make a significant difference in economic growth.

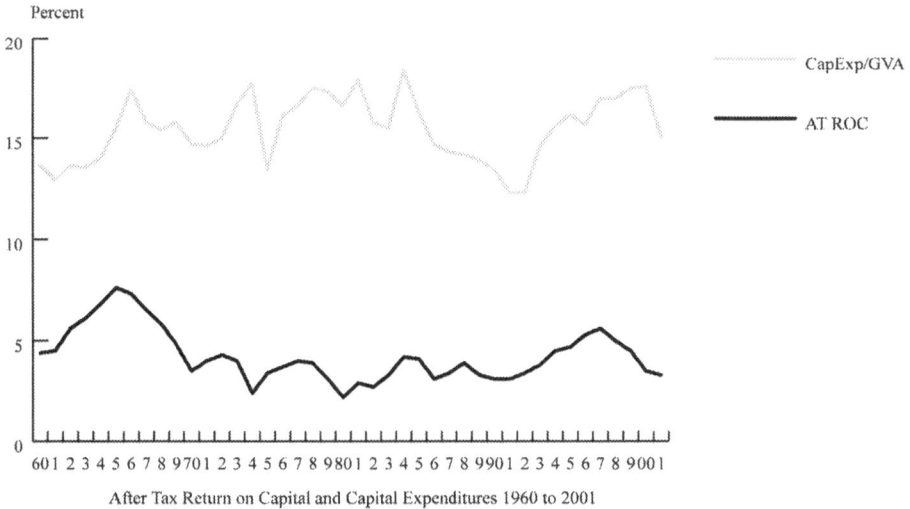

After Tax Return on Capital and Capital Expenditures 1960 to 2001

Figure 13.6 Earning and Investment Rates 1960 to 2001

Indirect Effects of Profits Taxes

Profits taxes also have a number of indirect effects that have a very serious negative impact on capital investment. These effects cause reduced competition in industry and increased perceptions of risk. When competition is reduced and risk increases, corporations have less incentive to invest. Other effects cause resources to be misallocated.

There are several effects which cause increased concentration and reduced competition in many industries. First, reduced returns to capital from high taxation of profits raise *barriers to entry* for an industry. With lower expected returns, potential entrants into an industry will decide not to make large investments needed to enter. Double taxation on capital may cause more profits to be retained and used for mergers rather than for capital investment. Several other effects also tend to induce more *merger activity* and increase concentration: 1) Companies that have difficulty borrowing may have to pay lower dividends and become easier targets for acquisition. Reduced earnings from taxation reduces the price of company stock and cheaper to buy. 2) Companies with tax losses become more attractive as acquisition targets so they can be used to reduce taxes, 3) Taxation slows the rate at which companies can grow. This makes expansion via acquisitions more attractive. Greater merger activity and greater barriers to entry lead to greater concentration in industries than would occur under minimal government taxation and regulation. Competition is reduced as a result. Companies then have less need to innovate. Less investment is needed to maintain market share. When competition is strengthened there is greater need to invest to maintain market share.

There are at least two effects of profits taxes that cause *increased risk*. First, the double taxation on capital makes financing by long term debt far preferable to financing capital investment from profits. But more debt causes interest rates to be higher than otherwise, which in turn causes reduced investment and worsens the relation between the returns to capital and interest rates further discouraging investment. *The increased debt in the economy increases risks.* Second, the existence of the corporate income tax encourages *frequent changes in the tax laws* to obtain political campaign contributions. This also causes increased instability and risk in the economy, since corporate executives are less able to project the consequences of their investment decisions. There is a greater tendency to put financial officers in charge, to maintain profits by cost cutting rather than trying to grow and innovate. More jobs are cut and less investment to improve productivity occurs. Fortunately during the past dozen years tax changes have become more infrequent and more economic stability has resulted.

There are at least two effects of corporate income taxes that cause substantial *misallocation of resources*. First, profits taxes permit increased government spending and taxation, whereas without it, business would spend the money instead of bureaucrats. Spending by bureaucrats causes more consumption and less investment.

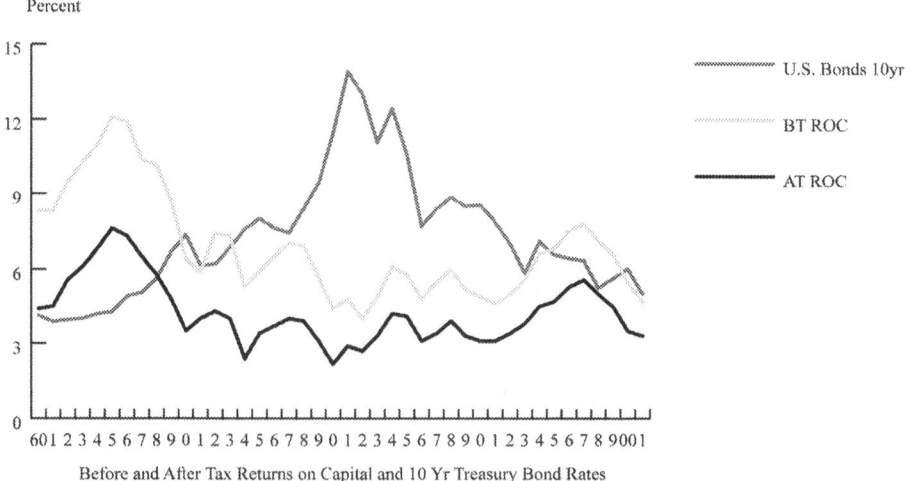

Figure 13.7 Returns on Capital Investment and Interest Rates

Second, *the reduced returns to capital cause more investment to go toward leveraged financial assets and real estate and less toward capital goods.* Figure 13.7 is illuminating.[8] It shows that interest on long term bonds was below the after tax return to capital until 1968. Then from about 1970 to 1993 it exceeded even the before tax returns on capital invested by corporations and after 1993 remains in excess of the after tax return on capital. When investors and corporations themselves can earn more from lending to the Federal Government the situation is not healthy for capital investment and economic growth. If profits taxes were removed, the incentives to make capital investments would greatly improve.

Corporations are also encouraged to move operations to foreign countries that have lower corporate taxes. Lower returns mean that less is invested in research and development and in training than would otherwise be the case. Having reduced returns to capital causes more cheap labor to be hired and less spent on capital investments to improve productivity and wages. Service industries will tend to expand since they are more labor intensive, and manufacturing industries, which are very capital intensive, will tend to shrink. The effect of misallocation of resources is that many resources are diverted from their most advantageous uses to less advantageous uses with resulting reduced growth in labor productivity.

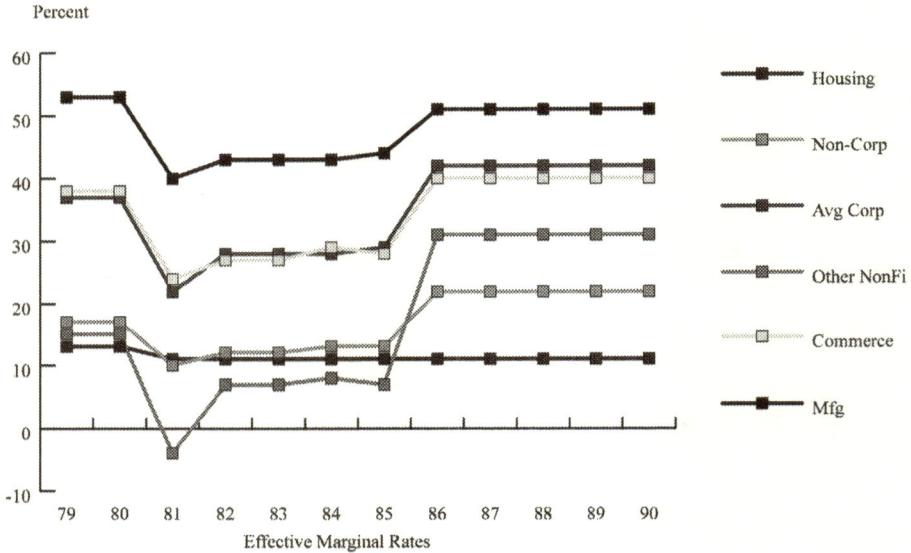

Figure 13.8 Effective Tax Rates on Six Different Groups

Figure 13.8 shows differences between effective marginal tax rates for different groups of corporate and non-corporate entities in the U.S.[9] The effective marginal rates are essentially the tax rates that would be paid if an additional dollar were invested by a member of a group of businesses or by individuals. We see here that additional investment in housing is taxed at about 11% throughout the period. Investment by non-corporate entities was taxed at 18% at the beginning, dropped to the 12% range for several years and finished at about 22%. The overall tax rate on corporations and on corporations involved in commerce track closely together beginning at 37% dropping about 10% for five years and finishing over 40%. The tax rate on the manufacturing sector was about 15% higher until 1986 when the rate on manufacturing was at 51%. For non-financial service industries including construction, the tax rate was considerably lower beginning at 15%, falling to 7% for several years and finishing at 31%. After 1990 tax rates have had little change.

Figure 13.8 evokes several observations. A first point is that *taxes on different sectors of the economy are unbalanced*. In the U.S. for non-financial industries other than manufacturing about 45% of the investment financing is by debt and in manufacturing about 20%. Manufacturing is very capital intensive and manufacturing corporations do not want to take on too much debt, so they fund primarily from retained earnings. This means that the effective rate in the corporate manufacturing sector is around 45% and the effective rates in the non-manufacturing sector are in the 30% range or lower. A large part of the tax rate is due to personal taxes on the dividends. The amount of financing by debt lowers the taxation by the corporate income tax.

A second point is that *if the corporate income tax in the U.S. were eliminated, the taxes on different sectors would become relatively balanced*. If the corporation taxes in the U.S. were removed, the overall reduction would be fairly small, because the personal taxes on corporate capital are the largest contributor. Nevertheless removal of corporate taxes would reduce the taxes on retained earnings from 60% to about 17%. The taxation of manufacturing corporations as well as competing service and commercial industries would be equalized at about 19% (in 1990 and a little higher under current rates).

A third observation is that it does not take a rocket scientist to figure out one of the main reasons that the U.S. has experienced a steadily shrinking manufacturing sector since the 1970's. It is not a result of the greed and venality of corporate leaders, but the incentives designed by lawmakers and bureaucrats. Many jobs and manufacturing plants have moved overseas. Service industries have expanded. Manufacturing is more heavily taxed and requires much more investment per worker than do service industries. It is not surprising that money has moved out of manufacturing and into the service sector.

Finally, as a rule of thumb, the effective rate of taxation of the U.S. corporate sector is about 40% and double the effective tax rate on the non-corporate sector (about 20%) which is double again the rate on owner occupied housing of about 11%.[10] Corporate taxation by introducing extra taxes obviously causes widely varying tax rates on different assets of industries and causes misallocation of resources. This is an example of government interference in the economy to misdirect investment, especially away from manufacturing into service industries.

We see here that while the corporate income tax causes misallocation of resources by itself, it can also result in different rates for different industry groups causing another kind of misallocation of resources. Democrats and labor unions have complained for years against free trade because it means our manufacturing companies will move plants overseas where they can take advantage of cheaper labor. However, we see from the great difference between the tax on the manufacturing sector and on the service sector that the corporate income tax encourages investment in the service sector in preference to the manufacturing sector. In fact the manufacturing rate was at 59% in the 1960's compared to 38% for the service sector and in the 1970's the manufacturing rate was at 58% compared to 34% for the service sector. Moreover, as has been noted, manufacturing industries require much greater investment in machinery and equipment per worker employed than generally is the case for service industries. Thus the tax incentives from the corporate income tax will tend to cause companies to invest in service industries rather than in manufacturing. It should not come as a surprise that there has been a shift in the U.S. over the past 40 years from the manufacturing sector to the service sector. It is not just greedy capitalists trying to increase their profits by building plants in foreign countries and moving operations to other countries. While some transfer of manufacturing to other countries may have been inevitable, the blame does not fall primarily on free trade but on the presence of the corporate income tax and the greater burden the corporate income tax places on manufacturing. Entrepreneurs follow incentives built into the tax code promoting investment in service industries in preference to manufacturing.

As was evident from Figure 13.4, an additional problem resulting from the corporate income tax is that different countries have different tax rates. The 52% rate imposed during the Truman Administration was very high, nearly expropriatory before 1954 when depreciation rules were liberalized. During the entire postwar period the effective rate of the U.S. corporate income tax has been higher than nearly all other countries. In recent years France and Germany have had higher tax rates. During the years following World War II the higher rates did not harm the U.S. much because our main competitors had been devastated by the war and were not very competitive against U.S. corporations. But after Japan and Germany had recovered from the war, the corporate income tax became disadvantageous. When U.S. corporations pay a higher rate on their profits, the price on U.S. goods must be a little higher. Foreign companies pay less and their goods are more competitive. This offers an incentive for our multinational corporations to move their operations to other countries.

Various schemes have been proposed to try to compensate for the disadvantage U.S. corporations face. *The simplest way to eliminate this advantage of foreign corporations is to eliminate the corporate income tax.* This would give U.S. corporations an advantage. Competition in global markets would tend to force other countries to reduce or eliminate their corporate income tax to the benefit of all countries.

All of the effects of the corporate income tax cited have consequences that directly reduce or misallocate the domestic investment needed to provide the greatest improvement in productivity and economic growth. The result is slower innovation. Many newer higher paying jobs, which would have been created if capital were not heavily taxed, are not created. Without investment and new job creation, pay will increase more slowly and some jobs may be eliminated. Less spending on training will occur. The net result is slower growth in productivity and in standards of living.

In an economic environment that is much closer to laissez-faire, businesses face much stiffer competition in the economy—especially for labor. They are forced by the market to invest more to make labor more productive and they must spend more on training to maintain market share and competitiveness. The result is much stronger growth in productivity and in standards of living especially for those with lower incomes.

High Tax Rates Promote Corporate Power Concentration

Traditionally Democrats have promoted concentration of government power in Washington. They have believed that many states were not providing some of the social services that they believed should be provided and that the services provided should be uniform across the country. They have believed that healthcare should be provided for everyone by the Federal government.

What is not realized by very many is that the policies of the Democratic Party promote concentration of corporate power in the hands of a few very large corporations. Democrats should consider the implications of the Three Fingers Rule with one finger pointed at the Republicans and three fingers pointing back at the Democrats. It seems that members of the Democratic Party believe that companies make excessive profits and should pay relatively high profits taxes. They tend to believe that corporations are run by greedy executives who try to exploit their customers and employees to increase profits and make huge salaries. They fail to perceive that corporations and their executives must respond primarily to market incentives including tax incentives imposed by government. If Republicans suggested that it would be very beneficial to the economy to eliminate profits taxes, Democrats would demogogue the issue to their public embarrassment and loss. The Republicans themselves do not understand the value of cutting profits taxes. In fact Republicans themselves were to blame for instituting corporate profits taxes in 1909. They advocate reducing capital gains taxes which would be helpful, but they do not appreciate the much greater positive impact of eliminating corporate taxes.

Democrats believe we need many laws and regulations to keep corporations in check. However, regulators and regulatory agencies tend to come under the control of the corporations they are to regulate. Very large corporations wield great political influence and get people on the regulatory boards who are sympathetic to their agendas. As a result the policies adopted tend to favor the largest corporations. The policies allow them to gain more power still, which they use to the detriment of smaller potential competitors. They are able by this means to reduce competition and concentrate power even more.

Although there are a considerable number of Democrats advocating free trade, most advocate protectionism to cater to their union supporters and to "save" American jobs. Protectionism however reduces competition allowing the largest corporations to maintain their power and influence. Another example is the Democrats desire to socialize health care. This would put the industry in the hands of a few large providers, as did Hillary Clinton's plan in 1993-4.

It is evident that the policies of the Democratic Party tend to encourage and help the largest corporations gain and maintain power. The least understood factor, yet probably the most important factor, is the corporate income tax or profits tax. The most authoritative studies of the corporate income tax up to the 1990's have shown the effective marginal rate to be about 60% on retained earnings.[11] The development of large multinational corporations was fueled by high profits taxes.

The 60% taxation of retained earnings, taxes away the primary source of funds that corporations have to expand and invest in new plants and equipment, to improve productivity. We may divide our corporations into three categories: 1) the large corporations that hold a large part of the market share of industries, 2) mid-size companies some of which are dynamic well-managed companies, and 3) small companies. The taxation of profits will not be a problem for companies in categories two and three that are not making profits and not doing so well. But well run companies in category two could do much more to expand, challenge, and compete with the large corporations, if they could retain all their profits and invest them to move into new markets and industries. The very large corporations in category one have already invested to dominate their industry. They have little incentive to innovate.[12] High profits taxes do not hamper large corporations from maintaining their market share. In fact high profits taxes help the large corporations maintain their market share. They act as a barrier to entry into the industry and markets for the smaller dynamic companies. If the smaller dynamic companies had more of their profits available, they would move into new markets, challenge the larger stodgy corporations, and "eat their lunch." We would see less concentration of economic power in large corporations if the corporate income tax were eliminated. The competition in many markets would be far stronger. We would have better products.

Knowledge of the history of corporate taxes and some economic statistics show that there are strong grounds for believing that high corporate income taxes cause greater concentration of economic power in very large corporations. We have statistics on the percentage of value added by very large manufacturing corporations to the total value added by all manufacturing corporations.[13] This is an appropriate measure of the share of production and share of the market possessed by very large corporations. Similar results come from examining relative percentages of assets. Figure 13.9 shows the percentage of value added by very large manufacturing corporations for the 50 largest, the 100 largest, the 150 largest, and the largest 200 U.S. corporations for a 50 year period from 1947 to 1997.

Percent

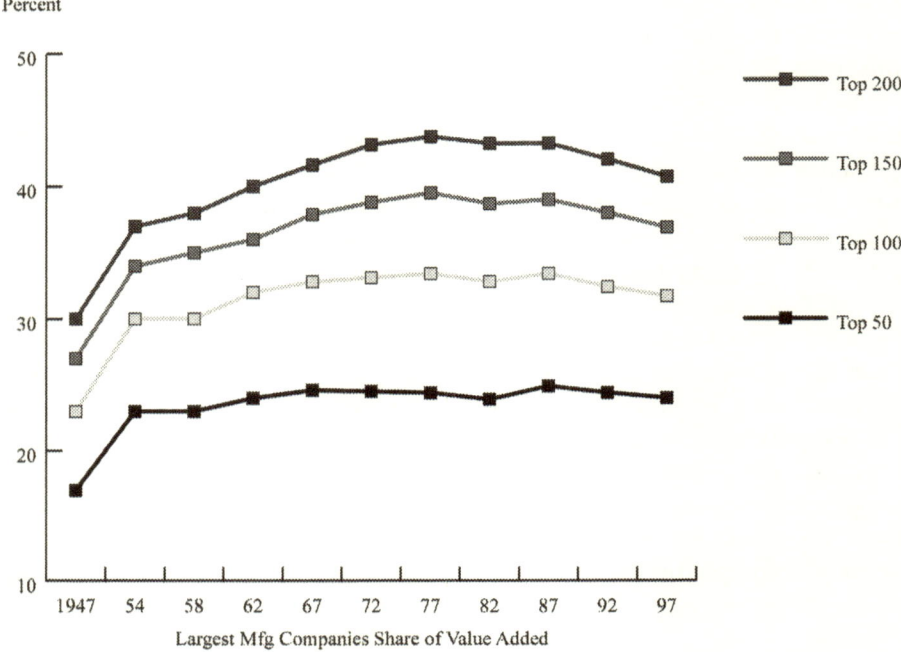

Figure 13.9 Concentration in Manufacturing

What we see in the figure is very interesting. During the Truman Administration when corporate income tax rates were so high, the share of manufacturing value added and income by the largest 50 U.S. manufacturing corporations rose from 17% to 23%. The share of the 200 largest rose from 30% to 37%. If we had comparable data for years prior to World War II we would probably see similar increases over that period. The largest 50 corporations increased by 6% accounting for nearly the entire increase. Another 1% increase is attributable to the 51st to the 100th largest manufacturing corporations. The total share of the 200 corporations approached 40%. After depreciation rules were liberalized effectively lowering profits tax rates in 1954 the share of the largest manufacturing corporations remained relatively stable with the 101st to 150th largest increasing share by 1%.

The investment tax credits given by the Kennedy Administration greatly favored the largest corporations which explains some increases in share of manufacturing from the 1958 figures to the 1967 figures. The increase for the 50 largest corporations went up 2% during that 9 year period. The increase for the 51st to 100th largest corporations went up 1% during that 9 year period yielding a 3% total increase for the 100 largest manufacturing corporations in the 1960's.

Since 1967 the share of the largest 50 has been relatively stable between 24 and 25 percent to 1997. The shares from 1972 to 1987 remained very stable with little change. During that period there was little change in corporate income tax rates. Since 1987 the shares of the largest 50 declined nearly 1% and the share of the next 150 corporations declined 1.6%. In 1997 the relative shares were not much different than in 1962. In the interim the share of the 200 went up 3% to a maximum of 43.7% in 1977 and then declined gradually to the value for the last published business census of 1997.

In evaluating the implications of the changes in share of value added over the 50 year period, we should realize that during this period the share of value added by manufacturing to the overall U.S. economy has declined.

> *It is very likely the decline in the relative size of the manufacturing sector over the years from 1970 to the present is closely related to the high corporate income tax rates.*

There is no doubt that some jobs would have gone overseas due to relatively free trade. However, I believe that there is sufficient evidence for believing that a significant amount of manufacturing that was sent overseas would have remained in the U.S., if corporate income taxes had been eliminated or reduced greatly. Much more money would have been available for investment to improve productivity.

An Example of Increasing Concentration: The U.S. Automobile Industry

The history of the U.S. auto industry illustrates many of the factors that produce industrial concentration. In the 1920's there were dozens of automobile manufacturing companies. When the Depression hit in the 1930's, sales fell off for many of the companies and many went bankrupt. The top companies, although they had some difficulty, did quite well in this environment. The rates on corporate income taxes were raised significantly in spite of the fact that most companies were struggling. Federal Reserve management of the money supply also dried up their source of financing. By the beginning of World War II less than 10 companies survived. During World War II the government gave large contracts to the major automobile manufacturers to manufacture weapons of war. They obtained windfall profits as a result, so the government imposed high profits taxes. Nearly all of the small struggling automobile manufacturers that did not receive war contracts went out of business.

After World War II corporate income taxes were set very high at near expropriatory levels. The IRS rules for depreciating assets meant companies had to report much higher profits than their true profits. As a consequence, the 52% tax on profits with the double taxation of dividends was really more like 100% of the true profits. The Big Three and several other companies survived past World War II. There were a couple of attempts to start new companies after World War II. By 1957 American Motors was the only surviving automobile manufacturer outside of the Big Three. It lasted another decade.

The United Auto Workers union also played a major role in reducing the number of automobile manufacturers. Its leader Walter Reuther wanted to have fewer negotiations and to play one company against the other two companies in the negotiations. He wanted no more than three companies to negotiate with.[14]

The net result of the reduction to effectively three corporations was an oligopolistic market structure. The Big Three had developed new innovations and had bought out some of their competitors in the 1930's to obtain the innovations. Yet by the 1950's and 1960's it was not in their interest to compete by innovation. This would have raised costs for all three market players and reduced their profits. They competed instead with style changes in cars and by advertising.

The only remaining means to restore true competition was to permit entry of foreign manufacturers into the competition. As Japanese automakers progressively cut into the market share of the Big Three, the American companies found it desirable to have the Federal government impose quotas during the early 1980's in order to "save American jobs." Labor also put pressure on the Democrats and Republicans to "save jobs." In fact, the quotas allowed the Big Three to raise prices and make higher profits. The higher profits meant plenty of money was available for investment. The high profits provided a justification to give executives big raises for the strong earnings. Because higher prices were charged, fewer consumers could afford to buy new cars. Sales in number of cars dropped. Fewer cars needed to be produced and hence fewer workers were needed. Tens of thousands of workers were laid off because the government, auto executives, and labor unions caused quotas to be imposed to "save American jobs." The money General Motors had available to invest ($5 billion) was spent acquiring Hughes Aircraft Company to obtain a little "synergy," not for producing better cars. Fat profits from fewer cars produced resulted in fewer workers employed. The high prices were unconstrained by competition. Relatively poor investment to secure a better production capability resulted.

The moral of the story is that trying to help companies maintain jobs by reducing competition through restricting trade of foreign competitors does not work even in the short run. Companies fail to take measures needed to remain competitive. When they can postpone action, they may fall so far behind competitors that they will not recover and may ultimately fail to survive.

In contrast with the U.S., the Japanese have a highly competitive local automobile market with nine companies building cars. The competition spurs innovation. By building better cars the Japanese eventually became highly competitive with the American automobile oligopoly. This is just another proof of the correctness of allowing free markets with open competition. It is not an example of the success of industrial policy. Quite the contrary. The industries the Japanese tried to promote, like shipbuilding, steel, and super-computers, performed poorly.

It is my contention that had the U.S. government with Congress and the Presidency controlled by the Democratic Party not intervened in ways which left the U.S. with only three companies, in particular, by imposing high profits taxes and by subsidizing the Big Three through war contracts, the U.S. automobile companies would have been far more innovative, and U.S. enterprises would have produced better and cheaper cars. Japan would never have made the inroads it did, nor would the U.S. have run a trade deficit of $139 billion in 2004 in automobiles and automobile parts.

The U.S. should have at least eight U.S. owned automobile companies. Once a company has a manufacturing plant capable of producing about 400,000 cars in a year there are no additional gains from economies of scale possible.[15] But because our policies reduced the number of companies, the second best solution was necessary: having Japanese owned companies build manufacturing plants in the U.S. The proper course is to reverse the policies which have led to the current situation. We should eliminate profits taxes so that the auto companies have an incentive to invest and also have the where-withal to be competitive. Under the current regime the Big Three are falling behind the Japanese in putting electronics in vehicles. In the long run we will continue to see erosion in our competitive position, if we do not take the measures suggested, namely, cut profits taxes and onerous regulations to improve the business environment in which businesses compete.

Conclusion

It is clear that there are strong grounds for believing that high corporate income tax rates tend to increase concentration in industry, especially in man-ufacturing, where considerable amounts of money are needed for investment. Interestingly reductions in tax rates if available only to the largest corporations like President John F. Kennedy's tax credits, can increase concentration as well. There should be a level playing field. We do not want taxes that discourage investment and improvements in productivity. There is no good justification for the corporate income tax. It should be eliminated.

In Chapters 2 through 8 we showed why the Social Security system needs reform with personal retirement accounts. It is only fair to American workers to provide a much better retirement income than is possible with a pure pay-as-you-go transfer scheme. A Social Security system with personal retirement accounts will also cause greater investment and growth. We would also be better off if burdensome bureaucratic regulations were eliminated. A relatively laissez faire economy will provide a much better standard of living for most people over the long term than the half-capitalistic and half-socialistic system that we currently have.

NOTES

Chapter 1

1. Jorgenson, Dale, *Tax Reform and The Cost of Capital* (Washington, D.C.: Brookings Institution, 1993), pp. 351, 353, and 355.

2. Darby, Michael R., *The Effects of Social Security on Income and the Capital Stock* (Washington D.C.: American Enterprise Institute, 1979); Feldstein, Martin, "Social Security, Induced Retirement, and Aggregate Capital Accumulation," *Journal of Political Economy*, 82:5 (1974): 905-26; Feldstein, Martin, "Social Security and Saving: The Extended Life Cycle Theory," *American Economic Review* 66 (1976): 77-86; Feldstein, Martin, "Social Security and Private Savings: International Evidence in an Extended Life-Cycle Model" in *The Economics of Public Services*, ed. by Feldstein, M. and Inman, R. (London: Macmillan, 1977); Feldstein, Martin, "Social Security and Private Savings: Reply to Barro," *Studies in Social Security and Retirement Policy*, (Washington, D.C.: American Enterprise Institute, 1978); Feldstein, Martin and Pellechio, Anthony J., "Social Security and Household Wealth Accumulation: New Microeconometric Evidence," *Review of Economics and Statistics*, 61:3 (1979): 361-68.; Feldstein, Martin, "International Differences in Social Security and Saving," *Journal of Public Economics*, 14 (1980): 225-44; Barro, Robert J, "The Impact of Social Security on Private Savings," *Studies in Social Security and Retirement Policy* (Washington, D.C.: American Enterprise Institute, 1978). Feldstein argued that Social Security had a very large negative impact on personal saving. Others like Barro argued that it had no effect. The consensus seems to be that it has some effect perhaps on the order of 10%. Even a 10% reduction has a significant negative impact on the economy. In addition Social Security induces people to retire earlier than they might otherwise have retired. Taxes on Social Security also induce people to produce less after retirement than they might have produced.

Chapter 2

1. References are cited in Footnote 2 for Chapter 1.

2. 2004 OASDI Trustees Report, Table IV.B7. gives an unfunded liability of about $10 trillion. The 2005 Trustees Report, Table IV.B7 gives $11.1 trillion. It illegitimately subtracts the $1.7 trillion "Trust Fund" debt as if it were assets. Thus the unfunded liability should be about $12.8 trillion.

3. In the 1950's and 1960's U.S. long term interest rates were lower than most industrialized countries except Switzerland. In the 1970's U.S. long term interest rates were lower than most industrialized countries except Japan and Switzerland (average 2.4% lower). In the early 1980's U.S. long term rates averaged about 12% and other industrialized countries were generally higher except the Netherlands (average 2.9% lower), Japan (average 4.2% lower), and Switzerland (average 7.1% lower). Since 1985 long term interest rates of the U.S. and other industrialized countries have remained roughly comparable except that Japan's rates have generally been about 3 or 4 percent lower than the rates in the U.S.

4. 2004 OASDI Trustees Report, Table IV.B1.(Intermediate) indicates estimated percents of covered payroll income through the year 2080.

5. Ibid., Table IV.B1.(Intermediate) indicates percents that Social Security retirement benefits of covered payroll that must be paid.

Chapter 3

1. 2004 OASDI Trustees Report, Table II.C1. The intermediate assumption for wage growth is 3.9% per year.

2. Tanner, Michael, "The Better Deal," Cato Project on Social Security Choice SSP No. 31 (Washington D.C.: Cato Institute, October 28, 2003): 12. Social Security actuaries have determined that persons can expect to earn an interest rate of 6.5% over the long term.

3. The current benefit formula for Social Security retirement has two bend points that are indexed to wage increases. So for an average wage earner, the formula will produce about 40% of the person's average monthly income. The bend points produce higher ratios of replacement income for lower income workers and lower ratios for higher income workers.

Chapter 4

1.2004 OASDI Trustees Report, Table II.C1. The intermediate assumption for wage growth is 3.9% per year.

2. Refer to Footnote 2 for Chapter 3.

Chapter 5

1.Calculations for this book were developed from the 2004 OASDI Trustees Report before the 2005 report was available. The differences in the conclusions in the Trustees Report from year to year are quite minor.

2. The numbers were generated before the 2005 Trustees Report was released. The demographic assumptions used for the calculations are the same in the 2005 report. There are some differences in estimates of benefits paid. The 2005 report has the trust fund being exhausted by 2043 instead of 2044. It seemed the differences are too slight to merit refiguring them.

3. 2004 OASDI Trustees Report, Table IV.B3. (Intermediate Assumptions). The bottom of the section indicates the "Trust Fund" will be exhausted in 2044. The 2005 Trustees Report shows the "Trust Fund" being exhausted in 2043.

4. Ibid. Table II.C1. (Intermediate Assumptions) gives a 5.8% Interest Rate.

5. Ibid. (Intermediate Assumptions) gives a 2.8% cost-of-living adjustment.

6. Ibid. Table IV.B2. (Intermediate Assumptions) gives a 2:1 ratio of workers to retirees in a few decades.

Chapter 9

1. 2005 Trustees Report Table IV.B7.

2. Evans, Paul, "Do Large Deficits Produce High Interest Rates?" *The American Economic Review*, 75: 1 (March, 1985): 68-87; Evans, Paul, "Interest Rates and Expected Future Budget Deficits in the United States" *Journal of Political Economy*, 95: 1 (February, 1987): 34-58; Evans, Paul, "Do Budget Deficits Raise Nominal Interest Rates? Evidence from Six Countries" *Journal of Monetary Economics*, 20 (1987): 281-300. These articles give evidence that there is no correlation between deficits and interest rates. Many attempts to link the movement of deficits and interest rates have proved fruitless.

3. Economic Report of the President 1990, (Washington, D.C.: GPO), Table C-76 gives the National debt—the money owed to the public and the Federal debt owed to other Federal agencies. The unfunded liability is my calculation.

4. The top marginal personal income tax rates for 1913 to 2003 can be found at www.truthandpolitics.org. The top marginal corporate income tax rates for 1909 to 2003 can be found at www.taxpolicycenter.org/taxfacts.

5. King, Mervyn, and Fullerton, Don, *The Taxation of Income from Capital* (Chicago: University of Chicago Press, 1984), p. 244; Jorgenson, Dale and Landau, Ralph, eds. *Tax Reform and the Cost of Capital*, pp. 351, 353-355.

6. Bureau of Economic Analysis, NIPA Tables 3.1 and 3.2.

7. Cato Institute, Cato Policy Analysis No. 225 (Washington, D.C.: Cato Institute).

8. Bureau of Economic Analysis, NIPA Table 5.1.

9. The rate of after tax return on capital comes from Bureau of Economic Analysis, *Survey of Current Business*, (September 2002): 17. Real Growth, Real

Interest, and 30 yr Treasury come from the 2005 Economic Report of the President (Washington, D.C.: GPO), Tables B-2, B-63, and B-73. Real Interest was calculated as the rate for 6-month Tbills minus the CPI-U consumer price index.

10. The tax on retained earnings and the effective corporation rate are from King, Mervyn, and Fullerton, Don, p. 244; Jorgenson, Dale and Landau, pp. 351, 353-355.

11. Bureau of Economic Analysis, NIPA Table 1.14 for gross value added for non-financial corporations. The rate of after tax return on capital comes from Bureau of Economic Analysis, *Survey of Current Business* (September 2002): 17.

Chapter 10

1. 2005 Economic Report of the President (Washington, D.C.: GPO), Tables B-2 and B-73.

2. Business Week, "Big Boom, Weak Profits," Aug 12, 2002.

3. Mellon, Andrew, *Taxation: The People's Business* (New York: MacMillan Co., 1924) Table II, p. 193. Adams, Charles, *Good and Evil* (Lanham, MD: Madison Books, 1993), p. 431.

4. The top marginal personal income tax rates for 1913 to 2003 can be found at www.truthandpolitics.org.

5. Mellon, Andrew, *Taxation: The People's Business*, Table II, p. 193. Adams, Charles, Good and Evil, (Lanham, MD: Madison Books, 1993), p.431.

6. Mellon, Andrew, Table II, p. 193.

7. Ibid, Table III, p. 201.

8. U.S. Bureau of the Census, *Historical Statistics of the United States: From Colonial Times to 1970*, Series Y 403, 406, and 407, p. 1110.

9. Feldstein, Martin and Feenberg, Daniel, "The Effect of Increased Tax Rates on Taxable Income and Economic Efficiency: A Preliminary Analysis of the 1993 Tax Rate Increases," in *Tax Policy and the Economy*, no. 10 (Cambridge, Mass.:The MIT Press,1996) ed. by Poterba, James M.: 88-117.

10. Kerry Blames Corporate Tax Code for Shipping Jobs Overseas, www.factcheck.org, July 28, 2004 gives arguments to show the "outsourcing" problem is not serious and the proposed Kerry tax cut will not deal with underlying causes.

11. Bureau of Economic Analysis, NIPA Table 1.14 gives gross value added for non-financial corporations. The rate of after tax return on capital comes from Bureau of Economic Analysis, *Survey of Current Business* (September 2002): 17.

Chapter 11

1. Adams, Charles, *Good and Evil* (Lanham, MD: Madison Books, 1993). Adams shows that the decline of civilizations is generally caused by excessive taxation.

2. Goodman, John C. and Musgrave, Gerald L., *Patient Power* (Washington. D.C.: Cato Institute, 1992). The book shows how medical savings accounts can solve the problems in the U.S. health care industry using market forces.

3. McGee, John S., "Predatory Price Cutting: The Standard Oil (N.J.) Case," *Journal of Law and Economics* (October, 1958). reprinted in Spulber, Daniel F., *Famous Fables of Economics* (Oxford: Blackwell Publishers, 2002), pp. 215-45. See also Folsom, Burton W. Jr., *The Myth of the Robber Barons* (Herndon, VA: The Young America's Foundation, 1991), 83-100.

4. Folsom, Burton W. Jr., *The Myth of the Robber Barons*, p. 90.

Chapter 12

1. Coase, Ronald, "The Lighthouse in Economics," *Journal of Law and Economics* 17 (1974): 357-76.

2. Klein, Daniel B., "The Voluntary Provision of Public Goods? The Turnpike Companies of Early America," *Economic Inquiry* 28 (1990): 788-812.

3. Liebowitz, Stan J. and Margolis, Stephen E., "The Fable of the Keys," *Journal of Law and Economics* 33 (1990): 1-25.

4. Liebowitz, Stan J. and Margolis, Stephen E., "Beta, Macintosh and Other Fabulous Tales," in Spulber, Daniel F., *Famous Fables of Economics* (Oxford: Blackwell Publishers, 2002), 111-116.

5. McGee, John S., "Predatory Price Cutting: The Standard Oil (N.J.) Case," *Journal of Law and Economics* (October, 1958) reprinted in Spulber, Daniel F., *Famous Fables of Economics* (Oxford: Blackwell Publishers, 2002), 215-45.

6. Akerlof, George A., "The Market for 'Lemons': Quality Uncertainty and the Market Mechanism," in Cowen, Tyler and Crampton, Eric eds. *Market Failure or Success* (Cheltenham, UK: Edward Elgar Publishing, 2002), 67.

7. Ibid., 71-72.

8. Coase, Ronald, "The Lighthouse in Economics," *Journal of Law and Economics* 17 (1974): 357-76.

9. Klein, Daniel B., "The Voluntary Provision of Public Goods? The Turnpike Companies of Early America," *Economic Inquiry* 28 (1990): 788-812.

10. Liebowitz, Stan J. and Margolis, Stephen E., "The Fable of the Keys," *Journal of Law and Economics* 33 (1990): 1-25.

11. Liebowitz, Stan J. and Margolis, Stephen E., "Beta, Macintosh and Other Fabulous Tales," in Spulber, Daniel F., *Famous Fables of Economics* (Oxford: Blackwell Publishers, 2002): 113-14.

12. McGee, John S., "Predatory Price Cutting: The Standard Oil (N.J.) Case," *Journal of Law and Economics* (October, 1958). in Spulber, Daniel F., *Famous Fables of Economics* (Oxford: Blackwell Publishers, 2002), 221.

13. McGee, John S., "Predatory Price Cutting: The Standard Oil (N.J.) Case,": 232, 239, 242.

14. Bond, Eric W., "A Direct Test of the 'Lemons' Model: the Market for Used Pickup Trucks," in Cowen, Tyler and Crampton, Eric eds. *Market Failure or Success* (Cheltenham, UK: Edward Elgar Publishing, 2002): 269-74.

15. Klein, Daniel B., "The Demand for and Supply of Assurance," in Cowen, Tyler and Crampton, Eric eds. *Market Failure or Success* (Cheltenham, UK: Edward Elgar Publishing, 2002): 172-192.

Chapter 13

1. Matthew 7:16.

2. Samuelson, Paul and Nordhaus, William, *Economics*, 12th Edition, (New York: McGraw Hill, 1985). The book has 890 pages. Profits are mentioned on pages 44 and 45, and in a few places after page 450, but the chapter discussing profits uses about 12 pages from pages 660 to 672.

3. Jorgenson, Dale, *Tax Reform and The Cost of Capital* (Washington, D.C.: Brookings Institution, 1993), Table 10-11, 355.

4. Ryan, John, *Current Depreciation Allowances* (New York: Fordham University Press, 1958).

5. Jorgenson, Dale, *Tax Reform and The Cost of Capital*, pp. 175, 252, 265, 294, 326, 355.

6. Jorgenson, Dale, *Tax Reform and The Cost of Capital*, 351, 355; King, Mervyn, and Fullerton, Don, *The Taxation of Income from Capital* (Chicago: University of Chicago Press, 1984), pp. 261, 263.

7. The statistics for Figure 13.6 come from the 2005 Statistical Abstract of the U.S., 1994 Economic Report of the President; Bureau of Economic Analysis, NIPA Table 1.14 for gross value added for non-financial corporations. The rate of after tax return on capital comes from Bureau of Economic Analysis, *Survey of Current Business* (September 2002): 17.

8. The rate for 10 yr Treasury Bonds is from the 2005 Economic Report of the President, Table B-73. The rates of before and after tax return on capital come from Bureau of Economic Analysis, *Survey of Current Business* (September 2002):17.

9. Jorgenson, Dale, *Tax Reform and The Cost of Capital*, 351, 353, 355.

10. King, Mervyn, and Fullerton, Don, *The Taxation of Income from Capital*, 365.

11. Jorgenson, Dale, *Tax Reform and The Cost of Capital*, Table 10-11, 355.

12. "For the whole 1953-73 period, the smallest firms produced about 4 times as many innovations per R&D dollar as the middle-size firms and 24 times as many as the largest firms." *Science Indicators* (Washington, D.C.: National Science Board, 1976), p. 118. Quoted with further examples in Adams, Walter and Brock, James W., *The Bigness Complex* (New York: Pantheon Books, 1986), pp. 52-54.

13. U.S. Census Bureau, *1997 Economic Census, Concentration Ratios in Manufacturing*, Table 1, p. 7; *1992 Economic Census, Concentration Ratios in Manufacturing*, Table 1; 1987 Economic Census, Concentration Ratios in Manufacturing, Table 1, 6-3; *Statistical Abstract of the United States*, 1978, Table 947, p. 576.

14. Adams, Walter and Brock, James W., *The Bigness Complex* (New York: Pantheon Books, 1986), 324. Details of the effectiveness of UAW negotiations are provided here.

15. Adams, Walter and Brock, James W., *The Bigness Complex*, 38.

Appendix I

The following tables give the calculations used in Chapter 3 to estimate the amount of pre-retirement income that would be replaced by contributions of 10.6% of wages or salaries to personal retirement accounts. The four tables are based on wages increasing at 3.9% per year for forty years. The average wage would then be about $35,000 x 1.039^{40} = $161,700 in 2045. Wages are assumed to increase at a rate of 5.34% from age 25 to age 50 and at the assumed rate of inflation of 2.9% to age 67. In each table Column 1 is the Age of a participant in 2005. Column 2 is the person's wages or salary for the year. Column 3 is 10.6% of the entry in Column 2. Column 4 computes the amount of money accumulated if the amount in Column 3 earns the assumed interest rate for the table to age 67 for regular retirement or to age 62 for early retirement.

25'	28700	3042	37772
26'	30233	3205	37361
27'	31847	3376	36954
28'	33548	3556	36551
29'	35339	3746	36153
30'	37226	3946	35759
31'	39214	4157	35370
32'	41308	4379	34985
33'	43514	4612	34604
34'	45838	4859	34227
35'	48285	5118	33854
36'	50864	5392	33485
37'	53580	5679	33120
38'	56441	5983	32760
39'	59455	6302	32403
40'	62630	6639	32050
41'	65974	6993	31701
42'	69497	7367	31356
43'	73209	7760	31014
44'	77118	8174	30676
45'	81236	8611	30342
46'	85574	9071	30012
47'	90144	9555	29685
48'	94957	10065	29361
49'	100028	10603	29042
50'	105369	11169	28725
51'	108425	11493	27754
52'	111570	11826	26816
53'	114805	12169	25910
54'	118134	12522	25034
55'	121560	12885	24188
56'	125086	13259	23370
57'	128713	13644	22580
58'	132446	14039	21817
59'	136287	14446	21079
60'	140239	14865	20367
61'	144306	15296	19678
62'	148491	15740	19013
63'	152797	16196	18370
64'	157228	16666	17749
65'	161788	17149	17149
66'	166479	17647	20015
67'	171307	18159	18159
			1388125
	13482	68.64%	6941
			9254

Table A1.1 Normal retirement at age 67; Interest Rate 6.5%

25'	27800	2947	30289
26'	29285	3104	29959
27'	30848	3270	29633
28'	32496	3445	29310
29'	34231	3628	28991
30'	36059	3822	28675
31'	37984	4026	28363
32'	40013	4241	28054
33'	42149	4468	27748
34'	44400	4706	27446
35'	46771	4958	27147
36'	49269	5222	26851
37'	51900	5501	26559
38'	54671	5795	26270
39'	57591	6105	25984
40'	60666	6431	25701
41'	63905	6774	25421
42'	67318	7136	25144
43'	70913	7517	24870
44'	74700	7918	24599
45'	78688	8341	24331
46'	82890	8786	24066
47'	87317	9256	23804
48'	91979	9750	23545
49'	96891	10270	23288
50'	102065	10819	23035
51'	105025	11133	22256
52'	108071	11456	21504
53'	111205	11788	20777
54'	114430	12130	20074
55'	117748	12481	19396
56'	121163	12843	18740
57'	124677	13216	18107
58'	128292	13599	17495
59'	132013	13993	16903
60'	135841	14399	16332
61'	139781	14817	15780
62'	143834	15246	15246
			911690
	11986	50.71%	4558
			6078

Table A1.2 Early Retirement at age 62; Interest Rate 6.5%

25'	28700	3042	45555
26'	30233	3205	44849
27'	31847	3376	44153
28'	33548	3556	43468
29'	35339	3746	42793
30'	37226	3946	42130
31'	39214	4157	41476
32'	41308	4379	40832
33'	43514	4612	40199
34'	45838	4859	39575
35'	48285	5118	38961
36'	50864	5392	38357
37'	53580	5679	37762
38'	56441	5983	37176
39'	59455	6302	36599
40'	62630	6639	36031
41'	65974	6993	35472
42'	69497	7367	34922
43'	73209	7760	34380
44'	77118	8174	33847
45'	81236	8611	33322
46'	85574	9071	32805
47'	90144	9555	32296
48'	94957	10065	31795
49'	100028	10603	31302
50'	105369	11169	30816
51'	108425	11493	29635
52'	111570	11826	28500
53'	114805	12169	27408
54'	118134	12522	26357
55'	121560	12885	25348
56'	125086	13259	24376
57'	128713	13644	23442
58'	132446	14039	22544
59'	136287	14446	21680
60'	140239	14865	20849
61'	144306	15296	20050
62'	148491	15740	19282
63'	152797	16196	18543
64'	157228	16666	17833
65'	161788	17149	17149
66'	166479	17647	20204
67'	171307	18159	18159
			1554064
	13482	76.84%	7770
			10360

Table A1.3 Normal Retirement at age 67; Interest Rate 7%

25'	28700	3042	14606
26'	30233	3205	14794
27'	31847	3376	14984
28'	33548	3556	15178
29'	35339	3746	15373
30'	37226	3946	15571
31'	39214	4157	15772
32'	41308	4379	15975
33'	43514	4612	16181
34'	45838	4859	16389
35'	48285	5118	16600
36'	50864	5392	16814
37'	53580	5679	17031
38'	56441	5983	17250
39'	59455	6302	17473
40'	62630	6639	17698
41'	65974	6993	17926
42'	69497	7367	18157
43'	73209	7760	18391
44'	77118	8174	18628
45'	81236	8611	18868
46'	85574	9071	19111
47'	90144	9555	19357
48'	94957	10065	19607
49'	100028	10603	19859
50'	105369	11169	20115
51'	108425	11493	19902
52'	111570	11826	19692
53'	114805	12169	19483
54'	118134	12522	19277
55'	121560	12885	19074
56'	125086	13259	18872
57'	128713	13644	18672
58'	132446	14039	18475
59'	136287	14446	18279
60'	140239	14865	18086
61'	144306	15296	17895
62'	148491	15740	17705
63'	152797	16196	17518
64'	157228	16666	17333
65'	161788	17149	17149
66'	166479	17647	19087
67'	171307	18159	18159
			821536
	13482	40.62%	4108
			5477

Table A1.4 Normal Retirement at age 67; Interest Rate 4%

APPENDIX 2

Table A2.1 includes the entries for all years 2005 to 2060 for both the current system (the first 15 columns) and the system of personal retirement accounts analyzed in Chapters 6 to 8. Tables 5.1, 5.2, 6.1, 6.2, 7.1, 7.2, 7.3, and 8.1 show various sections of this table.

Year Inc Cov Work	CovP	Ben %	Schd Ben	Con +Tx%	Net Con +Tx	Surpl/Def	TrustF Interest	SS Dbt	Ext Trust Debt	Ann SS Pay	Tot SS Debt Int	Tot Ann Int	Save	Red Rat	Red Ben	CP4%	Cont+ Tx%	Net Con /Def	Surp /Def	TrF Int	TF Debt	ExtSS Debt	Ann Int Pay	TotSS Dbt	Tot Ann Int	Tot Savd NoInt
	1.039						.058																			
2005	4757	9.11	434	10.9	519	85	85	1666	0	0	1666	85	0	1	434	162	7.49	356	-78	85	1503	78	5	1581	90	162
2006	4982	8.99	449	10.91	544	94	93	1854	0	0	1854	93	0	1	449	173	7.44	371	-78	87	1512	156	9	1668	96	335
2007	5234	8.94	469	10.92	572	103	103	2060	0	0	2060	103	0	1	469	185	7.38	386	-83	88	1517	239	14	1756	102	520
2008	5489	8.95	492	10.96	602	109	116	2385	0	0	2385	116	0	1	492	198	7.35	403	-89	88	1516	328	19	1844	107	718
2009	5755	9.03	521	10.95	630	109	130	2524	0	0	2524	130	0	1	521	212	7.27	418	-103	88	1501	431	25	1932	113	930
2010	6030	9.16	554	10.97	661	107	144	2775	0	0	2775	144	0	1	554	226	7.22	435	-119	87	1469	550	32	2019	119	1156
2011	6313	9.32	590	11.01	696	106	160	3041	0	0	3041	160	0	1	590	241	7.21	455	-135	85	1419	685	40	2104	125	1397
2012	6603	9.53	630	11.04	729	99	176	3316	0	0	3316	176	0	1	630	256	7.16	473	-157	82	1344	842	49	2186	131	1653
2013	6884	9.76	674	11.06	762	88	191	3596	0	0	3596	191	0	1	674	271	7.13	491	-183	78	1239	1025	59	2264	137	1924
2014 1.00622	7197	10.01	720	11.08	797	77	207	3880	0	0	3880	207	0	1	720	288	7.08	510	-211	72	1100	1236	72	2336	144	2212
2015 1.00622	7524	10.29	774	11.1	835	61	223	4164	0	0	4164	223	0	0.995	770	301	7.1	534	-236	64	928	1472	85	2400	149	2513
2016 1.00463	7854	10.6	833	11.12	873	41	242	4446	0	0	4446	242	0	0.985	820	314	7.12	559	-261	54	721	1733	101	2454	154	2827
2017 1.00463	8198	10.91	894	11.14	913	19	258	4723	0	0	4723	258	0	0.974	871	328	7.14	585	-286	42	477	2019	117	2496	159	3155
2018 1.00463	8557	11.22	960	11.16	955	-5	274	4992	5	0	4997	274	0	0.963	925	342	7.16	613	-312	28	193	2331	135	2523	163	3497
2019 1.00463	8932	11.53	1030	11.18	999	-31	290	5250	36	2	5287	292	0	0.953	981	357	7.18	641	-340	11	0	2671	155	2671	166	3854
2020 1.00463	9323	11.85	1105	11.19	1043	-62	305	5493	98	6	5591	310	0	0.942	1041	373	7.19	670	-370	0	0	3041	176	3041	176	4227
2021 1.00278	9714	12.14	1179	11.21	1089	-90	319	5721	188	11	5910	330	0	0.927	1093	389	7.21	700	-393	0	0	3434	199	3434	199	4616
2022 1.00278	10121	12.43	1258	11.23	1137	-121	332	5932	310	18	6241	350	0	0.912	1147	405	7.23	732	-416	0	0	3849	223	3849	223	5021
2023 1.00278	10545	12.72	1341	11.25	1186	-155	344	6121	465	27	6585	371	0	0.897	1203	422	7.25	764	-439	0	0	4288	249	4288	249	5443
2024 1.00278	10986	13.01	1429	11.27	1238	-191	355	6285	656	38	6940	393	0	0.882	1261	439	7.27	799	-462	0	0	4750	276	4750	276	5882
2025 1.00278	11446	13.3	1522	11.28	1291	-231	365	6418	887	51	7305	416	0	0.867	1320	458	7.28	833	-487	0	0	5237	304	5237	304	6340
2026 1.00257	11923	13.54	1614	11.3	1347	-267	372	6523	1154	67	7677	439	0	0.85	1372	477	7.3	870	-502	0	0	5738	333	5738	333	6817
2027 1.00257	12420	13.78	1712	11.31	1405	-307	378	6595	1461	85	8056	463	0	0.833	1426	497	7.31	908	-518	0	0	6256	363	6256	363	7314
2028 1.00257	12938	14.02	1814	11.33	1466	-348	382	6629	1809	105	8438	487	0	0.815	1478	518	7.33	948	-530	0	0	6786	394	6786	394	7831
2029 1.00257	13477	14.26	1922	11.34	1528	-394	384	6620	2203	128	8823	512	0	0.797	1532	539	7.34	989	-542	0	0	7329	425	7329	425	8370
2030 1.00257	14039	14.51	2037	11.35	1593	-444	384	6560	2646	153	9207	537	0	0.78	1589	562	7.35	1032	-557	0	0	7886	457	7886	457	8932
2031 1.0029	14628	14.65	2143	11.36	1662	-481	381	6460	3127	181	9587	562	0	0.762	1633	585	7.36	1077	-556	0	0	8442	490	8442	490	9517
2032 1.0029	15243	14.79	2254	11.37	1733	-521	375	6313	3649	212	9962	586	0	0.744	1677	610	7.37	1123	-554	0	0	8996	522	8996	522	10127
2033 1.0029	15883	14.93	2371	11.38	1808	-564	366	6115	4213	244	10328	610	0	0.726	1722	635	7.38	1172	-549	0	0	9545	554	9545	554	10762
2034 1.0029	16551	15.07	2494	11.39	1885	-609	355	5861	4822	280	10683	634	0	0.708	1766	662	7.39	1223	-543	0	0	10088	585	10088	585	11424
2035 1.0029	17246	15.22	2625	11.4	1966	-659	340	5542	5480	318	11022	658	0	0.69	1811	690	7.4	1276	-535	0	0	10623	616	10623	616	12114
2036 1.00317	17975	15.25	2741	11.4	2049	-692	321	5171	6173	358	11344	679	0	0.672	1842	719	7.41	1330	-512	0	0	11135	646	11135	646	12833
2037 1.00317	18736	15.29	2865	11.41	2138	-727	300	4744	6899	400	11644	700	0	0.654	1874	749	7.41	1388	-485	0	0	11620	674	11620	674	13582
2038 1.00317	19528	15.33	2994	11.41	2228	-766	275	4254	7665	445	11919	720	0	0.636	1904	781	7.41	1447	-457	0	0	12077	700	12077	700	14363
2039 1.00317	20354	15.37	3128	11.42	2324	-804	247	3697	8469	491	12166	738	0	0.618	1933	814	7.42	1510	-423	0	0	12500	725	12500	725	15178
2040 1.00317	21215	15.4	3267	11.42	2423	-844	214	3067	9313	540	12380	755	0	0.6	1960	849	7.42	1574	-386	0	0	12886	747	12886	747	16026
2041 1.00309	22110	15.39	3403	11.42	2525	-878	178	2367	10191	591	12558	769	0	0.586	1994	884	7.42	1641	-353	0	0	13240	768	13240	768	16911

Year	Inc Cov Work	CovP	Ben %	Schd Ben	Con +Tx%	Net Con +Tx	Surpl/ Def	TrustF Interest	SS Trust Dbt	Ext SS Debt	Ann Int Pay	Tot SS Debt	Tot Ann Int	Save	Red Rat	Red Ben	CP4%	Cont+ Tx%	Net Con	Surp /Def	TrF Int	TF Debt	ExtSS Debt	Ann Int Pay	TotSS Dbt	Tot Ann Int	Savd NoInt
2042	1.00309	23044	15.39	3546	11.42	2632	-915	137	1589	11106	644	12695	781	0	0.572	2029	922	7.42	1710	-319	0	0	13559	786	13559	786	17832
2043	1.00309	24016	15.38	3694	11.42	2743	-951	92	731	12057	699	12787	791	0	0.558	2061	961	7.42	1782	-279	0	0	13838	803	13838	803	18793
2044	1.00309	25030	15.38	3850	11.42	2858	-991	42	0	13048	757	13048	799	0	0.544	2094	1001	7.42	1857	-237	0	0	14075	816	14075	816	19794
2045	1.00309	26087	15.37	4010	11.42	2979	-1030	0	0	14079	817	14079	817	0	0.53	2125	1043	7.42	1936	-189	0	0	14264	827	14264	827	20838
2046	1.00267	27176	15.38	4180	11.42	3104	-1076	0	0	15155	879	15155	879	0	0.521	2178	1087	7.42	2016	-161	0	0	14425	837	14425	837	21925
2047	1.00267	28312	15.38	4354	11.42	3233	-1121	0	0	16276	944	16276	944	0	0.512	2229	1132	7.42	2101	-129	0	0	14554	844	14554	844	23057
2048	1.00267	29494	15.39	4539	11.43	3371	-1168	0	0	17444	1012	17444	1012	0	0.503	2283	1180	7.43	2191	-92	0	0	14646	849	14646	849	24237
2049	1.00267	30726	15.39	4729	11.43	3512	-1217	0	0	18661	1082	18661	1082	0	0.494	2336	1229	7.43	2283	-53	0	0	14699	853	14699	853	25466
2050	1.00267	32010	15.4	4930	11.43	3659	-1271	0	0	19931	1156	19931	1156	0	0.485	2391	1280	7.43	2378	-12	0	0	14711	853	14711	853	26746
2051	1.00244	33339	15.44	5148	11.43	3811	-1337	0	0	21268	1234	21268	1234	0	0.48	2471	1334	7.43	2477	6	0	0	14705	853	14705	853	28080
2052	1.00244	34724	15.48	5375	11.43	3969	-1406	0	0	22675	1315	22675	1315	0	0.475	2553	1389	7.43	2580	27	0	0	14678	851	14678	851	29469
2053	1.00244	36167	15.52	5613	11.44	4137	-1476	0	0	24150	1401	24150	1401	0	0.47	2638	1447	7.44	2691	53	0	0	14626	848	14626	848	30916
2054	1.00244	37669	15.56	5861	11.44	4309	-1552	0	0	25702	1491	25702	1491	0	0.465	2725	1507	7.44	2803	77	0	0	14548	844	14548	844	32422
2055	1.00244	39233	15.59	6116	11.44	4488	-1628	0	0	27330	1585	27330	1585	0	0.46	2814	1569	7.44	2919	105	0	0	14443	838	14443	838	33992
2056	1.00228	40856	15.64	6390	11.44	4674	-1716	0	0	29046	1685	29046	1685	0	0.457	2920	1634	7.44	3040	120	0	0	14324	831	14324	831	35626
2057	1.00228	42547	15.69	6676	11.45	4872	-1804	0	0	30850	1789	30850	1789	0	0.454	3031	1702	7.45	3170	139	0	0	14185	823	14185	823	37328
2058	1.00228	44307	15.75	6978	11.45	5073	-1905	0	0	32756	1900	32756	1900	0	0.451	3147	1772	7.45	3301	154	0	0	14031	814	14031	814	39100
2059	1.00228	46140	15.81	7295	11.46	5288	-2007	0	0	34763	2016	34763	2016	0	0.448	3268	1846	7.46	3442	174	0	0	13857	804	13857	804	40946
2060	1.00228	48048	15.87	7625	11.46	5506	-2119	0	0	36882	2139	36882	2139	0	0.444	3386	1922	7.46	3584	199	0	0	13658	792	13658	792	42868
								10234																			

Table A2.1

978-0-595-37153-2
0-595-37153-1